I0161720

Sculpturing
a
Masterpiece

by
Leanne
Hamilton

First published in the United Kingdom in 2023.
Copyright © Leanne Hamilton.
All rights reserved.

No part of this book may be reproduced, stored in a
retrieval system or transmitted by any other means
without prior and express written permission by the
author/publisher.

A catalogue record of this book is available from the
British Library.

ISBN 978-1-7398258-7-4

Cover © Leanne Hamilton

Published by © Newford Publishing

The characters in this book are imaginary.
Their names have no relation to those of actual people living
or dead—except by coincidence.

Contents

Chapter 1: *The Foundation* 5

Chapter 2: *Winning Over The Public* 11

Chapter 3: *Signed At Last!* 16

Chapter 4: *The Ideal Model* 18

Chapter 5: *Branching Out* 22

Chapter 6: *The Potential Big Break* 29

Chapter 7: *The Perfect Bass* 40

Chapter 8: *The First Major Display* 48

Chapter 9: *Creativity On Show* 62

Chapter 10: *Inspiration or Stark Warning?* 68

Chapter 11: *Engineering In The Works* 75

Chapter 12: *Bright Days To Dark Days* 84

Chapter 13: *Electric Feels* 102

Chapter 14: *Touring Further Afield* 113

Chapter 15: *A Broken Piece* 129

Chapter 16: *Repairing A Broken Piece* 134

Chapter 17: *Smoothing The Rough Edges* 145

Chapter 18: *Scaling The Heights* 156

Chapter 19: *Taking Shape* 167

Chapter 20: *Moulding Together* 184

Chapter 21: *Full Steam Ahead* 204

Chapter 22: *Crumbling Artwork* 212

Chapter 23: *Shards Of Porcelain* 238

Chapter 1:
The Foundation

Maria Mancini awakes to the sound of the birds singing and the summer sunrise. Her two sons have finished school for their summer break, and she has entrusted them as latchkey kids while she carries on running her business.

Maria was very tragically widowed nine years previously when her husband Armando was killed in an industrial accident aged just 24, leaving her to bring up their young sons Mario and Angelo aged four and two respectively on her own. Having moved to the United States from Italy with Armando to work and start their own business, Maria had no choice but to power through so she could build a better life for herself and her beloved sons, as going home just wasn't an option. Today, her ladies-only gym Ice Goddess Fitness Gym is thriving, and she manages a team of female wrestlers.

Maria counts her blessings every day and is forever grateful for all she has. As a single parent in the year 1971, she often reflects on how fortunate she is despite her previous hardships. At thirteen years old, her eldest son Mario is a fitness fanatic, a promising athlete and is expressing an interest in following in his mother's footsteps as a fitness professional. He is very street smart, wise beyond his years and Maria is hoping to send him to university to study and learn the trade now that she can afford to do so. Her youngest son, however, is the opposite of his brother. Young Angelo is an introvert who shows no interest in school or mixing with other children, preferring to stay in his room and play his guitar which he taught himself to play to a surprisingly high standard for a boy his age. He is a loner who has a strong bond with his brother, whom he has always idolised.

Maria gets showered and ties her long, silky, jet-black hair up in a bun before getting changed into her tracksuit. She goes into her sons' room to find that Mario is already up and dressed. "I'm going to work now, my love," she tells him. "I'll try not to be too late."

"We'll be OK, Mom," assures Mario, who is in the process of styling himself as the man of the house. "I'll get the fence whitewashed for you."

"Thanks, darling," smiles Maria as she hugs her eldest son. "Any problems, phone the gym, and I'll be home as soon as I can. Love you."

Mario: "I will. Love you, Mom."

Maria checks on Angelo, who is still fast asleep. "See you soon, my baby," she whispers as she ruffles his dark, curly hair and kisses him on the forehead before leaving for another day at her office.

It is almost lunchtime, and Mario is finishing off his whitewash. He had forgotten just how challenging this job was as he had to coat the fence several times before it looked remotely even. Thankfully, his talented little brother's singing and guitar playing had motivated him and helped speed up the job. Having been temporarily blinded by continuously working with the whitewash, Mario sits down to let his eyes refocus and recover as Angelo continues to play his guitar and sing.

"Hey," says a cheery, friendly voice.

Mario looks up, and the face of a small Hispanic boy comes into focus over the newly whitewashed fence.

"Hey, yourself," replies Mario with his crooked but warm smile. A difficult birth had left him with irreparable paralysis of one side of his face as well as part of his tongue, lips and chin, where doctors had pressed too hard on his head with the forceps, severing some facial nerves. He had been self-conscious of the imbalance as a young child but has grown to enjoy the uniqueness now that he is growing up. Mario is becoming a good-looking young man, and he knows it!

The little Hispanic boy looks at Angelo, who has now stopped playing and is smiling up at him. "Hey, you're really good," enthuses the boy. "Has anyone ever told you you look like Elvis?"

"Oh, shut up," scoffs Angelo.

"Come on, don't be like that," replies the boy. "It's a commitment and you really do!"

"Do you mean a compliment?" asks Mario.

"Yeah, yeah, that's the word," the boy laughs.

"Well, thank you," smiles Angelo.

"Do you want to come in or something?" asks Mario. "We're just about to eat. What's your name, kid?"

"Carlos," replies the boy. "I'm not a kid either. I'm eleven."

"You can't be eleven," laughs Angelo. "You're far too small. I'm eleven."

"I'm just small for my age," Carlos shrugs. "I start middle school after the break."

Mario puts out three bowls of minestrone that he had made the previous day, along with some fresh crusty bread. The three boys chat and laugh about all sorts of things as they eat, and, before they know it, the street lights come on, and that is Carlos' cue to go home.

"Where do you stay?" asks Mario.

"I've just moved into my papa's house at the end of the street with my mom," replies Carlos. "We moved here from Spain last week. Can I come round again tomorrow?"

"Sure," Mario and Angelo reply in unison as they bid their new friend good night. They both watch as Carlos walks to the two-storey house at the end of the street until he waves, letting them know he is home safely and closes the door behind him.

The following morning, Carlos turns up to the boys' cottage to find that they are not in the yard, and the door closed. He lets himself into the yard and shouts through the letterbox: "Mario. Angelo. Are you guys home? It's Carlos."

He hears the key turn in the lock, and Angelo lets him in. "Mario is at the gym with my mom doing some painting and stuff for her," he says, quietly. "I'm home by myself today."

"Do you want to come over to my house?" asks Carlos. "My mom is home and I have something really cool to show you."

"Really? What?" asks Angelo.

"It's a surprise, and you'll love it," smiles Carlos. "Bring your guitar."

Angelo doesn't need asked twice. He picks up his guitar and the two friends make their way over to Carlos' house.

On arrival at the house, the boys are greeted by a thick cloud of cigarette smoke from which Carlos' mother Antonia emerges. She is a petite, cheery woman with long, curly, dark hair, and she is overjoyed that her only son has found a friend. She gives the boys a glass of fresh orange juice and tells them to help themselves to some fruit and snacks before they go upstairs to Carlos' bedroom.

"Check this," says Carlos as he opens his bedroom door to reveal a small drum kit.

"Oh, WOW," enthuses Angelo. "You never told me you played."

"Well, you never asked," laughs Carlos. "Let's experiment."

Carlos sits down at his drum kit and begins to play and Angelo is surprised to learn that his new friend is, in fact, a very skilled drummer. He picks up his guitar and begins to sing along, making up his own guitar melody and lyrics as he does so. The boys finish performing their first-ever song together, and they are over the moon at how well it turned out. Singing and playing together just seems to come natural to both of them. They let out a huge, excited cheer and get up and dance around the room with each other.

Hearing all the noise from downstairs, Antonia bursts into the room to see what has happened. "Aaww, Mom," says Carlos. "You'll need to listen to the song Angelo and I just wrote."

"Really, love?" she asks, surprised. "You wrote a song on your own?"

"Yeah," smiles Carlos. "Wait till you hear it!" Not convinced, Antonia sits on Carlos' bed to listen as she puffs on her cigarette.

"OK," says Angelo. "This song is called…oh, I don't know!"

"Hangin' Out?" suggests Carlos.

Antonia chuckles and rolls her eyes. Carlos kicks off the song with the same rhythmic beat he had previously played and Angelo joins in with his guitar and vocals. The boys finish performing their track and look at Antonia to see that she has tears in her eyes and is covering her mouth.

"*MOM?*" asks Carlos, shocked, as Angelo stares at her with wide eyes.

"That was just…*AMAZING,*" cries Antonia, wiping away her tears. "You guys are fantastic! You'll need to let your father hear it when he gets home."

Carlos' father Jose Martinez, who works as head programme controller for local radio station Golden Plus FM, arrives home. Jose, also known as Papa Joe by his family and friends, also has vast experience managing bands, which was why Antonia wanted the boys to get his expert opinion. He is greeted, very excitedly, by his wife who tells him all about the afternoon she had spent with their talented son and his new friend.

The boys perform the three tracks they had written that afternoon, and Papa Joe is delighted as he has only ever heard his son play drum solos.

"I'm impressed. *VERY* impressed," enthuses Papa Joe. "What

you need to do now is go out busking together and see how the public like you, and we'll take things from there."

The boys are disappointed but take Papa Joe's advice on board. "I don't suppose it's going to happen overnight," says Carlos. "I suppose not," Angelo agrees. "We'll start tomorrow."

Thus begins the start of a new band as the young duo pledge to write more songs and perform them in front of strangers as they enter the world of music and showbiz.

Chapter 2:
Winning Over The Public

Early the following morning, Angelo and Carlos pack up their instruments and make their way to the town centre for their first-ever public performance. People are already beginning to stop and look at them as they unpack and get ready to play. The crowd starts gathering immediately as soon as they start to play. It's not long before the boys are well into their performance, and the crowd is genuinely cheering for them and throwing money into Angelo's guitar case. They play for almost two hours, and they decide to wrap things up for the day. However, every time they try to do so, the crowd shouts for more.

Finally, the boys sit down for a rest before they pack up their instruments to go home. "Well, what are you waiting for?" asks Carlos. "Count the takings."

Angelo looks at the mound of coins on his guitar case, and he begins to count. "OK," he says. "We have some empty soda bottles, candy wrappers and chip bags. Now for our pay. Oh, wait! There are some dollar bills in here too!"

Angelo looks up at Carlos and smiles: "Guess what we've made."

"Oh, come on," says Carlos. "Spill."

"$34," replies Angelo. "Not bad for our first shot."

"You *HAVE* to be kidding," cries Carlos.

Angelo: "Nope. Count it yourself if you want."

"No, no, I believe you," laughs Carlos. "We could really do something with this."

The boys go back to Carlos' house, where Antonia lets them sit on the sofa in the living room as they tell her about the success of their first gig. "Your father will be so proud," beams Antonia.

"Yeah," yawns Carlos as Angelo leans against him and closes his eyes.

Antonia prepares a light lunch of sandwiches and fresh orange juice but returns to find both boys fast asleep. "Aaww, adorable," Antonia chuckles to herself. "I suppose it's hard work being rock stars."

The boys carry on with their routine for the rest of the summer break, and they are proving to be extremely popular, with people even waiting for them at the spot they had regularly played. However, it's not all plain sailing for the young duo. Sometimes they go home with very little money, and there are times people jeer and steal from them. The boys resign themselves to taking the rough with the smooth.

When it's time to go back to school, Angelo and Carlos are delighted to learn that they are going to be in the same school *AND* the same class. After the summer they had had, school just seems more mundane and boring than ever. The weeks pass, and Angelo and Carlos continue to write new songs and rehearse at Carlos' house in their spare time as well as busking at the weekends.

One day, one of the monitors informs the teacher that the headmaster wants to see Angelo and Carlos in his office. "They're not in trouble, Miss," smiles the girl.

Still, the boys make their way nervously to the headmaster's office.

Mr Morgan, a well-spoken man in his mid-forties, sits at his desk alongside his deputy head teacher Mr Aitken. Both men smile as the boys enter the office, looking nervously at each other. "Please have a seat, boys," smiles Mr Morgan. "Make yourselves comfortable."

The boys are pleasantly surprised. As neither of them had ever particularly excelled in anything at school, they had never been spoken to in this manner by any teacher, let alone the head master.

"It has come to my attention," continues Mr Morgan. "That you boys are carving out a career as professional musicians. My wife and I heard you first-hand when we happened to be out shopping during summer break, and you really have something! Boys, my staff and I would be honoured if you would play a set for the school during assembly one morning next week. Do you think you could do that for us?"

Angelo and Carlos look at each other, still very surprised. "Yes, sir," the boys reply in unison.

"Fantastic," says Mr Morgan as he claps his hands. "What is the name of your band?"

"We don't have a name yet, sir," replies Carlos. "We're just new."

"That's your homework for next week," replies Mr Morgan. "Come up with a name and let me know when you have one, so I can announce it to the school."

Following the meeting with their headmaster, the boys decide to change their names in order to appeal to a wider audience and they come up with their band name Carl And Angel. Both agree that it is not very imaginative, but it's a start.

The morning arrives for Carl And Angel to perform in front of their entire school. They do so to be met by roaring cheers from their young audience, and they perform all the songs they had written during summer break as well as hit songs from artists such as Elvis Presley, The Beetles and The Beach Boys. Overall, Carl And Angel proved to be a hit with this age group as well as the teachers who are aged from their mid twenties to around fifty years old. The school even awards the boys with a payment of $10 each, which they are ecstatic about. They are rising in popularity with all age groups as they continue to busk on the streets for the next two years.

Presently, Maria and Antonia have become friends. The two women are enjoying coffee and the summer sunshine in Maria's backyard as they talk excitedly about their sons' developing music careers. "I am so glad things have worked out the way they have," smiles Maria. "My Angelo never keeps friends, and I have never seen him this happy or enthusiastic about anything before. I definitely have your Carlos to thank for that."

"What a lovely thing to say, my dear Maria," replies Antonia with sadness in her voice as she smokes her cigarette. "Carlos has trouble keeping friends too. He is hyperactive, and children tend not to stay long as they find him too wild and over-powering. He is supposed to be on a lot of heavy medication for his condition, but he's just not my boy when he's on it. I feel as though it does him more harm than good so I don't give it to him. Jose and I even split over my decision not to give Carlos his medication, which was why we went back home to Spain."

"You're his mother, and you know what's best for your boy," assures Maria. "I would never have known he was hyperactive as he is always fine when he is over here. I thought he was just very bubbly and full of fun. He has certainly brought Angelo out of his shell, which I am delighted about because my big boy will be leaving for university soon. Angelo would be lost without his brother otherwise. I just love having Carlos, and he is more than welcome at my house any time."

Antonia begins to well up. "That is so kind of you to say that," she says quietly.

"I mean it," Maria reassures her as she puts her hand over Antonia's. "I genuinely do. Remember, all children are different. Carlos is a terrific boy and very talented. He has found his calling now, and you should be proud of him."

"Thank you so so much," replies Antonia as she composes

herself. The two women hug as they pledge to continue to support their sons in their journey.

Chapter 3:
Signed At Last!

It is a Saturday morning, and Mario and Angelo have risen early because they both have a busy weekend ahead of them. Mario is competing in the schools' regional rowing championships, and Angel, now his preferred name, is going to Carl's house as Papa Joe has an important announcement to make before he goes to work.

The boys are talking excitedly about the day ahead when, suddenly, Angel stops mid-sentence and looks at his big brother in awe. He watches as Mario ruffles his thick, dark hair with an Afro comb which he is growing in order to be in line with the current nineteen-seventies fashion and his biceps and all his back muscles ripple as he does so. The now 15-year-old Mario had recently hit a growth spurt, is now standing at around 5 ft 8 and is still growing. He had also been working hard to build up his body using weights their mother had brought home, as he is still too young to go to a gym. He has filled out and is transitioning from a boy to a man. Even his voice has long since broken and evened out into a deep, manly drawl. Much to Mario's delight, the girls love it. "Aw, I wish mine looked like that," sighs Angel.

"Be patient and give it time, kiddo," assures Mario. "Neither of us are fully grown yet, and it will happen for you. You'll see. Right now, just enjoy being young and concentrate on that music career. Soon people will ask 'who is Elvis?'"

Angel laughs, the boys playfully wrestle with each other, and Mario finishes with a few playful biffs before giving his brother a non-awkward hug. "Good luck for today," Mario beams at his brother. "I can't wait to hear your news, and I have a feeling it's going to be great!"

"Thank you," replies Angel. "Good luck to you too."

Angel arrives at Carl's house to find Carl sitting on the sofa, looking nervous as Antonia holds his hand. "Angel," Papa Joe greets him without smiling. "Have a seat, son."

"Boys, I am just going to keep this short," continues Papa Joe. "I have watched you over the past couple of years. You have both worked extremely hard and stuck this out a lot longer than I ever imagined you would have. I can see you really are serious about a career in music so I have decided I am going to give you a chance, take you on and manage you. You will make some *REAL* money on a regular basis."

"*REALLY?*", Angel asks excitedly.

"*YES!!*" exclaims Carl. "*AT LAST.*"

"There is a catch, though," says Papa Joe. "As you are both only thirteen years old, you will only be legally allowed to play small, unlicensed venues such as cafes and malls."

Angel looks at Carl. "Well, we knew that anyway, and it's a start," Angel replies, maintaining a positive attitude. "Thank you, Mr Martinez."

"Please," replies Papa Joe. "It's Joe. If all goes well, I should be able to assign you to play at some outdoor festivals, too and get you a more exciting experience. Welcome to the jungle, boys."

Chapter 4:
The Ideal Model

In the year following, Carl And Angel see their success skyrocket as Papa Joe has them out working at all sorts of venues most weekends and at huge established festivals throughout the summer, in and out of state.

It is just after two o'clock on a Sunday morning, and Papa Joe drops Angel off at his mother's cottage following another successful gig at a large out-of-state festival. He turns to say goodnight to Carl to find that he is already asleep. Maria is already waiting for him to come home, excited to hear how the gig went. "It was amazing, Mom," Angel yawns as he struggles to keep his eyes open. "I am so tired, though. I need to go to bed."

"Alright, my superstar," beams Maria as she kisses him goodnight. "I'll hear all about it in the morning. Good night, baby."

Angel opens his bedroom door quietly so as not to disturb his brother but is hit by what feels like a gale-force wind, the room is freezing, and Mario is not in his bed. He notices that the window next to Mario's bed is wide open, and the curtains are blowing as the wind howls. Angel looks out of the window across the backyards and notices that the light is on in one of the bedroom windows with the curtains opened wide. Inside, he can make out the familiar figure of his brother, who is in full-on action with their 18-year-old neighbour Maryjane. Angel bursts out laughing. *"AW, YUCK,"* he says out loud, still laughing. *"FUCKIN' HELL, DUDE."*

He closes the window, leaving just enough of a gap so his brother can get back in, gets into bed and pulls the covers over his ears as he tries to block out what he just saw. Mario's antics are something that Angel gets used to in the year following, and he never once cracks a light to anyone about what his brother is getting up to.

During the summer break, Mario, now seventeen years old, gets an unconditional acceptance onto his degree course to study Health Sciences with Human Nutrition, and he has to move away. However, he is never a stranger as he makes the weekly commute home at the weekends, having acquired his motorcycle licence.

During one of the weekends, Maria invites the Martinez's over for their Sunday dinner, and all attention is on Mario. He speaks about his studies, sports teams he is part of, nightlife and, of course, girls. "So, do you have a girlfriend yet, Mario?" Antonia asks with a cheeky smile.

"Aw, yeah," grins Mario, now known as Moose at university and by most of his friends. "I have a new one every week." Everyone laughs at this except Carl, who continues to sit solemnly and quietly at the table.

Following yet another successful weekend of gigs, Carl And Angel wrap things up, and Papa Joe drives them home. Again, Carl is quiet prior to the gig and during the journey home as Papa Joe and Angel chat enthusiastically about the success of past gigs and about upcoming gigs. Noticing his friend's change in demeanour, Angel confronts Carl when they meet up for school the following morning. "What has been with you lately, dude?" asks Angel. "Have you been taking those pills your mom doesn't want you to have?"

"Of course not, buddy," replies Carl. "It's just...never mind. It's nothing."

"Well, you're not acting like this for nothing," presses Angel. "Is it something I've done?"

"No, no, not at all," replies Carl.

"Please tell me what's wrong then," pleads Angel. "We can't go on the way we are if something is bothering you, and I don't know what it is. We are supposed to be working as a team." There is about a minute of silence.

"Angel," Carl pipes up. "What are you noticing about our audiences?"

"They're super busy," enthuses Angel. "So good, in fact, that I'm thinking of not doing my exams."

"That aside," Carl continues being serious. "Do you notice who is in the audience?"

"Fuckin' Hell, dude," says Angel, frustrated. "Just get to the point, will you?"

"It only seems to be guys who like us," sighs Carl.

"What's wrong with that?" asks Angel. "We write and perform great stuff, and as long as we have audiences who like us, it shouldn't matter who they are. We still get our money, and Papa Joe gets his. Just what is the problem, dude?"

"Angel," Carl says, back in serious mode. "We need an image change. I mean, look at us. We are a pair of skinny, baby-faced boys, and the girls are hardly rushing to buy tickets to see us. Dude, we need to get your brother on board. He is a hit with the girls, and it will even out our audience."

"You're not serious," laughs Angel. "Moose isn't even musical. Forget it!"

"Could you not teach him a few chords on the guitar?" suggests Carl. "He might not be natural, but you could really help him get good. Didn't you teach me how to write good songs?"

"That's entirely different," says Angel, rolling his eyes. "You already had a base; Moose doesn't."

"Please try," pleads Carl. "Even if it's the last thing you do for me."

"OK," sighs Angel. "But if you hear hysterical laughter coming from my mom's house on Friday night, you'll know why!"

"Listen, we are off this weekend," says Carl. "How about we go to Norm's and pick an electric guitar and an amp? Moose is always saying how much he loves those guitar riffs, and we have enough money for a deposit. You never know; he might jump at the chance if it means more attention from the girls."

"*CARL*," exclaims Angel. "You are talking about changing our entire image when our own one is already working just fine! This could go very badly wrong."

"Dude," Carl rolls his eyes. "It is 1976, people's taste in music is changing and so are the styles. Electric is *THE* future. Look at the likes of The Rolling Stones, Queen and Eric Clapton. They all have that one thing in common, and they are all massive sellers."

"Let me talk to Moose when he comes home this weekend before we even think about buying anything," sighs Angel. "Just understand that I am taking no responsibility if any of this fucks up."

"Your big brother admires you, and you are a great teacher," Carl enthuses. "I have a great feeling about this."

"I don't," Angel shakes his head. "Hell will freeze over if I manage to get Moose to do anything musically."

"HELL FREEZE," cries Carl. "That will be our new name!"

"God, help me," groans Angel.

Chapter 5:
Branching Out

Friday evening rolls around and Angel and Carl are kicking a ball around the back yard of Maria's cottage when they hear the unmistakeable sound of Moose's motorbike as he arrives home for the weekend. The two friends make their way to the front to greet him. They both watch as a well-built, leather-clad Moose now eighteen years old dismounts from his bike. He removes his helmet allowing his long, dark, curly hair to cascade down his back.

"What are you waiting for?" hisses Carl. "Go talk to him. Listen I'll talk to you tomorrow, OK?"

"Alright, dude," smiles Angel. "Wish me luck."

Angel goes to greet his brother and is surprised to find that they are now almost eye-to-eye with each other. "Bloody Hell, bro," gasps Moose. "What has Mom been feeding you, in the name of God?"

"The usual," laughs Angel. "I just took your advice and it worked."

"See?" replies Moose as he playfully wrestles his brother to the ground. "I am *NEVER* wrong."

Having enjoyed a night and lots of laughs as a family, Moose and Angel bid their mother good night as they go to their room.

"Moose?" asks Angel, nervously. "I have a massive favour to ask you."

"Fire away, little bro," replies Moose, as he realises he won't be able to use this reference for much longer. "What's up?"

"Um, how would you feel about coming to work with me and Carl and Papa Joe?" asks Angel.

"I would be honoured, kiddo," enthuses Moose. "If I can fit all my studies in during the week, it certainly won't be a problem for me to come out with you guys at the weekends and help you with your heavy equipment."

"No, Moose, you've got me wrong," replies Angel.

Moose: "You've lost me." There is an awkward silence.

"Moose," whispers Angel. "You like all those crazy guitar riffs, don't you?"

"Fuck, Angel," Moose sighs. "It is almost two o'clock in the morning, I have had a long ride getting here, I'm drunk and you are talking in riddles. Get to the point, will you?"

"OK, here goes," says Angel as he clears his throat. "If I teach you the electric guitar, would you come on board and play for us?"

Moose bursts out laughing. "That's hilarious, bro," Moose continues to laugh. "Now, the punchline?"

"I'm serious," replies Angel. "Carl and I need somebody who can reel in the girls, and we know we can trust you. Come on, big bro. Be a sport."

"No," says Moose, flatly. "I am happy to come on board as one of your goons, not to play an instrument I can't play."

"Please, Moose," pleads Angel. "I can teach you."

"Angel," Moose says, putting his hands up. "The case is closed. I am doing enough learning as it is, and my tiny brain can only take in so much at a time. Do yourself a favour and find somebody competent. Like I say, I'll come on board as one of your goons, and that will have to be my final offer."

"No, Moose," Angel continues to protest. "You are NOT being a goon! Listen, how about you come to Norm's with Carl and I tomorrow and help us with our new guitar and *amp?*"

"Done deal," replies Moose as he gives his brother a few playful biffs. "Another thing: do yourself a favour. Look in the mirror and tell Carl to do the same. You both have your own good looks. Girls like the tall, athletic types like you as well as cute kids like Carl. Learn to enjoy it as it is a big thing when you are a performer."

"Thanks, bro," smiles Angel. "We owe you big for this."

The following morning, the brothers meet up with Papa Joe and Carl, and nobody has yet spoken to Papa Joe about the potential new member. They go into Norm's and Angel tries his hand on some of the electric guitars until he finds the very guitar that he and Carl both believe works the magic and will do so for years to come. Angel picks up a Fender Stratocaster and asks the assistant if he can try it with the amp they are intending to buy.

After performing three of Carl And Angel's favourite tracks and winning approval from Papa Joe, the boys leave the store content with their purchase. As soon as they arrive at Carl's house, Moose sets up the guitar and amp and sits back to listen to Carl And Angel's brand-new style. They finish their first track, and Angel gives Moose a crafty smile: "OK, big bro. Your turn."

"Hey, I told you no," protests Moose.

"Come on, Moose," Carl chimes in. "We need you."

"Guys," says Moose as he puts up his hands. "This is YOUR gig. I told you I am more than happy to be your goon. Honestly, I support you one hundred percent and I will always be proud of you."

"We know you are, Moose," replies Carl. "But we REALLY want you on board. Please, we will be an amazing trio."

"This conversation is just going round and round and round in circles," groans Moose.

Just then, Angel picks up the guitar and blasts out a powerful, hard-hitting riff that Moose recognises.

"Sounds banging, don't it?" enthuses Angel.

"Like everything you guys play," beams Moose.

"I could teach you that riff in under five minutes," Angel persists. "How about it, bro?"

"You're not going to take 'no' for an answer, are you?" asks Moose.

"Dude, we just want you to try," says Carl. "Please, just this once."

"OK," sighs Moose. "Just this once."

"Great," smiles Carl as he opens the door to leave Angel to his teaching. "Enjoy your lesson."

"First thing," says Angel, as he gets into his teacher mode. "You will either prefer sitting or standing. I, personally, prefer standing but that's up to you." Moose can't help laughing.

"What's funny?" asks Angel.

"You," Moose continues to laugh. "You and your serious teacher voice. You're like one of my crazy uni professors."

"Come on, Moose, apply yourself," Angel replies as he tries to remain professional.

Angel continues to show Moose exactly how to hold the guitar and then goes on to teach him some basic chords. "There you go," he exclaims as he slaps his brother on the back. "You're sounding like a veteran already."

"Are you shitting me?" asks Moose.

"NO," cries Angel. "You are doing a grand job!"

"You are doing a grand job of lying," groans Moose. "This just feels wrong."

Having heard all the practice from downstairs, Carl and Antonia enter the room.

"Sounds like you're getting the hang of it, dude," enthuses Carl as Antonia agrees.

"I'm not," Moose continues to argue. "My little brother is being far too nice...again."

"Mario," Antonia chimes in. "*NOBODY* is being nice for the sake of being nice. You need to remember this is Carlos and Angelo's potential livelihood and they wouldn't have you on board unless they really thought you were able for the job. Listen, why don't you get some rest and try again later? You had a long journey yesterday and a busy day today. Things will look better after you've slept. I promise."

"I suppose *I AM* tired," Moose yawns.

"Take the rest of the day off and we'll see you tomorrow," says Antonia as she hugs Moose and kisses him on the cheek.

"Thanks, Aunt Antonia," replies Moose. "See you tomorrow."

The weeks pass, and Angel continues to mentor Moose on his guitar playing until he is finally confident enough to rehearse unaided with his brother and Carlos. "You see?" Angel smiles cheekily. "I told you we would get there."

"Hell yeah," says Moose in his deep, manly voice as he playfully wrestles with his brother.

"Um, Moose?" Carl asks, nervously. "How are you fixed for two weeks time? We have a gig."

"Aw, shit," gasps Moose. "Is it a big one?"

"Just a small, local one where only everyone and their grandparents know us," replies Angel, quietly as he covers his face.

"I think I have a major dose of the shits," Moose whispers before running and locking himself in the toilet.

The evening arrives for the trio's very first gig under their new name "Hell Freeze" with new guitarist Moose, who seems to have been permanently glued to the toilet seat for the past fortnight. He eventually emerges with thirty minutes remaining before they are due to go on stage and perform.

"How are you feeling, dude," asks Carl, quietly.

"I feel as though I am shitting hot bricks," replies Moose, visibly sweating and his deep voice almost breaking. "What if I do something wrong out there?"

"There is *NO* wrong," assures Angel. "It's rock music, not classical, and it is *OUR* own material. If you play a bum note, you keep playing. The audience won't even notice as long as the three of us put on a good show for them. You are *MOOSE*

FUCKING MANCINI, our master of guitar riffs. We've got this. Trust me, bro, this gig is gonna be a blast!"

"Thanks, bro," replies Moose. "I suppose we'd best get a fucking move on!"

"YES," exclaims Angel as he slaps his brother on the back.

"Ladies and gentlemen," Papa Joe addresses the audience. "Please welcome to the world of rock and roll: *HELL FREEZE.*"

The audience erupts into a massive cheer as the long-haired, leather-clad trio takes to the stage and the crowd ascends into a wild roar as Moose and Carl play the introduction to their first song of the evening. Carl looks at the sea of faces in the crowd and is delighted when he realises that it is now a very mixed crowd of people who have turned out to see them, with many of them women of all ages that he had wanted to include as part of that dedicated group. His plan to recruit Moose has worked!

This is definitely the wildest gig the guys have played yet as girls in the front row get topless and try to climb on stage only to be pulled back by security staff.

Hell Freeze are ecstatic following their first gig as a trio, especially Moose who has surprised himself that he managed to keep his cool throughout the evening.

Backstage, Papa Joe congratulates the young trio on their debut. He wraps his arms around Moose's broad shoulders. "How are you feeling, son?" He asks. "You did a star quality job out there tonight."

"FUCK, YEAH," exclaims Moose. "I could get used to this, especially those girls in their birthday suits!"

"Well, we'll look forward to lots more," Papa Joe laughs out loud.

"FUCK, YEAH," Carl and Angel shout in unison.

"What's next then?" Carl asks Moose. "You'll be joining us full-time now, yeah?"

"No," replies Moose, quietly.

Angel puts a hand on Moose's shoulder. "You're not running out on us, are you bro?" he whispers.

"Of course not, guys," Moose assures them. "I do want to graduate before I do anything else. I promised I would help you guys all I can, and I stand by my word but I also want my degree."

"We're with you all the way, son," beams Papa Joe. "Brains and natural talent. What did I do to deserve you guys?"

"I make it party time," laughs Angel. "Come on, guys, we deserve it after the night we've had. We've earned it!"

Chapter 6:
The Potential Big Break

Following several weeks of sell-out gigs, Papa Joe has stopped booking Hell Freeze up for any further gigs for the time being. Moose and Angel are enjoying a well-deserved lie-in when Maria enters their bedroom, looking very excited as she holds up today's newspaper. "Look at this, boys," she enthuses. "Soul Food Records are scouting for their hottest new talent. The entire competition will be televised on a show called Band Stand-Off. The grand prize includes a cash prize of $500, a trip to Indianapolis to see Elvis Presley perform at Market Square Arena, flights and accommodation included, and...wait for it: **A RECORD DEAL WITH SOUL FOOD RECORDS!**"

"Aw, Mom," groans Angel. "We've no chance of winning that. There will be thousands of talented people from all over the world turning out for that competition."

"You certainly won't win anything if you don't try," replies Maria. "You are talented, good-looking young men who have several years of experience under your belts as well as lots of devoted followers. What have you got to lose?"

"Mom's right, bro," Moose chimes in. "They can only say no."

"But they could very well say *YES*," exclaims Maria. "Quick. Get showered and dressed. We're going to see Antonia, Papa Joe, and, of course, our superstar hitman Carl!"

The Mancinis arrive at the Martinez's house to find Papa Joe and Antonia looking very excited and Carl looking nervous as he sits on the sofa looking at the floor. "Oh, you already know," whispers Maria.

"Yes, my dear Maria," exclaims Papa Joe. "The boys are already entered. It will just need to be practise, practise, practise every weekend until our big contest. Our boys are well on their way to being stars now!"

Carl gets up and leaves the room, signalling with his head for Moose and Angel to follow him. The boys go to Carl's bedroom, and Carl closes the door tightly behind him. "I don't know about you guys, but I'm shitting myself," he tells the brothers.

"I'm scared too, dude," replies Angel. "For the first time in my life, I am absolutely terrified about performing. What if we fuck it up? Moose, we only see you for rehearsals at weekends. It's not enough, and we'll never be ready on time."

"We'll get our own place together," Carl smiles.

"It's not that simple, Carl," sighs Angel. "We can't just up and leave like that, and what about school?"

"WAIT," Moose gasps. "You're doing your exams after all?"

"Well, what else is there?" asks Angel, still apprehensive. "Our moms and Papa Joe will be so disappointed in us if we don't."

"For one, there's your music career," asserts Moose. "Two, our old folks will NOT be disappointed. Let me tell you something else. Mom and I have listened to you sing and play your guitar since you were any age. Mom knows fine that you have no intentions of going any further in school, and I'm sure your mom and Papa Joe believe that of you too, Carl. Look at it this way. Is putting yourself through all that stress for a pass in English or Math going to make you a better singer, guitar player or drummer?"

"Well…no," replies Angel and Carl shakes his head in agreement.

"There's your answer," Moose reassures his brother. "You know something else? As you grow up, I am seeing you more and more like how I remember Dad."

"Really?" Angel smiles.

"Yup," replies Moose. "He was very strong, determined, smart and hands-on. Just like you. He didn't need pieces of paper to get on in life either. It was his idea to come here to start a business, and he put the wheels in motion for Mom to keep going. It's all thanks to him; we have the life we have now. I just wish we'd had him for longer and that you'd got to know him. The trouble is that when God puts angels on this planet, He always wants them back early."

Moose goes to the bathroom before his emotions get the better of him as Angel and Carl look at each other, stunned by Moose's very rare show of emotion.

"OK, guys," Moose says as he re-enters the room and claps his hands excitedly. "Is it decided?"

"For sure," Carl and Angel exclaim in unison.

"As soon as I get back to my apartment, I'll start looking for a place. I'll definitely look forward to getting away from the three nerds I share with now!"

"This is gonna be some ride," enthuses Angel.

"We're almost into February, and our big competition is in November," says Moose. "If we all knuckle down, we'll be ready in no time."

Just then, Antonia bursts into the room. "Come on boys," she says excitedly. "We're going out for dinner to celebrate."

Carl and Angel exchange looks, and Moose puts a hand on each of their shoulders. "The ideal opportunity," he whispers. "We'll break the news to the old folks over dinner, while everyone's in a good mood."

At dinner, the boys are quiet as they try to determine how

they are going to tell their parents of their decision to move away. Angel and Carl look at Moose as they are relying on him being the spokesman for the trio. The parents are chatting happily when Moose calls for their attention "Mom, Papa Joe, Aunt Antonia," he addresses them.

"Is everything alright, love?" asks Antonia.

"Aunt Antonia, we have a suggestion," says Moose apprehensively. "You know the three of us are serious about this opportunity, right?"

"Yes..." replies Maria.

"The thing is, Mom," Moose continues. "Right now we're not really getting enough time to practice as a trio because I am away most of the time. Carl, Angel and I have decided it would be a good idea to get a place together close to the university so that I can continue my studies as well as getting more practice in for our big day."

"What?" cries Antonia. "But Carlos and Angelo are only babies. How will they cope out there on their own?"

"Come on, Antonia," says Papa Joe. "They are not babies anymore. Those boys stopped being our babies the day they decided to become professional musicians. They have become responsible young men who now know where they are going in life. As difficult as it is, we need to accept that our children are growing up rapidly and we need to let them go and see the world."

"But, but, what about school?" stammers Antonia, now on the verge of tears. "Carlos is doing so well."

"Mom, I'm not," Carl contradicts her. "All the teachers are saying is that I am more settled, and for the first time in my life they are not calling me a bad, unruly kid. Nobody has said that I am particularly good at anything, and I know I'm not because I can't sit still long enough to take anything in. Me and Angel have no interest in school, and the teachers know that. We don't want to go to college or university because we know it would just be a waste of our time and your money and for what? Just so we can do jobs we hate and don't want to do?"

"Carl is right, Antonia," assures Maria. "We must let our boys follow their dreams while they are young. They can always go back to school as mature students when they are older if they decide on a career change away from music."

"This is all so sudden," sobs Antonia. "My baby boy is going out into the big bad world to fend for himself."

"He won't be on his own, Aunt Antonia," Moose assures her. "Angel and I will be with him, and we will only be a bike ride and a phone call away. I promise, we will still be home to see you every weekend."

"You're doing the right thing, boys," beams Papa Joe. "This is the best plan of action, and we will still do gigs at the weekends wherever I can get them."

"Thanks, Papa Joe," says Moose, relieved. "I'll be able to get a cheap place for us. There are loads of great apartments up for sale near the university. I'll go out and look during the week."

"We'll leave it in your capable hands, baby," beams Maria as she hugs Moose and kisses him on the cheek.

"Thanks, Mom," replies Moose. "I'll keep you all in the loop."

The following Monday, after uni, Moose scours the local newspapers looking for potential accommodation for himself and his bandmates. He narrows his search down to five apartments on offer that are within the trio's budget, one of which looks far too good to be true. "Well presented ground floor apartment located close to university, schools and the mall," the advertisement reads. "Convenient for public transport. Three generously-sized bedrooms, lounge, kitchen, and bathroom with newly-installed shower. Fully air-conditioned. Communal drying area. Street parking."

Moose dials the number, and an elderly lady answers the phone. Not expecting too much, he arranges an appointment to see the apartment the following afternoon as he has an early finish from classes. That afternoon, Moose arrives at the address and is greeted by a lady in her sixties. "Oh, you're only a young boy," says the lady, surprised. "I heard the deep voice and was expecting somebody a lot older. Are you serious about this sale, son?"

"Of course, Mrs Sanders," replies Moose. "I liked the sound of the description, but the price just seems very low."

"Yes, son," Mrs Sanders replies with sadness in her voice. "It's a sad sale. This was my marital home, and I raised my children here. I have so many memories, but I am on my own now and will be moving to a retirement home, hence the reason I need the quick sale. This apartment is far too big for just me and it would be better suited to a family. Do you have family, son?"

"I don't," Moose tells her. "I am a student at the nearby university, and I am in a rock band. I thought the apartment would be ideal for myself and my two bandmates. I have the money here right now for a deposit if you need it?"

"You are a good boy, and I admire your honesty, son," smiles Mrs Sanders. "I'll show you where everything is, and you can let me know what you think."

Pleasantly surprised by what he sees, Moose thanks Mrs Sanders and arranges another appointment so that Angel and Carl can see the apartment.

"It's great," exclaims Carl when he sees his potential new residence. "We'll take it, please."

The trio proceed to pay Mrs Sanders her full asking price with cash up-front. "Thank you so much, boys," she says with tears in her eyes. "It was a pleasure doing business with you, and I wish you all the very best in your new home and in your career. Hopefully, I'll see Hell Freeze in concert soon."

Mrs Sanders leaves the young bandmates ecstatic with their purchase while she, herself, is relieved about her sale.

"This is just the shit," enthuses Angel. "I can't believe we have our own crib already!"

"Don't get too excited yet, guys," says Moose, lowering his tone. "You can't leave me high and dry. If you're not going to school, I need you both to get jobs and help me pay the bills. Remember, I'm only a poor student who works part-time in Walmart, and the pay we're making from Papa Joe's gigs doesn't stretch very far."

"Of course, bro," replies Angel. "We'll start looking tomorrow."

"Listen," says Moose. "I'm on good terms with my boss. I'll put in a good word for you, and they might be able to sort you out with something."

"Urgh, WALMART?" Carl grimaces.

"Well, the other option is that you go home, back to school and forget this competition," Moose replies, firmly. "This is our big chance, and we have to rehearse and give it our best shot. Sadly, we need some money to get us through it."

"We're with you, bro," assures Angel. "If you can put a word in for us, we'll start looking tomorrow too."

The following evening, Moose speaks to his manager regarding employment for his two bandmates. "Sorry, Moose," Big Shaun apologises. "I've just taken on a lot of new staff and have nothing just now. I have another idea, though. My wife is head of recruitment at Farrell's Pharmaceuticals in the industrial estate and they are crying out for workers right now. The rate of pay is good and they don't work weekends, the lucky buggers. Tell them to call into reception tomorrow and ask for Yvonne. I'll speak to her when I get home and tell her to expect them."

"Thanks, boss," replies Moose. "You're a pal, and we owe you big for this."

Early the following morning, Angel and Carl arrive at Farrell's Pharmaceuticals to enquire about employment. They enter the reception area to find two attractive blonde women in their thirties chatting and laughing with each other as they smoke cigarettes and drink coffee while they work. "Good morning, boys," the smaller of the two greets them as she puts down her cigarette. "Can we help you?"

"I hope so," replies Angel. "Can we speak to Yvonne, please?"

"That's me," smiles the taller lady. "Are you Angel and Carl?"

"Yes, that's us," replies Carl.

"Great," smiles Yvonne. "Thanks for coming in, boys. Let's go and have a chat."

They enter the canteen where are six members of staff are on their breaks who appear to be aged from their teens to late forties. The two women and four men stop chatting and look up briefly from their newspapers and puzzles before resuming their own business. Yvonne sits the boys down at an empty table, gives each of them a bottle of chilled water then sits down opposite them. "First of all, boys," Yvonne says with a serious, business-like tone. "Are you sure you want to do this? You're both VERY young. What about school?"

"We're finished with school, Yvonne," replies Carl assertively. "We're sixteen years old, we've just bought our first apartment and we have other things planned. We're actually..." Carl looks at Angel. "Am I allowed to tell her?" he asks.

"Yeah, go on," Angel smiles.

"We're in a band, and we play gigs all over California and sometimes out of state at the weekends," says Carl.

"Sounds interesting," smiles Yvonne. "You'll be glad to know we don't work weekends here, so that will free you up. What is the name of your band."

"Hell Freeze," the boys say in unison.

"Aaaww, I've seen you," Yvonne cries, and she looks at Angel. "You look like Elvis from a distance, and you sound a lot like him too."

"Thank you," says Angel as he blushes.

"You certainly know how to get a party going and keep it going," Yvonne continues enthusiastically. "My man and I

LOVE your gigs and always look forward to them!"

"Thank you," smiles Carl. "We love playing too."

"Yeah I can tell," Yvonne nods. "Right, back to the serious stuff. Guys, I like what I see and the jobs are yours if you still want them?"

"Thank you, Yvonne," replies Carl. "Yes, we still need the work as we are still not making enough money from our gigs to pay everything. Angel and I will do our best."

Yvonne looks at Angel. "What's wrong, handsome?" she asks him. "You're not saying much."

"I don't get the chance," he laughs and blushes.

"OK, guys, I'll get training organised for you for tomorrow," Yvonne says as she concludes their meeting. "You met Sharon briefly when you came in. She will be in charge of your training so if you come in tomorrow morning at ten o'clock, ask for her, we'll organise your overalls and get you started. You'll be finished for two in the afternoon at the very latest depending on how quickly you pick it up. All the very best with everything and please keep me posted if you're doing any more gigs."

"Thanks, Yvonne. We will," smiles Carl.

The following morning, the boys start their training with Sharon. She is a cheery woman who makes light of everything and always seems to be laughing, lifting everyone's spirits. "I wonder what would happen to Sharon if we really did say something funny," Angel whispers to Carl. "I worry that she's gonna croak one of these days."

The job is extremely fast-paced, and there is a lot of running involved, but the comic relief of Sharon and the chatter of the other employees as they work keeps everyone's spirits lifted. This is especially true when supervisor Marc joins his team on the shop floor. "Excellent joab, guys," Marc motivates the staff in his broad Scots-Glaswegian accent. "Yer all daein' crackin'! Whit a joab man, whit a fuckin' joab!"

"Whit a time tae be alive," exclaims Sharon as she buckles with laughter, and the other employees chuckle at her attempt at the Glaswegian accent.

"Holy fuck," Carl whispers to Angel. "She's gonna piss herself!"

"Never mind that," replies Angel. "What language are they speaking? I can't understand a damn word!"

"That guy's Scottish, I think," says Carl. "That must be Gaelic, but Sharon never said she was bilingual."

"Don't know," Angel shakes his head, confused.

"'Mon, guys, daein' brulliant," Marc interrupts the chatter as he smiles. "Whit a fuckin' joab!"

"Wait," Carl says to Sharon. "He's telling us to moan?"

By now, Sharon is almost on the floor with tears in her eyes as she laughs hysterically at her young trainees' confusion due to Marc's strong accent.

"Aw, man, I'm lost," sighs Angel. "I give up!"

Sharon finally calms herself down and puts a hand on Carl and Angel's shoulders. "Well done, guys," she says to them. "That was a great shift and you both did really well. This is our week of early shifts so I'll see you at five o'clock tomorrow morning and we'll be out of here for twelve."

"Suits us," smiles Angel. "That will free us up for rehearsals. Thanks, Sharon."

"Brulliant shift the day, bhoys," says Marc. "Whit a fuckin' joab. Well done and we'll see yeez the morra!"

"Brilliant shift, guys," Sharon translates. "Excellent job today. Well done and we'll see you tomorrow."

"It's not ideal," Carl says to Angel. "At least it's bearable until we hit the big time."

"Yeah," concurs Angel. "As much as that was a laugh, we need to remind ourselves to focus on the main prize. Music comes first and this job is only to pay the bills for now."

As the weeks pass, the three young bandmates are struggling as they juggle their workload and studies with rehearsals as well as their long bike rides home to see their parents. Moose s even surprised to pass his exams and be accepted into his second year at university. During one of their trips home, the trio are sitting in Maria's back yard having a beer. "I don't know about you guys," says Angel, on the verge of tears. "But I'm heading for burn-out. This is *SO* hard and I am exhausted. I don't even know if I can face this gig tomorrow."

"I'm bushed too, dude," replies Carl. "Nobody said it was gonna be easy but I didn't expect this!"

"Come on, guys," Moose chimes in. "We've all worked far too hard just to throw in the towel. We need to set ourselves apart from everyone else. Good things will come out of it. They just have to. Even if we don't win, we know we're good. We will be on TV and somebody, somewhere will give us a deal."

"You really think so?" asks Carl.

"It happens all the time," replies Moose. "You only need to read the stories of other musicians and bands who just happened to be in the right place at the right time and they make it big. All we can do is give it our best shot."

"Yeah," Angel nods as Moose puts a strong arm around his shoulders.

"We've got enough rehearsal hours in the bank, guys," reassures Moose. "We'll have an early bath tonight and we'll feel more up for the gig tomorrow. We've got this."

Chapter 7:
The Perfect Bass

A very busy summer comes and goes, and it is time for Moose to return to university for his second year. His first class of the semester is Scientific Study, a large module that is expected to last the entire school year for all the students. Moose enters the huge lecture theatre, which is already busy with enthusiastic students from various science-based disciplines. He notices a half-empty row of seats near the front of the theatre, and he makes himself as comfortable as possible. The attractive red-haired girl next to him gives him a welcoming smile, and he nods to her in acknowledgement as they settle down to listen to the lecture and prepare to take notes.

"Good morning, ladies and gentlemen," the well-presented lady in her late thirties addresses the students. "I am Dr Joanna McKenzie, and I will be your main consultant for your Scientific Study module. These are my colleagues Dr Gillian Lane and Dr Andrew Hamilton, both of whom will also be on call should you have any questions or require any assistance. The three of us will now split you into groups, and you will be presented with your subject matter for your study, and I strongly recommend that you nominate a chair person once you have been allocated your group. Can I please request that you be patient as there are over a hundred students present, so your allocation may take some time. Please bear with us."

The lecture theatre gradually empties as all the students leave in their groups to start work on their studies in the library. It is now Moose's turn to receive his subject matter and find out who his colleagues are. "Hello, ladies and gentlemen," Dr Hamilton greets the students who are seated in Moose's row. "One, two, three, four, you five are a group and your subject matter is 'Kenyan endurance athletes. Do they have an advantage?' Good luck."

"Fuck," Moose thinks to himself. "I haven't a bastard clue!" He looks at his peer group, which consists of three attractive girls: a blonde, a brunette and the red-head he met earlier as well as a tall, skinny boy with long, spiky red hair. The three girls look like deer caught in the headlights, and Moose imagines he does too, but the guy is smiling confidently. "How are you doing, folks?" the quietly-spoken boy greets his colleagues with a poetic British accent that Moose is struggling to place. "I'm Ronnie Buchanan."

Moose introduces himself and gives Ronnie and the three girls a firm handshake. "I'm Jan," says the blonde girl.

"Marty," smiles the redhead.

"My name's Betty," says the dark-haired girl.

"Where are you from, Ronnie?" asks Jan as she bats her eyes. "I *LOVE* your accent."

"Isle Of Skye, Scotland, hen," Ronnie laughs. "I'm here to make my fortune." This makes the three girls chuckle and even Moose can't help smiling.

"Folks, I know this stuff," Ronnie continues. "I compete in cross country and have had the misfortune of coming up against these Kenyan athletes at international level. They're just not human! If OK with all of you, I'll be chairman. I studied this very subject at school because it irked the Hell out of me. I'm a highlander and I *STILL* can't compete with these people!"

Moose is slightly peeved by Ronnie's boldness as he seized the role as chairman but, at the same time, he is relieved that somebody in the group is familiar with the subject. Ronnie proceeds to give each girl a small chapter of the subject to research then he comes to Moose. "Moose, your department is 'the effects of altitude in endurance training', and I will take 'safe acclimatisation in altitude training'," he concludes.

Noticing the worried expressions on his classmates' faces, Ronnie puts everyone at ease. "Don't worry, guys," he assures them. "Honestly, it sounds a lot worse than it is and I will tell you exactly where to look for your info because I still have everything noted from my high school study. Please, just beware of plagiarism and remember to reference absolutely everything. I'll give you all my phone number in case you run into any problems or have any other questions."

"What a nerd this guy is," Moose thinks to himself. "At the same time, I don't know whether to throw my arms around him or whether to punch him."

"If we all get tore into this together," Ronnie continues. "Our sections should be no more than 1500 words each. That's not much, right?"

"Yeah, that sounds manageable," replies Betty as the rest of the group nod in agreement.

"Bugger wasting the entire school year on this pish," says Ronnie. "I plan to be finished and have the whole lot typed up and handed in for just after Christmas at the very latest so we can spend our Monday afternoons in the Union sinking pints. Does that sound fair to you guys?"

"You know what, dude?" says Moose. "I'm into that. Why don't we check out the Union right now? I think we should relax a bit before we hit the books."

"Sounds good to me," exclaims Marty. "Let's go try some of these pints Ronnie is talking about."

The following weekend, Hell Freeze have time off performing having wowed the audiences of several sell-out gigs over the past few weeks. Rather than make the journey home, the trio decide to stay at their apartment and recharge their batteries as they feel that working long hours and seven-day weeks is getting to them.

As Moose feels he has energy to expel, he arranges to meet some of his classmates at the Union because there is a popular band from the university playing their very last gig before they break up. "Ladies and gentlemen," the middle-aged female band manager calls for everyone's attention. "For the very last time for their farewell gig, please welcome FLAMES!"

The four long-haired, leather-clad band members enter the stage, waving as they take their places and prepare to perform. "Hang on," Moose says to himself, surprised. "There's somebody I know! No, that can't possibly be right..."

Moose continues to listen to Flames perform. They are an excellent rock band and it is apparent that they have years of experience under their belts. They also have something that Hell Freeze are missing: a powerful, hard-hitting bass. Moose looks at the tall, slender figure of the bass player and he is surprised to realise that it is, in fact, nerdy Ronnie from Scientific Studies. "I'll catch him after the gig," Moose says to himself as he continues to enjoy the music and cheer them on.

After the gig Moose approaches the band manager, a maternal-looking lady who looks to be in her early forties, and asks for permission to speak to Ronnie. "Of course, honey," she smiles as she escorts him backstage.

"Hey, it's Moose," Ronnie laughs as he strides over and high-fives his classmate and gives him a firm handshake. "Great to see you here, pal. How are you doing, my man?"

"All the better for seeing you," says Moose as he gives Ronnie a few playful biffs. "That was a great gig. You guys sure know how to rock!"

"We're finished now, man," Ronnie says with sadness in his voice. "The lads are finding things tough trying to juggle studies, jobs, girlfriends and everything else that comes with being a student. I would love to keep playing but the guys are knackered and feel it would be best for us just to break up."

Moose looks over his shoulder at the lead singer who is now crying uncontrollably, mourning the demise of his music career as he is consoled by his manager. The poor boy looks frail, tired and ill. "That could easily be Angel and Carl," Moose thinks to himself. "I'll keep an eye on them."

Moose snaps back to the reality of Ronnie's predicament. "That's too bad, man," he sympathises. "What's on the cards for you now then?"

"Walmart or McDonalds it will need to be, pal," replies Ronnie. "I still have bills to pay and beer tokens to buy."

There is a few moments' silence.

"Ronnie," Moose says as he breaks the silence. "I'm in a band too, and we may very well have a vacancy..."

"Jesus, man," laughs Ronnie. "You're a right dark horse, you! I never had you down as the musical type."

"I'll never cut it as a singer with this voice but I hold my own with the electric guitar," Moose chuckles. "We don't have a bass player and you guys have that edge that we don't. There's one other tiny thing though. We have entered Band Stand-Off, and the competition is in November."

Ronnie's eyes widen. "We were going to enter that just before we all decided to call it a day," he cries.

"Listen, Ronnie," says Moose. "Why don't you come to mine tomorrow for dinner and meet my friend and my brother? My little brother is an amazing singer and guitar player and my friend Carl is a master when it comes to the drums. I make a mean lasagne and we always have beer in our fridge."

"You're on," smiles Ronnie. "See you tomorrow, pal. I'll look forward to meeting the lads."

Unable to contain his excitement, Moose wakes Angel and Carl as soon as he gets home. Both disheveled and yawning, they put on their bath robes and go into the living room to hear what Moose has to say.

"A BASS PLAYER?" Angel asks, his eyes wide with excitement and disbelief.

"Dude, we can't get those for love nor money," cries Carl. "This is the shit!"

"There is a downside though," says Moose, lowering his tone. "It's nerdy Ronnie from my class."

"That's the least of our worries," says Carl. "We can always kick him into shape if he starts any of his crap and tries to take over."

"Look, the main thing is that the guy can play," asserts Angel. "It might just give us the edge we need for this competition. He knows we've entered, right?"

"Yeah, he says he's ready," assures Moose. "Right, let's get to bed. We'll phone Papa Joe tomorrow and tell him."

The next morning, Carl phones his father to tell him about Hell Freeze's potential new addition. "It all seems too good to be true, son," says Papa Joe. "I've been on the look-out for a bass player since we took on Moose but to no avail. Can the boy definitely play bass guitar?"

"I've not met him yet, Dad," replies Carl. "He is in Moose's year at uni and his band have just broken up. He is shit hot, according to Moose."

"I'd like to meet him," says Papa Joe. "I'll see you all tonight. We are slowly sculpturing the perfect masterpiece in the form of this band."

That evening, Ronnie arrives at Hell Freeze's apartment having borrowed his roommate's car so that he could transport his bass guitar and amp. He is greeted on arrival by Moose who introduces him to Papa Joe, Angel and Carl. "Good to meet you, Ronnie," says Carl. "We actually work with a dude from your neck of the woods but he has the broadest accent in the world, and Angel and I still struggle to understand him sometimes."

"Make that most of the time," Angel laughs.

"Really?" asks Ronnie. "Is he from the Scottish highlands too?"

"He's from Glasgow and his name's Marc McLauchlan," Carl tells him. "Do you know him?"

Ronnie laughs out loud. "Well, for me to get to his place from my old folks' house, it would be about an hour in the car, a ferry trip, then about another two or three hours in the car, depending on the driving conditions, but chances are I'll know him to see among thousands of people!" All the guys laugh at this, and Ronnie continues to keep them amused with his tales of working on his parents' croft in Isle Of Skye to drunken nights in Glasgow with his friends to, gigging all over Scotland and his decision to migrate to the States with the help of his parents. By the time Papa Joe and the boys finish eating, their sides are sore from all the laughing at Ronnie's hilarious stories.

"Are you up for a jam, Ronnie?" Papa Joe asks with a cheeky smile.

"Och, aye, of course," replies Ronnie, enthusiastically.

Moose helps Ronnie into the living room with his guitar and amp and they begin to play. Angel smiles as Ronnie sings along with him to the three songs they had chosen to perform.

"Hey, that was amazing," cries Angel. "You can really sing too!"

"Thanks, big chap," smiles Ronnie. "I was backing vocalist for Flames, and I loved doing it."

"How would you feel about doing it for us?" Moose asks. "As

I've already told you, I'm no expert but I think your two voices harmonise really well together. What do you think, Carl?"

"Listen to you," Carl beams at Moose. "You've learned a lot in this really short time. Yeah, I totally agree with you, dude. I loved that audition."

"Ronnie," Papa Joe says with a serious, business-like tone. "We would *LOVE* you to come and work with us. You are an extremely talented young man, full of great stories and very funny. You will be an asset to our band."

"Welcome aboard, brother," smiles Moose as he gives Ronnie a playful slap on the back.

"How are you fixed for next weekend?" asks Papa Joe. "We have a gig, and we are sold out for Saturday *AND* Sunday."

"I'm well up for it," replies Ronnie. "If OK with you guys, I'll leave my kit here so we can rehearse when Moose and I finish our classes."

"Sounds like a plan, brother," smiles Carl as the quartet continues to discuss their future plans with Papa Joe.

After some more jamming and talks with Papa Joe, Ronnie bids his new bandmates and manager good night and heads for home. "Hey," Angel whispers to Moose. "Is this the same nerdy guy you were talking about? I think he's mad cool and I really want to go and see Glasgow more than ever now!"

"What can I say, bro?" replies Moose as he puts his hands up. "I got him very far wrong, and I can only apologise. I hope he sticks with us to the end."

Chapter 8:
The First Major Display

The weeks pass, and the young bandmates continue to fit their rehearsals and gigs in between their shifts at work, school days and studying. They finish another productive rehearsal night, and Angel fetches four beers from the fridge as they settle down to relax after practise.

"Not for me, brother," Ronnie yawns and stretches. "I need to hit the road and get to bed for uni tomorrow."

"Wait," says Carl. "Where do you stay?"

"I share an apartment with two guys from the other uni," replies Ronnie. "It's about a ten-minute walk from that one."

"That's miles away," exclaims Angel. "Moose?"

"We could make room for you here, bro," says Moose. "Angel, you and I could share and give Ronnie your room."

"Och, naw," Ronnie shakes his head. "I don't want to put you guys out."

"Honestly, you're not," replies Angel. "There's plenty of room here. You heard what Moose said. We don't mind sharing a room."

"Listen, dude," asserts Moose. "We have a very busy schedule, and you can do without the long drives and bike rides after after-classes and rehearsals. It's a very long day, and how long can you work a seven-day week like that? We're worried about your safety. What if, one of these nights, you crash your car or bike and don't make it home? How would we tell your old folks? Please think about it."

"OK, guys, you've convinced me," says Ronnie as he looks at Angel. "As long as you don't mind?"

"Definitely not," assures Angel. "We'll get everything organised during the week."

"Thanks, guys," smiles Ronnie. "That's another thing less to worry about."

It is now November and Hell Freeze have just under two weeks to get everything exactly right for Band Stand-Off. "We've done all we can possibly do," Moose assures his bandmates. "All we can do now is get out there and show them what we're made of."

On the Friday evening prior to competition weekend, Hell Freeze arrive at Papa Joe and Antonia's house to discuss final preparations. Even Ronnie's parents Donald and Margaret have made the trip from Scotland to support their son. "I never got the chance to tell you before you left," Donald tells Ronnie. "I am proud of you, son. I wish I had told you more often."

"No need, Da," assures Ronnie as he hugs his father. "You always said a lot more with your actions. The fact that you let me travel all this way to study and funded it, then turned out to support me says it all. By the way, me and the lads really appreciate you and Ma being here."

Hell Freeze are scheduled to play on the Saturday. They arrive in Papa Joe's van and three burly sound engineers help them set up their equipment on stage. It is now their turn to perform in front of the studio audience. "Best of luck, guys," the assistant whispers to them. "Get out there and blow them away!"

The crowd goes wild as Carl and Moose open with a hard-hitting beat and powerful guitar riff. They play three of their best songs, and the panel decides that they have heard enough to judge the band on; even the audience continues to cheer and cry out for more. "Hell Freeze, thank you," cries the middle-aged male presenter as he rises to his feet and claps his hands. His female co-presenters follow suit, and the audience keeps chanting, *"Hell Freeze, Hell Freeze, Hell Freeze."*

Happy with their performance, Hell Freeze exit the main stage and are greeted by the assistant who had helped them earlier. "Guys, that was awesome," she cries. "That was possibly the *BEST* performance we have seen this weekend so far!"

"Really?" asks Carl.

"You see that old man who stood up and clapped for you at the end?" she asked. "That's Giles. I have worked with him for ten years and have *NEVER* seen him genuinely smile that much. There will be a major injustice done if you guys don't, at least, get placed."

"Thank you," smiles Angel. "Here's hoping..."

After the show, the boys are reunited with their parents in the venue's restaurant. "Well done, boys," cries Papa Joe. "You did us all proud. That was the easy bit. Now for the hard bit: the waiting game."

"When do we find out, Dad?" asks Carl. "I forgot to ask."

"Next Saturday, son," replies Papa Joe. "It will take them all that time to count all the votes."

"Aw, man, that's a lifetime away," sighs Angel.

"Patience, baby, patience," soothes Maria as she hugs her son. "You'll get your turn. You'll see."

The week following does indeed feel like an eternity to the young musicians as they continue to concentrate on their studies as well as their main jobs in order to help the time pass quicker. The eve of the big show arrives and Moose, Angel and Carl make the bike ride to their parents' house. Rather than allow him to watch the results being broadcast alone, Papa Joe invites Ronnie to stay at his house for the weekend. Hell Freeze are understandably unable to sleep that night. It is now time for the main broadcast, and the Mancinis and Ronnie are watching at the Martinez's house. They all cheer with excitement as a thirty-second clip of Hell Freeze's performance is shown among some real star performances and some really dreadful ones as well as some young musicians completely falling apart due to nerves on stage. It is now time for the results. "Ladies and gentlemen," says Giles. "In third place, we have THE MARALYNS. Well done, ladies."

A minute-long clip is shown of a group consisting of three pretty teenaged blonde girls singing and dancing to a backing band.

"Tonight's runners-up are THE BAKER BROTHERS. Congratulations, gentlemen," says Giles as he presents a minute-long clip of their performance. The clip shows a well-groomed five-piece boy group aged from their teens to their early twenties sitting on tall bar stools as they sing along to a backing band.

"Now, ladies and gentlemen," Giles builds the excitement. "The moment you have *ALL* been waiting for..."

"Gawd, this is torture," Moose groans.

"THE WINNERS OF BAND STAND-OFF 1976 ARE... STYLISTS!! Well done, ladies and gentlemen," cheers Giles. A young quartet of two boys and two girls in their teens are shown for the duration of what they had performed on-stage at their audition. Again, the group played no musical instruments but sang and danced along to a backing band.

"Oh no," groans Moose as he looks at Ronnie, who is cupping his face in his hands.

"We didn't even get a mention..." whispers Ronnie.

Meanwhile, Angel and Carl are crying uncontrollably as their mothers, Margaret and Donald console them.

"Listen boys," says Papa Joe. "It was only one opportunity. ONE. I know it's difficult but try not to dwell on it too much. Right now is just not your time."

"What did we do wrong?" asks Angel through his tears. "We played the best we have ever done, and we had everything going for us. Everyone said they liked us. Did they lie?"

"NO, nobody lied," exclaims Moose as he jumps to his feet.

"Did anyone notice anything about the people who were placed?"

"I wasn't paying attention to be honest," replies Carl as he dries his tears, waiting for Moose to give a magical answer.

"They were all pretty boys and girls with not a musical instrument being played between them," indicates Moose. "Look at *US*. We are rough and rugged, we have our own on-stage characters *AND* we play our own musical instruments. Those guys and gals are pretty, polished dancing clones. No offence to them if people like that sort of thing but they are a completely different style to what we are."

"What are you saying, Moose?" asks Angel.

"Look at the likes of Thin Lizzy, the Rolling Stones, The Who and Black Sabbath," Moose continues. "*THOSE* are the guys we should be looking at for inspiration. As Papa Joe says, we have had *ONE* set-back and we'll probably have many more. Let's not let it get to us. We're just not what Soul Food Records are looking for. Does anyone remember She-Devil, the six girls who played just before us? Those girls gave it their all too, with all their talent. That dark-haired girl who was singing and playing the guitar was a dead ringer for Janis Joplin and the other five were shit-hot rock musicians too. I was actually worried about *THEM* beating us...even though I secretly wanted to..."

"Aye, Moose, we can imagine what you wanted to do," laughs Ronnie as he stands up and puts an arm around his broad shoulders. "If I'm honest, so did I!" Even Angel and Carl can't help laughing at this.

"*RONNIE*," gasps Margaret, surprised by her son's cheek as Donald lets out a loud guffaw.

"You're spot on, though, brother," Ronnie continues. "Nobody has said we're bad. In fact, we are drawing huge crowds everywhere we go. It will happen for us one day. We just need to keep plugging away. I just hope She-Devil and the rest of those great bands who auditioned and didn't get a mention are all bearing up alright..."

"That's the spirit, kids," cheers Papa Joe. "I am proud of you boys for what you have achieved. We may not be mega rich at the moment but people are getting to know who you are."

"The waiting game continues," smiles Maria. "You boys should be holding your heads high. You will get your turn, I promise."

"I'm tired," Angel yawns. "I'm having an early night. See you all in the morning, everyone. Night and God bless."

Moose gets up and mouths "night" to both families as he puts a strong arm around his brother's shoulders and guides him out.

"Good night, my darling Angelo and Mario," smiles Antonia. "See you tomorrow. Once again, we are proud of you. Please be proud of *YOURSELVES*."

The Mancinis arrive home to find that the phone is ringing. "Hello?" Maria answers. "Oh, hello, Yvonne. How are you?"

Angel looks at his mother, surprised. "Yes, they're very disappointed but definitely not for giving up," Maria continues her telephone conversation. "Oh, definitely...yes, that's exactly what my Mario said...yes, he's here...thanks so much, love... same to you...here he is." Maria hands the receiver to Angel.

"Hi, handsome. How are you doing, superstar" Yvonne cheers down the phone as Angel blushes. Moose notices this and chuckles to himself.

"Aw, I don't feel very super right now, Yvonne," Angel replies in a depressed tone. "I suppose you saw us play?"

"*I DID,*" exclaims Yvonne. "It looked like you played the performance of your life, and you and your band were definitely robbed. I doubt those so-called winners could do what you do live!"

"I suppose," replies Angel.

"Anyway, superstar," continues Yvonne. "I'm proud of you and so is Shaun. I'm glad you're at your mom's just now. Why don't you stay there for the week and I'll put you and Carl down for some holidays? You could do with recharging your batteries."

"That would be amazing, Yvonne, thanks," smiles Angel. "I'll tell Carl in the morning."

"You're very welcome, babe," replies Yvonne. "Oh, here's Shaun. Can you put your brother on, please?"

Angel passes the receiver to Moose. "How ya doin', big guy?" asks Shaun as Moose greets him.

"Aw I'm OK, thanks, boss," replies Moose. "I'm just gutted for my brother and his pal. After all, it's their gig."

"No, it's *YOUR* gig," asserts Shaun. "You're very much part of it, too now. Listen son, like Yvonne just told your brother, we are super proud of you guys. If OK with you, I'll give you this week off with full pay and I'll see you next week. The run-up to this competition must have been tough."

"Yeah, that would be great," smiles Moose. "I really appreciate it, boss. Thanks."

"Any time, dawg," replies Shaun. "Well, you enjoy the rest of your well-deserved break and I'll see you next week. As always, keep us posted on your upcoming gigs."

"Thanks, Shaun," says Moose as they conclude the phone call. "See you next week."

The following morning, the Mancinis arrive at the Martinez's house having been invited for breakfast which Ronnie is making in his own Scottish style. Antonia answers the door and the aroma of a combination of bacon and sausage meat wafts into the hallway, masking Antonia's cigarette smoke. "I'm barred from my own kitchen," giggles Antonia. "Come into the living room and let's not disturb the chef."

Everyone is chatting when Ronnie pops his head around the door. "Breakfast is served," he smiles. "C'mon give me a wee hand, lads." he signals for his bandmates to follow him.

The boys take plates of what looks like mountains of food and hand them to their parents before settling down with their own food.

"Ronnie, what *IS* this?" asks Moose.

"That, my old pal," replies Ronnie. "Is a good old fashioned full Scottish breakfast. We only eat this on Sundays as a special treat after mass. It's tradition in my country. The only thing missing is the black pudding because I couldn't get my hands on the ingredients."

Moose looks at his plate which contains a combination of bacon, fried egg, sausage, tomatoes, mushrooms, toast, baked beans and two other things he doesn't recognise. He holds up a well-fried, triangular piece of food. "Ronnie?" he asks.

"Tattie scone, pal," laughs Ronnie. "Just braw!"

"And this?" Angel points at a piece of square meat.

"Sausage, my man," replies Ronnie. "Square sausage. It's my wee Ma's own recipe. As they would say in Glasgow: cannae beat it! A roll and square sausage washed down with a glass bottle of Irn Bru is *THE* sworn hangover cure."

"This is just the shit," exclaims Carl. "Ronnie, you'll need to promise you'll take us on a tour of Glasgow when we hit the big time."

"Oh, I will," laughs Ronnie. "Don't worry about that."

As soon as they finish eating, everyone sits back to relax as they reflect on the past few weeks and what Papa Joe has planned for Hell Freeze next. The chat is disturbed by the phone ringing. "Yes?" Papa Joe answers the phone. "Yes, speaking," he says in a serious tone as he signals for Antonia to empty the living room.

Antonia feels herself turn pale as Papa Joe usually takes this tone when he is about to discipline one of his workers. Antonia leaves the door slightly ajar so that she can hear what is going on. "I see," Papa Joe continues his telephone conversation. "Oh, alright, I didn't realise that...Yes, I understand...tomorrow?...Yes, the boys are all here. They are very disappointed but I suppose we can't have it all ways... That's kind of you to say so, sir...I really appreciate what you're doing...Yes, I'll tell them and make sure they're ready... Thank you...Of course, see you tomorrow."

Papa Joe enters the kitchen where everyone, except Antonia, are chatting and laughing. "Come into the living room," he says, excitedly. "I have an important announcement."

"What's wrong, honey?" asks Antonia, nervously. "Has something happened at work."

"No, no, my love," smiles Papa Joe. "That was Giles on the phone."

"You mean Giles as in...?" asks Carl, his voice rising in pitch.

"Yes," Papa Joe nods. "He has requested that he come here tomorrow and meet with you guys. A friend of his, who owns an established record label, was in the studio audience the day you played and he is interested in giving you a deal along with two other acts he saw that day."

"What is the record label?" Angel asks quietly.

"Satanic Productions," replies Papa Joe. "I trust you boys know them?"

"That *CANNOT* be right," exclaims Carl. "They're huge!"

"Yes, son," smiles Papa Joe. "They only want the best! What I suggest, for now, is for you boys to relax and enjoy a chilled night. We'll see what this person has to say tomorrow."

"It all sounds too good to be true," says Angel, apprehensively. "I don't know who to trust anymore."

"It's a very fickle industry, baby," soothes Maria. "One day, everyone will love you. The next, nobody will know who you are. Strip everything back to when you were busking on the streets as Carl And Angel. Can you remember what you came home and told me one night when you got booed and came home with practically no money?"

"We'll have to take the rough with the smooth," Angel and Carl say in unison.

"Nothing has changed," Antonia chimes in as she stubs out her cigarette. "You boys know you're excellent at what you do. You just need to find the people who fully appreciate your work. The person from this record label is not making this visit for nothing. He means business so I suggest you all get a good night's sleep tonight and show him the REAL Hell Freeze when he comes here tomorrow. Just remember to take the rough with the smooth. You never know, it might just be ALL smooth tomorrow. Just be you."

The following afternoon, the Mancinis arrive at Papa Joe and Antonia's house where the three families wait patiently for their visitors. Eventually, they hear a car pull up outside the property and Papa Joe looks out of the window to investigate. Giles is helped out of the back passenger seat of a chauffeur-driven Limousine and an athletic, well-presented man, who looks to be in his mid to late thirties, emerges from the other side. The chauffeur gets out of the car and knocks on the door. "Goodness, it all looks very official," laughs Papa Joe as he goes to greet his visitors. Papa Joe enters the living room with his guests, where all three families are waiting, Hell Freeze sitting side-by-side on the three-seater sofa as they wait nervously to hear what the person from Satanic Productions has to offer them. "Good afternoon, ladies and gentlemen," Giles greets his audience. "Please allow me to introduce my friend and managing director of Satanic Productions, Mr Cameron Barrett."

"Good to meet you, Mr Barrett," says Papa Joe. "Thank you both very much for taking the time to come and meet with us."

"I have seen these magnificent boys perform live," Mr Barrett smiles warmly. "I can assure you the pleasure is all ours."

"Ladies and gentlemen," asserts Giles. "Before I hand you over to Mr Barrett, I feel it is my duty to apologise for any distress caused by Saturday's results. I am afraid they were out with my control which is why I endeavour to get Hell Freeze the fair treatment they deserve. Cameron."

"Thank you, Giles," Cameron smiles. "Also, thank you, Mr Martinez, for the opportunity. Boys, I cannot stress enough how impressed I was with your performance last week. Soul Food Records specialise in pop which is intended for much younger audiences, whereas you gentlemen appeal to a much wider market. At Satanic Productions, we work with artists of all age groups and genres include everything from hard-hitting pop to country to heavy metal. It would, therefore, give me great pleasure to offer you a record deal. Your prize will include a $750 cash prize as well as a trip to see Elvis Presley perform at Market Square Arena, Indianapolis."

"Is this real?" Angel whispers to Moose.

"Seems to be," replies Moose.

"Mr Martinez," continues Cameron. "As the band's manager, do you believe this sounds like a fair deal?"

"It's a far better deal than we expected, Mr Barrett," replies Papa Joe. "What do you think, boys?"

"Mr Barrett?" asks Carl, timidly. "Is there a catch?"

"Now you mention it," Cameron continues.

"Aw, naw," Ronnie whispers to Moose. "Here we go."

"There is something very minor," says Cameron. "Last Saturday, I saw several super-talented acts and I couldn't possibly stop at just one. I am also proposing to give contracts to two other young bands who auditioned last week: She-Devil and A.X.E. Do you know who they are?"

"Yes," exclaims Ronnie. "She-Devil played just before us and we were chatting to them in the waiting area and I've seen A.X.E play at different places ever since I moved here to study. I'm glad they're finally getting a shot too."

"Right," says Cameron. "Well you can see why my choice was difficult with three such talented acts playing back-to-back. Now for the catch, as you called it. These boys and girls will be accompanying you on your trip to Indianapolis when the time comes. I hope this isn't a problem?"

"No, no," cries Carl. "We'll be looking forward to catching up with She-Devil again! PARTY TIME IN INDIANAPOLIS!"

"Sorry, son," Cameron apologises. "There is one more catch. If management of She-Devil and A.X.E accept my offer, there will be a party of thirteen of you going on this trip. Unfortunately, as you are all under the age of twenty-one, we can't allow alcohol."

"That's cool," says Moose. "The main thing is that we have our contract. The other prizes are a bonus we didn't expect. One drink and I'm anybody's anyway..."

"Moose, you're anybody's anytime *WITHOUT* the drink," says Ronnie as the whole room falls apart with laughter at his unexpected cheek.

"It has been a pleasure doing business with all of you," says Cameron. "Welcome aboard, Hell Freeze. I'll look forward to working with you in the very near future."

Meanwhile, Ronnie is in serious, authoritarian mode as he is rushing to submit his projects for university before he goes home for Christmas break. "Come on, my man," he says to Moose. "I *REALLY* need your submission before I go home. Remember the promise we made ourselves?"

Moose grits his teeth but tries to think positively. He has been finding student-rockstar life tough, but, at the same time, he doesn't want to let either team down. "I'll have it for tomorrow, Ron," he says. "I promise."

Meanwhile, Ronnie gets on the phone to the three girls in order to try to hurry things along. Thankfully, all four students manage to write up their submissions and hand them to Ronnie just in time. He loads his things into Papa Joe's car and bids both families a Merry Christmas. "I'm sorry if I was an arse to you, Moose," he apologises. "I've borrowed my ma's typewriter and will have this all done quick smart. I hope this means we can kick back and relax now."

Moose squeezes Ronnie's shoulder. "No apologies needed, big guy," he reassures his friend. "You did a far better job than I ever could have, and the four of us really owe you big for this, whatever the result. Have a good rest and a whiskey on us, will you?"

"Sure, pal," replies Ronnie as he hugs Moose tight. "See you when I get back."

Christmas time seems to pass in a flash and Ronnie is no sooner home until the grind of work, study, rehearsals and gigs resumes.

Moose and Ronnie are both in their separate classes one morning when they are called to Dr McKenzie's office. Moose arrives to find that Ronnie and the three girls are already there, their faces white with fright. "What's going on?" asks Moose.

"The moment of truth," replies Jan. "We were first to submit our scientific study, and we get our final result today. Dr McKenzie wants to speak to us."

Just then, Dr McKenzie emerges from her office and the five students are struggling to read her body language.

"Good morning, ladies and gentlemen," Dr McKenzie greets them, her facial expression serious. "First of all, thank you for your submission and for being so prompt with it. It was a very challenging project, the biggest one you will do for this year."

The students continue to listen in anticipation and Moose can feel a bead of sweat rolling down his forehead as his stomach is churning.

"Secondly," Dr McKenzie continues as she begins to smile warmly. "Massive congratulations are in order. You have passed on your first attempt. Your submission was very well-presented, easy to follow and very thorough and informative. The five of you have scored an A plus for your group project."

All five students sit quietly for a moment before erupting into a loud cheer. Moose and Ronnie get up, pick Dr McKenzie up and whirl her around as the three girls laugh.

"It has been a pleasure being mentor to you five," smiles Dr McKenzie once everyone sits back down. "Once again, congratulations and I wish you all the best with the rest of your studies. If you require any assistance in any of your other subjects, please do not hesitate to come to me. My door is always open."

Chapter 9:
Creativity On Show

Having finally achieved their record deal which they have dreamt of for so long, Hell Freeze continue to study and work in their regular jobs as they continue to write and record new songs. The time has now come for the young band members to compile their very first album, "Rocket Launch". On one of their very rare weekends off from recordings and gigs, the boys go to their parents' houses for the weekend and Ronnie stays with Papa Joe,

Antonia and Carl as he has done for the past year now. Moose and Angel make their way to The Papa Joe's house to tune into the Top 100 Chart Show, having been advised by Cameron that their single "Power Through" had done really well. They all watch nervously as each song from massive artists all over the world is played. "Straight in at number eighty-nine," says the well-spoken presenter in his deep, smooth voice. "We have a group of young newcomers with their brand new single. Ladies and gentlemen, I give you Hell Freeze with 'Power Through.'"

Carl and Angel get up and storm out of the room with Carl slamming the door so hard that it almost comes off its hinges and go into Carl's room. "I can't believe the fuckin' bastard lied to us," yells Carl. "He said we did well and we didn't."

"I am so bloody angry," replies Angel. "I am sick, fed-up of being conned and taken for a fool. Fuck this shit, I ain't doin' it no more!"

"You ain't doing what no more?" Moose asks as he storms into the room. "Dude, you had *BETTER* not be talking about running out on us. We have come too far and achieved too much just to throw it all away."

"Our single flopped, bro," says Angel, fighting back the tears. "We've achieved damn all! I feel as though I have failed as a songwriter *AND* a performer. I just want to go to my job at Farrell's and forget about everything. It's just not for us."

"*YES IT IS,*" exclaims Ronnie. "Listen, pal. I have played in lots of different bands and played all over the place since I was just nine years old and I'm nineteen now. Never before has any band I have performed in had a song in the charts. *EVER!* Our single *DID NOT* bomb. That's our feet finally in the door now, even if it's by the toenails."

"Ronnie's right, bro," soothes Moose. "You need to remember we are just new to the industry."

"Moose, we're not new," wails Carl. "Me and Angel have been playing together for six whole years. That fucker Cameron lied to us. I feel so used…"

"Carl," Ronnie chimes in. "It might seem hard to believe but six years isn't long. People back home in Scotland don't know who I am. People even still walk past Moose and I with their noses in the air at uni and at work. What does that tell you?"

"We're shit," exclaims Angel.

"Make that *THE* shit," Moose corrects his brother. "What Ronnie is trying to tell you is that people don't even know who we are, yet we have a song in the charts."

"But what about our gigs?" asks Carl. "We are still selling out…"

"…which means we can't possibly be shit," replies Ronnie. "People who know who we are locally are buying our tickets because we put on a great show every God damn time! The next step is a big one for us. We need to prove ourselves nationally as well as globally as recording artists. We've not done that yet. The fact that enough people who don't even know us have heard our debut single, liked it and bought it so that it actually gets into the charts is *NOT* a fail. In fact, it's a big win! We just need to keep going."

"Oh, I never thought of it like that," says Angel as he begins to smile.

"Right," affirms Moose. "So forget about giving up. Yes, by all means go to work as usual but remember better things are coming. I promise. We still need to hear from Cameron about our royalties too."

"Fuck, I forgot about that," cries Carl as he jumps to his feet.

Just then Papa Joe, Maria and Antonia enter the room. "Are you boys alright," Maria asks, quietly.

"Never better, Mom," smiles Angel. *"WE HAVE A SONG IN THE CHARTS!!"*

Everyone cheers.

"That's a much better attitude," exclaims Papa Joe as he puts his arms around Angel and Carl. "Very proud manager and father here! Moose and Ronnie, what would I do without you boys? Bloody Hell, you're old for your ages!"

"You too," Moose replies with a cheeky smile as the room falls apart with laughter.

The next day, Cameron calls Papa Joe and Hell Freeze for a meeting in his office to discuss future plans for the band. Cameron's office is situated within a state-of-the-art building in the middle of the city centre. Papa Joe parks his car nervously as he observes all the classic cars parked in the car park. Manufacturers range from Mercedes to Jaguar to Porsche. *"WOW,"* enthuses Carl. "If this isn't a sign we are on our way up, I don't know what is!"

Papa Joe and the band take the glass elevator to the fourth floor where Cameron had said his office was and he is already waiting in the foyer. He greets Papa Joe with a firm handshake and then proceed to his office where he offers them all a freshly, brewed coffee.

"Good morning, gentlemen," Cameron greets his guests as they make themselves comfortable on the large, white leather sofas. "I think we can all agree that congratulations are in order on your recent chart success."

"We only got to number eighty-nine," exclaims Carl in confrontational mode.

"*CARLOS,*" hisses Papa Joe.

"Carl, my dear boy," soothes Cameron. "Number eighty-nine is a fantastic result! You need to remember that you haven't quite broken through as recording artists. Yes, you are great performers. I recruited you boys because I have faith in you. You are one of the most talented bands I have met in years, and I see numerous bands. 'Power Through' is the first single you have ever released and you have made it into the Top 100. That only ever happens once in a blue moon. You boys should be proud of yourselves. I know I am and so is your manager."

Papa Joe nods in agreement as Moose and Ronnie look at Carl and give him the thumbs up and Angel gently squeezes his friend's arm.

"What you boys should do now is take a well-earned rest from the music scene," Cameron continues. "I understand that the past few months have been brutal for you as you are not only producing music but working and studying too. Take a week or two off and I will get to work on compiling your first album. You have more than enough quality goods to do that now. Is that alright with you, Mr Martinez?"

"Definitely," concurs Papa Joe. "Thank you for your time, Mr Barrett. We will see you in a couple of weeks' time."

The following Monday, Angel and Carl return to their work, a late shift, at Farrell's Pharmaceuticals to be met with a welcoming reception complete with balloons, party poppers and a selection of food and drinks. "Congratulations on your chart success, guys," cries Yvonne as the rest of the workers cheer. "We are so proud of you!"

"Well done, bhoys," says Marc. "Whit a joab, man. Whit a fuckin' joab! I hope you remember us when you leave this place."

"It won't be for years yet," replies Angel, modestly. "How could we possibly forget you crazy lot, Marc?"

"TO HELL FREEZE," cheers Sharon as she pops open a bottle of champagne and the celebrations commence and continue throughout the shift.

By the end of the shift, Carl and Angel can barely stand unaided. "Dude, you're gonna need to drive us home," slurs Angel. "I'm totally shit-faced!"

"So am I, dude," replies Carl through his hiccups. "Let's phone Moose."

Just then, Yvonne enters the staff room. "Come on, superstars," she whispers. "I'll take you home."

Throughout the car journey, Carl chats excitedly to Yvonne while Angel sits in the back seat trying not to be sick as he feels his head swim. At last, Angel is relieved when Yvonne pulls up outside their apartment and bids both boys good night. Angel suddenly feels the colour drain from his face. "What's up, dude?" asks Carl.

"Carl," Angel says quietly, his voice rising in pitch. "I've pissed in the back of Yvonne's car! Oh, *FUCK*. I can't show my face at Farrell's again!"

Carl's legs buckle under him as he laughs hysterically at Angel's predicament. Hearing all the noise from the living room, Moose and Ronnie run out into the street to find Angel slumped against a lamppost and Carl on the ground still laughing. "I've had a little accident, bro," Angel whispers to Moose as he goes to give him a fireman's lift.

"Your secret's safe with me, kiddo," Moose chuckles as he signals to Ronnie to help him carry Angel indoors. Moose and Ronnie lie Angel on his bed and Moose goes back out and carries Carl in as though he is a child.

"What a bloody state to get into," laughs Ronnie.

"Damned apprentice rock stars, dude," replies Moose. "They've got a lot to learn."

The weeks pass and Hell Freeze continue with their lives as rock stars as they juggle, work, studying, gigs and recording. Meanwhile, they watch in anticipation as their single "Power Through" ascends in the charts. It is now May and it has reached number thirty-two. The revelation has given Moose and Ronnie the lift they need as they sit the exams that will determine whether or not they will be accepted into their final year of study.

A very busy May passes rapidly for both students and Ronnie meets up with Moose following his final exam and they go to the union for beers to celebrate finishing their exams. "How do you think you did?" Ronnie asks Moose, quietly.

"Hard to tell, dude," replies Moose. "This year just seemed too easy. I hope I've not missed anything out."

"I feel the same way," concurs Ronnie. "Surely somebody would have contacted us if something was missing?"

"You know, dude," says Moose. "This might just be our year. You know what's next? Elvis!"

"I'm buzzing, pal," smiles Ronnie. "It's all starting to feel real now!"

Chapter 10:
Inspiration or Stark Warning?

The time has finally arrived for Hell Freeze's long-awaited trip to Indianapolis to see one of their biggest inspirations, Elvis Presley, perform live. The band arrive at the airport with Papa Joe to meet up with A.X.E, She-Devil and their managers before their flight. They enter the lounge to find that A.X.E are already waiting with their manager and both parties greet each other and chat excitedly among themselves as they wait for She-Devil to arrive. Shortly afterwards, She-Devil run excitedly into the lounge as fast as they can and greet all the members of both bands. It is now time to board their plane.

"*WOW*, this is neat," exclaims Carl as they board their private jet. "I could get used to this!"

All the band members of the three bands make themselves comfortable on the large, white leather chairs of their magnificent aircraft and chat among themselves as they enjoy a selection of snacks, Pepsi and root beer provided by their hostess while Papa Joe and the other two managers indulge in whiskey and beers.

Following a short coach trip, the three bands and their managers arrive at their five-star hotel. Their host, a well-groomed gentleman in his thirties dressed in a tuxedo, escorts them to their rooms. The entire hotel is like a lap of luxury as they cross the white, marble floor of the magnificent foyer, which also hosts a water fountain, to the brass-framed glass elevator. Moose, an art enthusiast, looks in awe at all the original paintings from American and European artists that he recognises as they make their way along the corridor to their rooms. "Holy shit," he whispers to Ronnie. "I didn't expect all this!"

"I know, pal," replies Ronnie. "This will definitely be a once-in-a-lifetime opportunity for us to tell our old folks and future generations about!"

Even the rooms are impressive. Angel estimates that they are around the same size as his mother's cottage with each room comprising of a king-sized bed, television, an en-suite bathroom and every main wall decorated with dark blue velvet tiles.

The evening finally arrives for their long-awaited gig with Elvis Presley and Hell Freeze arrange to meet the members of the two other bands in the foyer. The boys dress smart but casually in their jeans and tee shirts as they make their way downstairs to meet with the other two bands who are all waiting already. They make their way to Market Square Arena on foot, chatting and laughing excitedly among themselves as they go to join the massive queue of hysterical Elvis fans.

After what feels like forever, the stewards finally open the doors allowing the hoards of dedicated Elvis fans to flood the arena. The members of all three bands hold onto each other in order not to be separated as they make their way as far to the front as possible. At last, they all find they have a great view of the stage although some young men and women in the audience are so overwhelmed with the excitement that they have to be carried out by first aid staff.

It is now time for Elvis to perform as he walks on stage, dressed in a white diamonte jumpsuit and cowboy boots as he waves to his fans. Everyone lets out a massively excited cheer and young fans scream as Elvis greets them. Moose, however, is ill at ease and is feeling nauseous and anxious in a way that he has never felt before. "Maybe it was the seafood I had at dinner," he thinks to himself as he tries to relax but to no avail.

Elvis opens his gig with a very energetic performance of "C.C Rider" as the crowd goes wild. Moose continues to watch his bandmates, who are all embroiled in the atmosphere, with one of the girls from She-Devil resisting the urge to faint as Carl and Angel prop her up. Moose tries his best to enjoy the gig as Elvis goes on to sing "I Got A Woman/Amen" followed by "Love Me" but he just can't relax because something feels very far wrong and he can't think what it is. He can see Carl and Angel are safe, as are all six girls from She-Devil as well as Ronnie and the three guys from A.X.E. "Everyone is OK except one person," Moose thinks to himself. "I don't feel well either."

Elvis continues with his breath-taking performance and Moose still can't enjoy it as he feels overwhelmed by feelings of anxiety and nausea. Elvis begins to sing "Fairytail" and appears to be looking at Moose as he does so. "I don't feel well," Moose whispers to Ronnie. "I'm going back to the hotel. Please keep an eye on Angel and Carl."

"You're walking out of an Elvis Presley gig?" hisses Ronnie. "Are you nuts?"

"Maybe I am, dude," replies Moose. "But I can't do this. Sorry. See you in the morning."

"OK, pal," says Ronnie. "I hope you feel better soon. See you in the morning."

Ronnie watches as Moose is ushered to the exit by a young, female first aider before continuing to enjoy Elvis' magnificent performance.

Moose gets back to his hotel room, immediately falls onto his bed and bursts into tears. "Everything about all of that was just wrong," he tells himself. *"SO* wrong!"

He composes himself enough to get on the phone to his mother. "Hello, son," Maria greets Moose as she answers the phone. "That was a short gig. Are you alright?"

"No, Mom, I'm not," replies Moose. "I just couldn't enjoy that gig. There is something very wrong with Elvis. The poor guy needs help."

"Oh my goodness," gasps Maria. "Listen, baby, I'm sure Mr Presley will get all the help he wants if he really needs it. All the best medical professionals will be looking out for him."

"I'm not sure about that one, Mom," replies Moose, as he tries to fight back the tears. "Elvis may be a millionaire but he looked so vulnerable, sick and lost on that stage. Yes, there will be medical professionals there but I'm not sure they have his best interests at heart because all they see are dollar signs as they give him drug after drug. Elvis was definitely not well and that gig should have been cancelled."

Moose can't hold back the tears anymore and he begins to cry uncontrollably. "My darling Mario," Maria soothes. "I'm sure you're reading to much into this."

"I'm not," sobs Moose. "Elvis Presley's days are numbered, Mom. I can feel it in my bones. That man is not being cared for properly. My real worry is that it could very well be Angel standing in those shoes one day."

"I doubt it," Maria tries to assure Moose. "Angel will always have you and I trust you will protect your brother throughout this journey, just as you have done since he was a baby. I still remember the day you held him for the very first time as soon as your father and I brought him home. I knew baby Angelo had a protector for life..."

"Yeah," Moose sighs.

"Listen, baby," soothes Maria. "Try to relax for the rest of tonight and try to put this concert to the back of your mind. I know it's hard because of what you have seen but try to trust the professionals. I'm sure Mr Presley will be looked after and that he appreciates all the love and support he gets from you and the rest of his fans."

"I hope so, Mom," replies Moose. "Good night and God bless. Love you and I can't wait to see you."

"Love you too, my darling Mario," replies Maria. "Good night, God bless and I'll see you very soon."

Exhausted from the stress of that night, Moose gets into bed, falls asleep almost immediately and begins to dream. "Help me, Moose," he can hear Angel slur as his tired, croaky voice fades to a whisper. An image of his painfully thin, sickly-looking brother flashes through his mind, his greasy, long hair hanging over his shoulders like rats' tails and his skin pale and dry. "Moose?" This time his brother's voice is louder, clearer and more prominent, followed by knocking. Moose sits up quickly as he hears the knocking continue. He opens his room door to be met by his young brother who, although looking very confused, is the picture of health with his long, shiny, dark curly hair, lightly tanned skin and naturally slim, athletic physique which he has grown to accept and enjoy. Relieved, Moose throws his arms around Angel, hugs him tight and pulls him into the room. "What happened, bro?" asks Angel, oblivious to what Moose had seen that night. "That was a once-in-a-lifetime chance to see Elvis Presley perform. Why did you walk out?"

"I just couldn't enjoy it," replies Moose. "Elvis is a very sick man and that gig should never have been allowed to go ahead."

"Come on, Moose," says Angel as he sits on the bed. "Elvis is surrounded by the best possible people taking care of him. OK, he may be a few pounds heavier but I suppose that's to be expected when you are older, eating on the go and can't get to the gym because you are on tour. Remember he is about the same age as our old folks..."

"No, Angel," Moose cuts his brother off. "I'm not talking about the weight because that's the least of his worries. He was sweating profusely, slurring his speech, he kept forgetting his words and he just wasn't his usual bubbly, happy self. Something's wrong..."

"Like I said, Moose," says Angel as he rolls his eyes. "He's probably tired from performing and touring and you know how hot it gets on-stage with all the lights. How many times have we had to perform shirtless for that reason? We'll probably see press coverage of him jogging with his personal trainer over the next few days once he's had a rest. You'll see!"

"I doubt it, dude," replies Moose. "I just don't see it and I feel sick to my stomach thinking about it..."

"Well I'm going to Carl's room for a few beers," Angel changes the subject as he realises that Moose has made up his mind. "Why don't you join us and cheer yourself up? You might even be in with a chance with one of the girls from She-Devil. That cute, little, blonde one *REALLY* likes you."

"It's tempting, pal, but no thanks," replies Moose. "I'm going to sleep and I just want to forget about that gig."

"Suit yourself," shrugs Angel as he heads for the door.

"Angel," Moose calls his brother back. "I'm sorry, kiddo. Please don't take anything from anyone. Do you know what I'm sayin'?"

Angel nods. "Night, bro," he whispers as he closes the door behind him.

The following day Hell Freeze return home and continue with their routine of work, recording and gigs. As they are still on their summer holidays having been accepted into their final year at university, Moose and Ronnie take on extra shifts at work in order to make up their money for bills and food.

One Tuesday night, Hell Freeze are chilling out before they get tore into their rehearsals for that evening. It is just before 4 p.m. and there is a news flash on television. **"ELVIS PRESLEY HAS DIED,"** the announcement rings out.

Moose feels his entire body go numb as he looks at his bandmates. Ronnie is sitting on the sofa with his head in his hands as Angel and Carl are crying uncontrollably. "Jesus Christ," Moose mutters to himself as he fights back his own tears. "I knew it. I bloody knew it!"

"Our Father who art in Heaven," Moose begins to pray as Ronnie joins in but Angel and Carl are unable to speak as they hang their heads and listen amid their sobs.

The death of Elvis Presley makes Moose and Ronnie all the more determined to protect their younger bandmates as they continue their own journey in the world of rock and roll.

Meanwhile, Hell Freeze see their own success improve as their debut single, "Power Through" peaks at number thirty-two in the charts. "Excellent result, boys," enthuses Papa Joe. "It's been a challenging year for you but you're getting your rewards. Here's to many more in the future."

As a special treat for Ronnie, Papa Joe and Antonia invite his parents over for Christmas. "I really can't thank you enough for everything, Papa Joe and Antonia," says Ronnie.

"Your parents are very much a part of this too, darling," replies Antonia. "We appreciate that it's difficult for them as they are so far away. We are trying to keep them in the loop as much as possible. After all, their boy is our superstar bass player."

"We should definitely do Glasgow for Christmas and New Year next year," enthuses Ronnie. "The Glasgow folk know how to party and you will all love it!"

"Whit a joab, man," shouts Carl. "Whit a fuckin' joab!"

"What?" Papa Joe and Antonia ask in unison as Ronnie laughs.

Chapter 11:
Engineering In The Works

The year following the demise of Elvis Presley proves to be a struggle for the four young bandmates, especially Moose and Ronnie, who are preparing to graduate from university. Ronnie is quietly confident that he will pass everything, although Moose admits that this year has been mentally, emotionally and physically challenging.

Realising just how fatigued his bandmates are, Papa Joe lightens their workload as he organises fewer gigs and urges them not to make the long journey home. By now, the bandmates have all acquired their driving licences and still insist on going to see their parents at the weekends.

It has now come to the final hurdle for Moose and Ronnie as they submit the last of their assignments and finish their exams. Moose walks to the university and anxiously waits outside the hall where the final exams are being held as Ronnie finishes up.

Visibly sweating, Ronnie finally emerges from the hall having finished his Immunology exam. "How did you get on, dude?" asks Moose, nervously.

"A Hell of a lot better than I thought," replies Ronnie. "*TOO* well, in fact."

"Well, we've both done it now," affirms Moose as he rubs

Ronnie's back. "All we can do now is wait. Come on. Let's go to the union."

Determined to take their minds off their pending results, Moose and Ronnie ask Papa Joe for more work. Surprised by the request, Papa Joe happily obliges.

Hell Freeze arrive back at their apartment one Sunday evening following a weekend of successful gigs with Papa Joe to find two A4 envelopes lying on the doormat addressed to "Mr Mario Mancini" and "Mr Ronald Buchanan." The young men lift their envelopes and Angel and Carl watch, nervously, as Moose and Ronnie go to their bedrooms. After what feels like an eternity, they exit their rooms with blank expressions on their faces. "Well?" Ronnie asks with a faint smile shining though.

"*I PASSED,*" Moose yells, excitedly.

"*SO DID I,*" cheers Ronnie as he dances around the hallway with his bandmates.

"*FUCK, YEAH,*" the four of them shout in unison.

"Next up, *GRADUATION,*" laughs Ronnie. "*WE HAVE OUR DEGREES!*"

It is now prom night and Moose and Ronnie are getting ready as they get showered and iron their best suits. "*WOW,*" gasps Carl. "You guys are lookin' mighty sharp!"

"Thanks, dude," replies Moose. "Is Angel not up yet?"

"Nah, he volunteered to work overnight tonight," sighs Carl. "It's the annual night audit and I suppose he couldn't resist the double money. I'll wake him after I drop you guys off."

"You're a pal, Carl," smiles Ronnie. "Thanks a lot."

Having picked up their awards, Moose and Ronnie return their mortar boards and gowns and go to the huge assembly hall where refreshments are being served and is being used as a temporary dance floor. The new graduates buy their first drinks of the night and observe the hall, which is packed with other ecstatic graduates dancing, chatting and drinking. Moose is scanning the room when he spots a table. "Hey, Ronnie," he whispers. "There's a couple of empty seats over there. Let's go ask those girls if we can join them."

Before Ronnie has a chance to reply Moose is striding over to the table which is already being occupied by two tall, stunning girls, one blonde and one brunette. "Good evening, ladies," Moose greets them. "Are these seats taken?"

"Yes, they are," replies the brunette in a deep, husky but very sexy voice. "By you two cuties! How are you doing?"

"Hey, thanks," laughs Moose. "They call me Moose and this is my good pal Ronnie, our oracle who has come all the way from the Scottish highlands."

"Good to meet you," the blonde girl smiles sweetly. "I'm Debbie and this is Andrea. We are so looking forward to this night after all the grind of the exams!"

Ronnie can't take his eyes off Debbie. "She's stunning," he thinks to himself.

"What are you girls drinking?" asks Ronnie.

"Vodka and orange for me, please," replies Andrea.

"Come on," says Debbie. "I'll help you, honey."

Ronnie and Debbie continue to chat as they go to collect their drinks while Moose stays at the table and chats to Andrea. "Debbie is not only very beautiful, she is so easy to talk to," Ronnie says to himself. "I hope I can see her again."

After several drinks, the four are in good spirits as they dance the night away. Andrea, who is significantly taller than Moose, holds him close as she tilts his chin upwards to kiss him and he allows it to happen. Moose looks out of his peripheral vision and notices that Ronnie is having the same luck with Debbie.

"Do you wanna split, baby?" Andrea whispers as she winks at Moose.

"Yeah," smiles Moose.

He goes into his shirt pocket, takes out a ten dollar bill and presses it into the palm of Ronnie's hand. "Here you go, dude," he winks at Ronnie. "Take that beautiful lady somewhere nice and enjoy your night."

"Cheers, pal," he smiles as he leads Debbie to the exit. "See you tomorrow."

"My roommates are out tonight," purrs Andrea. "Let's have a wicked time to ourselves! It's just a five-minute walk from here."

"Can't wait," enthuses Moose.

Finally, Moose and Andrea arrive at the two-storey house she shares with her three roommates. She closes the door behind her, pins Moose against the wall and they kiss passionately. "Let's go to bed," whispers Andrea. "It's more comfortable."

They head upstairs, stripping off as they go. "This is fuckin' amazing," Moose whispers between the kissing as he feels Andrea's hands all over his body and they go on to have very well-needed, loud, energetic sex.

Meanwhile, Angel is working his nightshift at Farrell's when he feels his head swim. "Whit a joab, guys," Marc says in his usual motivational manner. "Whit a fuckin' jo...hey, Angel. Are you awright, mate? Yer no lookin' too clever."

"I'm sorry, Marc," groans Angel as he runs to the toilet. He just makes it before projectile vomiting into the toilet bowl then sits down. The other end isn't any better as he feels everything run from him and he feels as though he has been kicked full force in the stomach by a race horse as his head continues to spin. Angel sits for about ten minutes until he feels brave enough to stand up and go back to work. Marc is already waiting for him outside the men's toilets. "Get yersel' up the road, mate," Marc tells him. "You've done a lot the night and we'll manage the rest."

"I'm sorry, Marc," Angel apologises again. "I swear, I was fine when I came in."

"There's a lot of wee bugs gawn aboot the noo," assures Marc. "My missus and my two weans are no well either. Away hame tae yer bed and phone the work the morra if yer stull no well. Kin a get ye a taxi?"

"I'll be OK to drive, thanks, Marc," replies Angel. "Thanks for understanding. See you soon."

Back at Andrea's house, she and Moose are finishing their session. They share a shower before getting into bed and settling down, kissing as they go. They lie in bed and pull the duvet over themselves, which doesn't last long as it is a warm night and the body heat of the two fitness fanatics is not helping. They kick the duvet off and Andrea continues to spoon Moose as she entwines her legs and feet into his, occasionally kissing his muscular shoulder and the back of his neck until she falls asleep. Everything is just perfect. Moose closes his eyes and he can still very faintly smell Andrea's perfume. All of a sudden, Moose has the urge to look down as he hears Andrea's deep breathing as she sleeps. He looks down his naked, muscular body, at Andrea's large hand as it cups his pectoral muscle, at their toned legs and, finally, at their feet. "Fuck," Moose thinks to himself as he suddenly sobers up. "I don't exactly have small feet but her's...I gotta get outta here!"

He gently lifts Andrea's arm and slides off the bed and onto the floor as he plans his escape. He quietly opens the window, picks up his clothes, throws them out and puts on his boots to help his grip. Still naked, he begins to climb down the drain pipe.

Presently, Angel is driving home still feeling ill but confident enough that he's not going to throw up in their car or worse. He rounds the corner to be met with a very unusual sight as his headlights appear to highlight what looks like a very well-toned, bare backside. Sure enough there is a well-built, naked man descending the drain pipe of one of the nearby houses. Angel's heart is in his mouth as he pulls over and continues to watch. "If this guy falls, I'm gonna need to call an ambulance," he thinks to himself as he spots a call box outside one of the neighbouring houses.

At last, the muscular, long-haired man makes it onto the lawn safely. He looks up briefly, gathers his things then sprints towards the car. Angel is about to start the car and speed off when he suddenly realises something. "Wait," he gasps. "I know him!"

Just then, the naked man opens the passenger door, gets in and Angel immediately forgets how sick he is as he goes into hysterical laughter. "Oh my God, Moose," Angel shrieks. "The sights you see! I thought you were a burglar."

"Wise guy, eh?" growls Moose. "How many naked burglars have you seen in your time? Get out, I'm driving."

"By fuck you are," exclaims Angel. "You're totally shit-faced, bro. I'll drive. I want to get home in one piece!"

"Hey, man, fuck you," says Moose. "Do you want to be quick about the driving? It's damn cold."

"Can you please do us both a favour and put your clothes on?" asks Angel as he starts laughing uncontrollably again and continues to do so with tears in his eyes throughout the drive home.

Moose and Angel arrive home and Angel muffles his laughter in order not to disturb Carl. He finally calms himself down enough to ask Moose how he got himself into that predicament and about Ronnie's whereabouts. "Ronnie got lucky and won't be home tonight," Moose smiles warmly. "I'll tell you the rest tomorrow."

"Ronnie got lucky?" laughs Angel. "It looked like you had a lot of fun too!"

"It was OK," Moose replies, sheepishly. "Like I said, I'll fill you in later. Do me a favour, kid? Keep this between us, OK?"

"Alright, bro," Angel laughs quietly, now feeling a million

times better. "See you in the morning."

The following evening, Ronnie arrives home with Debbie in tow. "Hello again, Moose," she smiles as she hugs Moose and kisses him on the cheek. "Aw, I *LOVE* your apartment."

"Thanks," replies Ronnie. "It does the job for us. Please meet Angel and Carl, my other two bandmates and really great friends."

"Hi, guys," Debbie greets each of them with a firm handshake and a hug. "I can't believe I'm in Hell Freeze's apartment. I have followed you guys for years and you look even better close up. I must apologise, Moose. I'm afraid I didn't recognise you and Ronnie at the dance. I just wasn't expecting to see you there, of all places!"

The bandmates and Debbie continue to chat among themselves as Moose serves up some of his home-made tomato and basil soup. "This is absolutely delicious," enthuses Debbie. "I love to see men who do for themselves."

"Thanks, Debbie," smiles Moose. "So what were you studying at uni?"

"I was just coming to that," says Debbie. "My degree is in Technological Sciences with Sound Engineering."

"*WOW,*" Angel and Carl say in unison, pleasantly surprised.

"As Moose helped me get together with this one," Debbie continues as she hugs Ronnie. "I was thinking I could help you with your sound at your gigs as well as the set-up of your equipment. I even have my own van."

"That's fantastic," enthuses Moose. "Well, that side of it is neither our strong point nor Papa Joe's. We would love you to come and work with us. We just need to run it past our manager, although I have a feeling he will be delighted."

"I would be honoured, babe," says Debbie. "I already have lots of experience doing this kind of work and I love it. Being able to spend more time with Ronnie is an even better bonus."

Debbie gets up, lifts all the dirty soup bowls to take to the kitchen and Moose follows her. "Debbie," he whispers, looking sheepish.

"What's wrong, darling?" she asks.

"Um, Debbie," Moose says quietly. "I feel I need to apologise for what happened with Andrea the other night."

Debbie looks confused. "I didn't really know Andrea," replies Debbie. "I was only sitting next to her and we got chatting because we were both separated from our friends and I've not seen or heard from her since. Dare I ask what happened?"

"It's kind of embarrassing..." Moose begins.

"Babe," Debbie whispers. "If you had a problem getting it up, don't worry. These things happen to guys after a few drinks."

Moose lets out one of his childlike, gurgling laughs. "That part was fine and it was all going really well until..." Moose blushes and looks at the floor.

Debbie raises her eyebrows.

"We were lying relaxing in bed afterwards and I just happened to look down," Moose continues. "Debbie, I'm not exactly a small guy but that girl's hands and feet! Bloody Hell, they were MASSIVE compared to mine. She REALLY scared me and I had to escape. I climbed down the drain pipe in all my glory and poor Angel had the misfortune of seeing it all. He'll be traumatised for life, the poor boy! I'm so sorry..."

Debbie bursts out laughing, throws her arms around Moose and hugs him tight. "Aw, Moose, that's hilarious," she continues to laugh. "She did tell me she is a volleyball player just before you and Ronnie joined us. You should tell that story over our main course. It will give the guys a good laugh as it has made me laugh."

Moose and Debbie continue to chat and laugh as they serve up their main course of chicken in white wine sauce with a selection of vegetables.

The following week, Hell Freeze have a weekend of sold-out gigs in one of their local venues. Having informed Papa Joe of their new recruit, they help Debbie load up her van as they head for their parents' houses. After chatting with Debbie as everyone assembles at Maria's cottage, she is welcomed aboard by Papa Joe and Antonia happily agrees to accommodate her as well as Ronnie while they are there for gigs.

Papa Joe is impressed by how smart Debbie is with her set-ups with sound and lighting. From then on, she works hard as sound engineer and stage manager for Hell Freeze.

It is late one Sunday afternoon and Hell Freeze have just finished performing. Debbie gets to work immediately as she safely unplugs all the electrical equipment and dismantles it in record time. Papa Joe unlocks the van and the guys help Debbie carry all the heavy equipment into the back. "She's amazing," Papa Joe whispers to Carl. "She is an absolute whizz at everything I have struggled with over the years. I tell you, Debbie is an unexpected addition to our band but I'm not complaining."

"Right," Carl agrees. "Ronnie is a very lucky guy and we are lucky to have her. Talk about fate!"

Chapter 12:
Bright Days To Dark Days

After months of hard graft between live performances and recording in the studio, Hell Freeze finally see the production of their very first studio album. However, as the young band are still fairly unknown in the world of rock and roll, their debut album doesn't make it into the charts. "Take the rough with the smooth," Moose reminds his colleagues as Debbie smiles and gives him the thumbs up.

"Listen," says Debbie. "We're really not in that bad a place. You guys are building your reputation as a rock band, we are making not bad money considering people don't really know Hell Freeze yet, the three of us have our degrees and we all have work to go to."

"Spot on, Debbie," smiles Moose. "In fact, I have a job interview tomorrow."

"Oh, *WOW*," enthuses Angel. "Mom will be ecstatic if you get this job."

"WHEN," asserts Ronnie. "Not IF. Have faith, my friend."

Angel nods in agreement.

"Where is the interview for, Moose?" asks Carl

"Trojans' Fitness Gym in the town centre," replies Moose. "I really hope I get it."

"I might go with you and offer them my services," says Ronnie. "They might even have a room I can rent."

"It won't do any harm to try, babe," says Debbie. "People who work out regularly are always on the lookout for somebody who can fix their broken bodies. It would be ideal."

"Angel?" asks Ronnie. "Do you fancy trying out one of my treatments? I've just qualified as a Reiki master and am looking for bodies to practise on while I look for a job and I want to try out my new massage table. Come on. It's free."

"What exactly is that?" Angel asks, nervously.

"It's nothing to worry about, pal," assures Ronnie. "You're our leading man so I'm not going to hurt you. It's a treatment that involves minimal contact and you will be fully clothed apart from your shoes. I know you've been feeling under the weather recently so I thought this would be a nice one to heat you up and help you sleep."

"You're on," smiles Angel.

Ronnie closes the living room curtains and Moose, Debbie and Carl go to Carl's bedroom to watch T.V. while they wait for Ronnie to finish his treatment on Angel. Ronnie finishes the treatment to find that Angel has fallen asleep. "That was amazing," Angel yawns as he stirs. "I feel like a new man. Thanks, dude."

"You're welcome, pal," Ronnie says as his friendly smile suddenly turns wicked and he cracks his knuckles. "Right. Moose's turn."

Angel laughs as he gets up and calls Moose into the temporary treatment room.

"For you, my friend," Ronnie smiles at Moose. "A good old-fashioned sports massage. I'll do your full body."

"Just what I need," enthuses Moose. "I've been working hard in the gym now that I've finished uni."

"Right," says Ronnie. "Strip down to your underpants, lie face down on the table and cover yourself with a couple of towels."

Moose follows Ronnie's instructions and relaxes as he feels him remove a towel so he can start on his top half. Ronnie oils up his hands and smoothes it all over Moose's back, shoulders and arms before moving to his bottom half. "This isn't so bad,"

Moose thinks to himself.

"You're full of knots," Ronnie whispers. "I'm going to have to work deep to get rid of these bad boys. Here goes..."

Moose grimaces as he feels Ronnie run his elbow down one side of his back. This continues for what feels like an eternity as Debbie, Angel and Carl laugh at Moose's muffled screams which they can hear from across the hallway while Ronnie works all the way down his entire body to the soles of his feet.

Just over an hour later Ronnie oils up his hands again again gives Moose a final, relaxing full-body massage, during which he falls asleep. "Moose," Ronnie whispers into Moose's ear but he doesn't answer, which Ronnie is delighted with as Moose is a very light sleeper.

Happy with his work on two very different clients, Ronnie covers Moose with dry towels and leaves him to sleep before washing his hands to join his friends and girlfriend in Carl's room.

"I think I'll draw the line at Reiki treatments," Angel laughs.

"Ach you're a lot tougher than you think, pal," smiles Ronnie. "You're next for the sports massage."

"You'll get a job in no time," Angel smiles sweetly.

"Don't try to butter me up," laughs Ronnie as he rises to his feet. "I'm serious."

Just then Moose walks in yawning but smiling. "How are you feeling, brother?" asks Ronnie.

"Like a new man," smiles Moose. "Thanks, Ron. I can't wait for my next one."

"Bonkers," Carl shakes his head. "Stark bloody bonkers!"

The next day, Moose arrives at Trojans' Fitness Gym accompanied by Ronnie. They check in at reception where Barry the sales manager greets them and escorts them to the office where the interviews are being held. Moose waits with the other two young candidates who are already waiting and Ronnie goes to the cafe to wait until the manager is free. Moose looks at his competition who both look to be around his age. The first guy is tall, fair-haired and extremely muscular. He looks as though he could easily walk onto a stage and win any body-building competition of his choice. The other guy is very burly with Latin looks and Moose is struggling to figure out what his sport may be. A well-dressed, fit-looking man in his forties emerges from the office. "Good morning, gentlemen," the man greets the three candidates. "My name is Charles Davidson, owner of this fine establishment. Thank you very much for coming in and apologies for the slight delay. Please come into the office and have a chat."

They enter the office and Charles tells his candidates to help themselves to a cold drink from the fridge. "Please tell me a bit about yourselves," Charles smiles, warmly. He starts with the tall, fair-haired guy. "Hello everyone," he greets the group. "My name is Lukas Brietner. I only moved here to the U.S. from Austria having graduated with my degree in Health Sciences with Human nutrition. I'll be honest, I only began studying these subjects for my own benefit but the more I looked into other people's needs and behaviours, the more it made me want to coach and help others to a better quality of life. Bodybuilding is my forte when it comes to sports. I compete locally as well as worldwide and have won several awards. I hope I can continue to do so for years to come."

"Very interesting, Lukas," enthuses Charles. "I see you are hungry for success and the fact that you have the desire to drive others forward is an even bigger plus. What about you, son?" Charles looks at the young Latino man. "Hi, guys," he smiles warmly. "My name is Marco Pieraccini. I have taught different disciplines in martial arts, mainly to children, since I won my junior black belt in Karate when I was fourteen years old. I have also just graduated with my degree in Sports Sciences with Human Nutrition. I enjoy working out in the gym as I compete all over the United States and have also travelled to

Australia and the United Kingdom. I hope to open my own martial arts school one day."

"Thank you, Marco," smiles Charles as he looks at Moose. "Tell us a bit about yourself, son."

"Hi, everyone," says Moose with his warm but crooked smile. "My name is Mario Mancini but I go by the name Moose..."

"NO WAY," exclaims Marco as Charles raises his eyebrows. "You're that dude from Hell Freeze!"

"Yes..." smiles Moose nervously.

"Dude, you guys have *REALLY* got it going on," says Marco. "Your live shows are something else!"

"Definitely," says Charles. "I originally only bought tickets for your shows because it was my daughters who wanted to see you. Now I sneak out to buy the tickets for myself!"

The three guys laugh at this. "I'm kidding about the last bit, of course," smiles Charles. "I buy tickets for all of us. So what brings you to Trojans'?"

"Sports coaching and fitness training are my professions," says Moose. "My mom owns Ice Goddess Fitness Gym and I have helped her out with classes and personal training since I started studying. I only joined Hell Freeze as a favour for my little brother but then I got the bug..."

"Well, I would love to have you on board here at Trojans'," enthuses Charles as Lukas and Marco hang their heads. "Don't worry, guys. I want all three of you!"

All three of the young candidates' faces light up. "Congratulations, boys, and welcome aboard," says Charles. "I'll look forward to working with you and I hope the three of you will be friends."

"I hope so," smiles Lukas as he shakes hands with Moose and Marco. "Thank you so much for the opportunity, Charles."

"Thank you," Moose and Marco say in unison.

"Does anyone have any other questions?" asks Charles.

"I do," asserts Moose. "Do you plan to do sports massage or anything like that here in the future?"

"You are a step ahead of me, son," Charles laughs. "I was going to advertise for somebody to deliver those services as I have had a lot of enquiries this year alone. Do you know of anyone?"

"My friend is waiting in the cafe," says Moose. "We graduated at the same time. Ronnie's degree is in Physiotherapy with Immunology and he really knows his stuff. He's been picking up odd bits of work independently and he's looking for something permanent now."

"That's beautiful," exclaims Lukas. "If he starts here, it means I can book him instead of having to travel to the opposite end of town. I need *A LOT* of treatments!"

"Me too," Marco concurs.

"Lukas, Marco, Moose," Charles addresses his new recruits. "Thank you, again, for your time. I will look forward to working with you from Monday and also seeing what skills and services you can offer Trojans'. Moose, can you send your friend in now, please?"

"Thanks, Charles," Moose smiles warmly. "I'll go get him."

Satisfied with his interview with Ronnie, Charles recruits him as resident physiotherapist and masseur for Trojans' Fitness Gym.

The success stories don't stop there for Hell Freeze. It is six o'clock one Tuesday morning and the year is now 1982. Papa Joe receives a phone call at home. "Jose Martinez speaking," says Papa Joe in his serious business-like tone.

"Hello, Mr Martinez," says the caller. "It's Cameron Barrett."

"Greetings, Mr Barrett," replies Papa Joe. "To what do I owe the honour?"

"Mr Martinez," says Cameron. "I am calling you with some excellent tidings. Hell Freeze have gone straight into the charts at Number twelve with their latest single 'Intuition.' May I take this opportunity to congratulate you and your boys? That is an outstanding achievement!"

"It is indeed, Mr Barrett," smiles Papa Joe. "This is definitely cause for celebration. Thank you so much for the news and I trust we will see you very soon."

"Indeed," replies Cameron and they conclude their phone call.

Having received the news from Cameron, Papa Joe calls Hell Freeze's apartment to break it to whichever members he can get a hold of. "Hello," Debbie answers.

"Debbie, my darling," Papa Joe cheers down the phone. "How are you, my love?"

"I'm fine, thanks, Joe," replies Debbie. "Moose, Carl and Angel are out early and Ronnie and I are just getting ready for work now. More importantly, how are you and Aunt Antonia?"

"Antonia has a bit of a cough," says Papa Joe. "But it's winter time and I'm sure it will pass if she rests. My wife is a tough little lady."

"She is indeed," smiles Debbie. "She's amazing. Anyway, you're early this morning. Is everything alright?"

"More than alright, my baby girl," enthuses Papa Joe. "Hell Freeze have just gone into the charts at number twelve with 'Intuition'."

"That's fantastic news," gasps Debbie. "The guys will be ecstatic, especially Moose as it's his first ever composition."

"That boy is more talented then he gives himself credit for," says Papa Joe. "He has come into his own as a guitarist now he is proving himself as a very powerful songwriter along with the other three guys."

"I am so lucky to be sharing this journey with all of you," smiles Debbie. "Here, I'll let you talk to Ronnie."

Debbie kisses Ronnie before handing the receiver to him. Elated by the news, Ronnie and Debbie head for work. "There he is," cheers Marco as Ronnie enters the reception area at Trojans'. "Our other superstar has arrived!"

All the members of staff and all the gym members stop and cheer as Charles holds up Moose and Ronnie's arms. "This calls for a night out," exclaims Charles. "All members and staff members are invited. Having members of staff in the charts is a once-in-a-lifetime opportunity. Let's say this Saturday.

There will be a buffet and a free bar on us!"

Ronnie is over the moon but he can't help but notice that Moose looks solemn and he remains quiet for the remainder of his shift. Ronnie expresses his concerns to Lukas and Marco who agree that Moose has been unusually quiet since they got the news about the chart success very early on. Lukas watches as Moose finishes up his session with a personal training client and follows him into staff room. "Moose?" asks Lukas. "Is everything OK, my friend?"

"Of course," replies Moose with a weary smile.

"Surely you're not disappointed with the result of your single?" presses Lukas. "I think it's great after all your band's struggles and it will probably climb higher."

"I know, Lukas," replies Moose. "I'm happy. Really, I am."

"You don't look happy, my friend," says Lukas. "Is something bothering you? Come on, you can tell me in confidence. I promise, it won't go anywhere."

Moose sighs. "If you get a chance, Lukas," Moose replies. "Listen to the song, especially the lyrics. I'm gonna need to go home soon."

"Very cryptic," sighs Lukas. "Well, I'm here if you ever want to chat. In the mean time, try to enjoy your success. Once again, congratulations, my friend. I am beyond proud of you."

Lukas gives Moose a friendly, non-awkward hug before heading back to the gym floor to greet his next client.

In the week following, Debbie and the other bandmates of Hell Freeze are becoming increasingly concerned about Moose's behaviour. "I don't know what's gotten into him recently," Angel tells Debbie. "He is constantly on edge about everything and very clingy with me. Mom even called me at work to see if everything was alright here because Moose is constantly on the phone to her, Antonia and Papa Joe."

"I noticed he has been like that with me too, Angel," Carl nods. "Just as he was after the Elvis gig."

"He's a popular personal trainer at the gym and his classes

are constantly packed out," says Ronnie. "It could be that he is subconsciously stressed with the workload and the demands. I think we'll go to your folks' houses next weekend. It will do us all good to get away from work and relax."

"Yeah, I'm up for that," Carl agrees. "I'll look forward to it."

The following Friday evening, Debbie and the guys pack up the van and make their commute to Papa Joe and Maria's houses. Having arrived later than usual Moose and Angel bid Carl, Ronnie and Debbie a good night as they go to Maria's cottage. Moose is relieved to see his mother still looking strong, happy and in excellent health. He runs to her and gives her the tightest hug. "What's all this?" Maria asks, surprised.

"I've missed you so much, Mom," replies Moose. "I'm just glad to be home."

"I miss both of you too," replies Maria as she hugs Angel and kisses him on the cheek.

They sit up late chatting and Angel notices Moose is looking a lot more relaxed. "Thank God," Angel thinks to himself as he gets ready for bed and settles down to sleep. Moose, however, is still unable to sleep. Every time he feels himself beginning to drift off, something jolts him awake and he can't think what it is. He looks across the room at Angel who has long since fallen asleep and is singing softly, which he has done ever since Moose can remember. This has never bothered Moose as it gives him comfort knowing that his little brother is content and relaxed. Moose sighs with frustration at his own inability to sleep as he picks up a nutrition book and torch and reads until he eventually drifts off into a broken sleep.

At breakfast the following morning, Moose's anxiety is no better as he is constantly watching the clock so that he can go to Papa Joe's house. By now, Angel is getting irritated. "Will you calm the fuck down, dude?" he hisses at Moose. "You're spending too much time with them crazy, hippy yoga chicks. You're *REALLY* getting on my damn nerves with your yins and your yans or whatever the fuck they are!"

"I'm sorry, bro," Moose apologises. "Something just feels off..."

"What can possibly be off?" presses Angel. "We are doing well financially, we're riding Harley Davidsons, we have decent cars, great clothes and we are finally able to help Mom and Papa Joe do all those repairs and upgrades in their houses. We've never been so comfortable. I don't get it?"

"Are you ready, my loves?" Maria interrupts.

"Coming, Mom," replies Moose as they head for Papa Joe's house.

The Mancinis arrive at the Martinez's house to be met by the usual thick cloud of Antonia's cigarette smoke. "Ola," Antonia greets her friends in her typical cheery manner. "I'm just making the coffee. Please come in and make yourselves comfortable."

Maria and Angel go into the living room and Moose follows Antonia into the kitchen to help her with the coffee. Suddenly, Antonia erupts into violent coughing fit and Moose's entire body goes numb. He runs the water, pours a glass and gives it to Antonia.

"Thanks, my darling Mario," she says after taking a sip of the cold water. "Aaww, that's better. Here's a tip for you: *NEVER* shout at the T.V. when you're not completely over the flu!"

"Oh," Moose smiles as a feeling of relief washes over him and Antonia continues to giggle.

Both families enjoy a pleasant afternoon before deciding to go out for dinner. They are just heading out for the evening when Ronnie whispers in Moose's ear: "How are you feeling, brother?"

"A million times better, thanks, dude," Moose replies with his warm, crooked smile. "Maybe Angel is right. I need to stay away from them damn yoga girls. They're making me paranoid."

Ronnie playfully slaps Moose on the back as they both laugh and continue to walk to the nearby, family-run Italian restaurant for dinner as everyone else follows behind, chatting among themselves as they go.

The following week, Hell Freeze are elated to see 'Intuition' climb to number six in the charts then reach number one in the next few weeks in the U.K charts as well as the U.S charts. By now, people are getting to know Hell Freeze and they have several interviews lined up for television as well as popular teenage magazines. The band members, however, are still not confident enough in their future as full time musicians so they carry on doing their regular jobs. Charles is also delighted to see membership sales at Trojans' at an all-time high when people realise they can be trained by super-fit Moose or get a massage from Ronnie Buchanan. The future is currently looking brighter for everyone involved in the journey of Hell Freeze.

However, the elation of having a number-one single in the charts does not last long. It is now week seven of "Intuition" being at number one when Carl receives an unexpected mid-week phone call from his father. The conversation starts off happily as Carl is always pleased to hear from his father, to whom he has always felt inferior and like a burden due to his condition. Suddenly the conversation turns sour. "No, papá, no," says Carl as he breaks down in tears. "Por favor dime que están mintiendo. Por favor dime que están mintiendo!"

As the conversation continues in Spanish, Debbie and the bandmates get wind of Carl's heartbreaking news. Angel's legs buckle under him where he is standing as he bursts into tears, Debbie runs to pick him up and comforts him, Ronnie cries quietly to himself and Moose sits still and dumbstruck, unable to take in what he has just heard from the one-sided telephone conversation.

"Everyone, pack a bag and get them into the van," Debbie quietly commands the group. Moose and Ronnie guide Carl out, Debbie puts an arm around Angel as she supports him as they walk to the van and they head for Papa Joe and Maria's houses.

Moose reflects on what he has felt for such a long time. He knew something was wrong at home but he was unable to fathom what it was. Now he has his answer. Antonia has cancer, doctors are unable to do anything for her except make her as comfortable as possible in her final days and she is not expected to see her forty-third birthday. Moose sits at the back of the van where he thinks he will be neither seen nor heard and cries quietly to himself as he prepares for the worst of what is in store for the strong lady he classes as an aunt as well as a manager.

As soon as they arrive home, Hell Freeze go straight to the Martinez's house. A very distraught Maria greets them on arrival having been there since early morning comforting Papa Joe and helping to take care of Antonia, who is now very weak and sick.

"Call Farrell's and tell them what has happened," Moose advises Angel. Angel nods, composes himself as best as he can and gets on the phone to his workplace.

"Hello, superstar," Yvonne greets Angel cheerily as she answers the phone. "How are you, darling?"

"Not good," Angel breaks down and is unable to say anymore. Moose sits his brother down and takes the receiver from him.

"Hello, Yvonne, it's Mario," Moose continues the call. "I'm really sorry about that. We've just had some real bad news at home and Carl and Angel won't be at work this week."

"Goodness," replies Yvonne. "It's not like those two not to be at work. What has happened?"

"Carl's mom has been diagnosed with terminal cancer," Moose informs her. "She doesn't have long left."

"I'm so sorry, babe," sympathises Yvonne. "What a blow. Tell the boys not to worry about work and I'll sort all the finances from my end. If there is anything more Big Shaun and I can do, please get in touch with me again on this number. I send my deepest condolences to all of you at this time as I know how much Carl's mom means to you. Please take care, superstar."

"Thanks for everything, Yvonne," Moose says, relieved. "We really appreciate all you're doing for us and we owe you big. Please tell Big Shaun I said hello and that I'll catch him for a beer very soon."

"Will do, my love," replies Yvonne as they conclude the phone call. "Look after yourselves."

The weeks pass, and "Intuition" remains high in the charts. Everyone returns to work with the exception of Carl, who has been granted long-term leave so he can help his father and Maria care for Antonia.

Hell Freeze go back to their parents houses one more time in order to visit Antonia, hoping to see her in her final hours. They enter her bedroom and they are shocked at how unrecognisable she now looks. She is very small, frail and old. Her once thick, dark hair has now gone and she wears a head scarf to retain some heat. She wakes up on hearing the dulcet tones of everyone she has grown to love like a family and manages a smile, which doesn't quite reach her tired, deep, brown eyes and she beckons Moose and Angel forward. She pulls her oxygen mask down, looks them both in the eyes and manages to utter: "Please take good care of my baby."

"Yes, Aunt Antonia," says Moose, just retaining his composure and no more as Angel cries uncontrollably.

"Ronnie and Debbie," Antonia continues. "My adopted babies. Thank you for being there and bearing with us. My dear Maria, thank you for being a real friend and accepting us for who we are. Jose. Good night, my love. Stay strong and keep going for my baby. Carlos, my baby boy. Keep doing me proud. I love you all…"

Antonia closes her eyes and her laboured breathing finally

ceases. Moose removes her oxygen mask and pulls the bedsheet over her face as everyone cries quietly as they pray to themselves. Carl picks up Antonia's cigarettes and offers them around. Only Angel and Ronnie accept one as they go to the living room and light them up. Neither of them find their first cigarette pleasant but smoking, somehow, gives them comfort as they mourn Antonia's passing.

"I can't bear to stay in this house tonight," Papa Joe says quietly as they sit in the living room.

Moose looks at his mother. "Papa Joe," he says as he puts a strong arm around his shoulders. "Come back with us for a few weeks, even if it's just until after the funeral."

"Thanks, son," replies Papa Joe, relieved. "I'd like that."

Two weeks after Antonia's funeral, Papa Joe and Carl go back to work. "Are you sure you'll be alright, dude?" Angel asks Carl.

"I need to get back up sometime, bro," replies Carl. "I just want to take my mind off everything and get back on the road again as soon as possible. I promised my mom."

"Carl," says Angel, looking his friend in the eyes. "For what it's worth, you made your mom proud and let her see what you were really capable of. She was the first person to genuinely cheer us on when we played our first ever song together when it was just the two of us. You proved your dad wrong too. He really admires you for all you've achieved and for the man you have become."

"I don't know where I would be without you, Angel," Carl says as he begins to cry. "You were my first real friend and you never once abandoned me."

"Likewise," replies Angel. He puts an arm around his friend's shoulders as they both head for their shift at Farrell's.

The weeks roll into months and Papa Joe is still staying at Hell Freeze's apartment.

"I have a feeling your dad doesn't want to go home," Debbie tells Carl.

"He can't stay here forever," replies Carl. "I'll talk to him when he gets in tonight."

"Please don't," pleads Moose.

"What?" Carl asks surprised.

"Grief is a dreadful thing, Carl," says Moose. "My worry is that he goes back to that house and does something bloody stupid. I know he's working and powering through but what happens when he's alone and trapped in that house with his own thoughts and all the memories of your mom?"

"You've been hanging around them yoga girls again, you dirty devil," Carl laughs.

"I'm serious, Carl," Moose replies firmly. "We'll talk to your dad tonight. It's not as if we don't have room."

"I suppose," says Carl. "Thanks, Moose. You're a real friend."

"It's just not home anymore," Papa Joe says with sadness in his voice when discussing the current situation with the group over dinner.

"Why not just sell the house?" suggests Carl. "To be honest, I couldn't really face going back there either."

"I couldn't do that to you, son," Papa Joe shakes his head. "I don't want to be a burden."

"I'm with Carl, Joe," Debbie chimes in. "The house has been lying empty for months now and you clearly don't want to go back. You would be as well selling it and staying here permanently."

"Papa Joe," says Angel. "We're worried about you. Anyway, things are working fine as they are and Carl enjoys having you here."

"You're sure y'all don't mind?" Papa Joe asks, quietly.

"Never," says Moose. "Anyway, it will be better for my anxiety if I can keep an eye on you."

"You and them damn yoga girls," laughs Carl as Moose playfully wrestles him to the ground.

It is Halloween night and Hell Freeze get news from Papa Joe that they have been nominated for several awards for their number one single "Intuition." These include best new-comer, best breakthrough artist and best rock song and the entire event has to be televised just before Christmas.

Awards night arrives quickly and Papa Joe, Debbie and Hell Freeze get dressed in their best attire for their big night. Papa Joe drives them to the venue where they show their passes and are escorted to the VIP entrance. They enter the large, dark hall which is decorated with neon lights and are almost star struck as they observe the sea of famous faces of other huge stars who are already seated and awaiting news of their wins. Hell Freeze take their seats and are offered champagne and a selection of high quality snacks by staff.

A huge cheer erupts as a well-groomed middle-aged male presenter in a tuxedo takes to stage with his co-host, a willowy blonde woman in her mid to late twenties who wears an extravagant-looking, deep blue prom dress. "Ladies and gentleman," the male presenter greets his guests. "Welcome to our awards ceremony. May I take this opportunity to thank you all for turning out. I wish you all the very best of luck and I hope you enjoy your evening, whatever the results."

"First up," continues the stunning female presenter. "The nominations for Best New-Comer." Clips of five new bands, approximately twenty seconds long, are shown on the giant screen on stage.

"The Best-New Comer award goes to…," the male presenter builds the excitement as he opens the envelope. "HELL FREEZE!"

Debbie shrieks with delight as she kisses Ronnie and proceeds to congratulate the rest of her colleagues.

"What a start to the night," enthuses Carl. "At least we're not walking away empty-handed."

Hell Freeze enjoy the rest of the awards ceremony when the female presenter takes to the stage. "Next up," she smiles.

"Nominations for best breakthrough artist." Again, around a twenty-second clip is shown of five artists, including solo artists.

"The winner is…," the female presenter proceeds to open the envelope. "HELL FREEZE!"

"*FUCK*," exclaims Moose. "*TWO?*"

"You deserve them, honey," smiles Debbie as she squeezes Moose's muscular thigh. "Thousands of people have voted for you."

"Ladies and gentlemen," the male presenter calls for everyone's attention. "I give you the nominations for best song of 1982." He proceeds to play twenty-second clips of the five nominees.

The female presenter opens the envelope. "The winner is HELL FREEZE WITH 'INTUITION'."

The entire audience erupts in a massive cheer and Debbie hugs Moose and kisses him on the cheek.

"Ladies and gentlemen," the female presenter continues. "Performing their award-winning single live for you tonight, I give you Hell Freeze with 'Intuition'."

As Hell Freeze stride confidently up to the stage Moose looks over his shoulder, catches Debbie's eye and solemnly shakes his head.

The lights are turned down low as Hell Freeze perform for an excited studio audience. Moose watches as Angel, Carl and Ronnie give it their all and he is thankful that nobody is able to see his silent tears as he reflects on his reasoning behind his composition. Hell Freeze play the massive outro of 'Intuition' as the audience continues to cheer. Unknown to his bandmates, Moose walks off stage very quietly as he hopes nobody will notice. However, his actions do not go unnoticed by Debbie, who rushes backstage to talk to her colleague. She walks in to find Moose with his head in his hands. "Let it out, babe," she whispers as she pulls Moose close. "You've bottled all of this up for far too long."

"Debbie," Moose says quietly. "The whole Elvis Presley and Antonia instances. I saw them coming. I knew they were happening and it's still not any easier to deal with. I can't even enjoy the success of my own creation because of it."

"I know," whispers Debbie. "Just let everything go, babe. Let it out."

Moose holds onto Debbie as he continues to cry quietly as she consoles him. Debbie hugs Moose, allowing him to cry for a good while, before handing him a bottle of chilled water from the fridge which he gratefully accepts as he composes himself. Oblivious to the interaction between Moose and Debbie, Papa Joe and the rest of the bandmates join them backstage. "Are you young 'uns ready for the off?" asks Papa Joe.

Angel nods as he struggles to keep his balance and stay awake having drunk too much champagne.

"Thanks for everything tonight, Debbie," Moose smiles warmly. "You really are something else and we are so lucky to have you."

"You're very welcome, babe," soothes Debbie. "You did really well. Remember, having a good cry doesn't make you any less of a man. I hope you feel better now and will get a decent sleep tonight. I'm always here if you ever want to talk."

Moose nods with his genuine, warm smile as he picks his brother up and carries him out to Papa Joe's car in a fireman's lift.

Chapter 13:
Electric Feels

Having taken a break from recording and live gigs following Antonia's passing, Hell Freeze decides that now is the time to get back to recording and touring. The year is 1984, and popular music has changed drastically.

Angel and Carl are working away at their job in Farrell's when this song with a bold, hard-hitting keyboard synthesiser intro comes on the radio. "Aww, Sharon, can you please turn that up?" asks Carl.

Sharon smiles and happily obliges as she laughs heartily and dances along. "That's fuckin' crackin'," exclaims Marc. "Who is that?"

"I believe it's Van Halen, and the song is called 'Jump'," enthuses Carl. "I'm *REALLY* into that keyboard. It's an art form in itself!"

"Sure is," concurs Angel. "You got something in mind?"

"You bet," exclaims Carl.

From there, Hell Freeze start scouting for a potential keyboard player. "One of my presenters tells me his brother plays," says Papa Joe. "I've given our details to my presenter so please listen out for the phone if I'm not home."

"Sounds great, Dad," enthuses Carl. "I can't wait to meet him."

"I've got a brand new keyboard kit in the van," says Debbie. "It was bought by the management of another band I worked for when I was studying, but the band went through a very messy break-up, and the kit was never even opened. I've tried to send it back to them, but the manager won't return my calls."

"Ah, well," smiles Papa Joe. "That's a gain for us, sweetheart. I'll leave it in your capable hands."

The following afternoon, Ronnie finishes work early. He has a personal training session with Moose then he goes home so he can spend some time with Debbie. Ronnie and Debbie are cuddling up on the sofa when the phone rings. "I'll get it, babe," says Ronnie.

"Hello?" Ronnie answers. "Hiya, pal. How are you? Thanks for getting back to us... We're still looking, aye...Tomorrow night? Aye, that's perfect... That's smashing...Naw, naw, just yourself. We've got all the kit here and my girlfriend will have it all set up for you coming...She does all our sound and engineering and she does the work of *TEN* men...Looks as well as brains, aye…Ha ha ha, aye, well let's just say I'm a very lucky man... Alright, pal...See you tomorrow...Ta-ra for now."

"Nice work, darling," Debbie whispers as she cuddles up to Ronnie again. "I am so lucky to have you. I love you so much."

"I love you too, babe," says Ronnie. "Let's go to bed. We're going to be busy tomorrow."

"Let's," smiles Debbie as Ronnie leads her to their bedroom by the hand.

The following afternoon, Debbie comes home from work early and gets started on the set-up of equipment as she prepares for the arrival of Hell Freeze's potential new keyboard player. She opens several boxes and assembles the trio of keyboards onto their stands then realises that she has run out of plug sockets in the living room, which are already occupied by guitar amps and various pieces of sound equipment. She calls Angel in and asks him to wire up the plug of one final piece of equipment and plug it into the socket in the hallway and he happily obliges. Presently, Carl is taking Debbie's unused tools back to her van when a new red sports car pulls up outside the apartment block. The driver gets out and approaches Carl. He is a handsome guy with fair hair, tanned skin and he looks like he's into his fitness. He also must be at least six foot three because he is even taller than Ronnie. "Hello," the fair-haired guy greets Carl. "Are you Ronnie?"

"Ronnie's not home yet, dude," Carl informs him. "I'm Carl. Are you Finn?"

"Sure am," smiles Finn as he and Carl shake hands. "I'm here to audition for the keyboard player gig."

"That's awesome, big guy," smiles Carl. "Thanks for coming along. Please let yourself in and Debbie will sort you out with a drink. I'll be in shortly for a chat before your audition."

"Cheers, little dude," replies Finn as he enters the apartment.

Meanwhile, Angel is crouched down in the hallway with his back to the door as he wires up the plug like Debbie has asked him to and doesn't react when Finn enters the hallway because he is expecting it to be Carl. Instead, he remains focused on the job. Finn stares at Angel for a few moments as though he is a snack. He takes in his super trim, athletic body and his curly, dark hair which is cascading down to the middle of his back. He then proceeds to crouch down behind him, grabs his buttocks and whispers in his ear: "Hey, sexy. How about a steaming hot mug of coffee for your new man? Things could get hot and steamy between us, yeah?"

Shocked, Angel freezes for a minute as he digests what has just happened. *"WHAT THE FUCK ARE YOU DOING?"* yells Angel as he jumps to his feet and spins round. *"WHO THE HELL ARE YOU?"*

"Sorry, buddy," stammers Finn, who is equally as shocked to be faced by a man. "I just saw the long, curly hair and the cute, little, tight butt and thought you were Debbie."

"Well obviously I ain't," Angel snaps, his face red with rage and humiliation. "You clearly have no respect for a lady if that was your behaviour towards me. Anyway, you were told that Debbie is already spoken for so keep your dirty fuckin' mitts off, or else!"

Finn bursts out laughing when he realises who he is talking to. "Angel Mancini?" he continues to laugh. "Fuckin' Hell, dude, you are an even prettier boy in real life and you're cute when you're angry! I'm Finn. I'm here for the keyboard player gig."

Finn outstretches his hand to shake Angel's but he declines, looks Finn up and down with disgust and shakes his head. "Get out of my sight before I change my mind," he hisses angrily as he continues to glare at Finn. "The audition is in the living room and Debbie is waiting for you."

"Come on, kid, it was an honest mistake and you do have a great butt," laughs Finn.

"I don't swing that way and you are skating on *VERY* thin ice, pal," Angel replies. "I would strongly advise you not to say any more and to stay the Hell out of my way."

"Little faggot," Finn mutters under his breath as he turns to walk into the living room.

"Dick," Angel mutters simultaneously.

Angel shudders and goes back to what he was doing before he was interrupted by Finn. He plugs in what he believes is one of the keyboards and, suddenly, he hears a tremendous bang coming from the living room. Startled and believing the bang is related to the piece of equipment he has just plugged in, Angel bursts into the living room in a panic and sees Finn lying on the floor with his face in his hands. "What just happened?" Angel asks, wide eyed. "Was that me?"

"That, my darling, is what happens when you put your filthy hands where they don't belong," Debbie yells, angrily. "HOW DARE YOU? Now get out of here before you REALLY get hurt."

"You fuckin' whore," Finn mumbles as he scrambles to his feet, continuing to hold his face where Debbie had smacked him.

"Hey, don't speak that way to my girl," yells Angel as he gets ready to fight.

"What you gonna do, you little faggot?" Finn asks as he tries to intimidate Angel.

"He ain't gonna do anythin'," Moose shouts in his deep, gravelly voice. "But I sure as Hell will."

Moose takes off his leather jacket, throws it on the floor and Finn claps his eyes on his well developed fore arms and biceps. "Forget it," yells Finn. *"YOU'RE ALL FUCKIN' LOSERS."*

He locks eyes with Angel one last time. "See you later, you little faggot," he sneers before pouting at him and slamming the door on his way out.

"Are you both alright?" asks Moose.

"All fine, babe," smiles Debbie as she gently puts an arm around Angel's waist. "That was eventful though!"

"And how," exclaims Angel as he grimaces. "I won't be able to sit down for a month now. That guy has hands like cast iron vices. My butt cheeks will be black and blue because of how hard he grabbed them. I feel violated!"

"WHAT?" asks Moose, wide-eyed.

"It ain't what it sounds like, bro," Angel says, sheepishly. "He came up behind me and groped me because he thought I was Debbie."

"DIRTY BASTARD," Moose curses. "I hope the damage ain't too bad, kiddo."

"Aaww, babe, I'm so sorry," Debbie apologises as she gently hugs Angel. "Thanks for saving me. Honestly, though, are you OK?"

"I'll be cool, thanks, sister and you did most of that yourself," Angel winks at Debbie. "Thanks for getting rid of him. We'll start looking for keyboard players again tomorrow."

"Oh wait," smiles Debbie as Carl and Ronnie join the group. "There's a girl at my work who says she plays. I'll get her in tomorrow."

"Good shout, Debbie," Angel laughs nervously as he lies on the floor on his front. "At least she'll be a bit more gentle if she decides she wants to grope me!"

"What did we miss?" laughs Carl. "Did you finally get lucky, Angel?"

"Very *UNLUCKY* that time, bro," scowls Angel. "It will certainly be an interesting dinnertime convo!"

The following evening, Debbie arrives home with her work colleague who had claimed to play keyboards. This audition proves to be another disaster as the young girl plays a selection of nursery rhymes as she sings out of tune. "I take it this is only your warm-up?" asks Debbie.

"That's all I know just now," smiles the young woman. "But I thought you guys could teach me to play. What an honour it would be to be trained by Hell Freeze."

"Sorry, ma'am," says Carl. "We need somebody who knows what they're doing. We have neither the time nor the resources to train anyone up."

"Your loss," the girl shrugs as she walks out.

In the week following, Hell Freeze go on to see several other auditions with not a single candidate being suited to the position.

"This is no use," Debbie sighs, dismayed.

"Don't sweat it, sister," soothes Angel. "Carl and I will put an ad into the university on Monday after work. There are a lot of talented kids there and we're sure to find somebody who can play."

The following Tuesday evening, Papa Joe, Debbie and Hell Freeze are having dinner when the phone rings. Only Moose is absent as he is teaching evening classes at work. "Hello?" Debbie answers the phone with her fingers crossed. She furrows her brow and looks more and more confused as she listens to what the caller has to say.

"Sorry to interrupt," Debbie apologises. "Can you please hang on? I'll let you speak to my partner."

"What's wrong, babe?" asks Ronnie.

"It's a guy from the uni phoning about the keyboard position," says Debbie as she covers the mouthpiece. "But I can't understand a damn word. I think he's from your neck of the woods."

Ronnie laughs and takes over as Angel and Carl exchange

looks.

"Hello, this is Ronnie speaking," he greets the caller. "Aye? When did you move here?"

There is a few moments' silence as Ronnie listens, looking hopeful. "That sounds smashing, pal. What are you doing at uni? LAW and you say you've done all this before?...Aye, aye, I like the sound of that...Och, aye! When can you come in?... Tomorrow night is good for us if it's good for you...Awright, pal, see you tomorrow...Naw, we've got everything here...Ha ha ha, *LOVE IT*...Thanks, ma man...See you then."

Ronnie chuckles as he concludes the phone call. "Well?" Papa Joe asks, nervously.

"I have a great feeling about this one," Ronnie tells the group as he rubs his hands together. "His name is Willie McLarnon and he is studying law. He says he was in a band back home and he only left when he moved here at the beginning of the year. He's a Glasgow lad so I'm sure we'll have great fun with him."

"Wait," says Angel. "A Glasgow guy who is studying law who is an experienced keyboard player? Sounds too good to be true…"

"Aye," enthuses Ronnie. "I can't wait to meet him."

"Whit a joab, man," Carl cheers. "Whit a fuckin' joab?"

Papa Joe looks confused. "I beg your pardon?" asks Debbie as Carl, Ronnie and Angel laugh.

The following evening, the entire band insist on being present for Willie's audition in case of any further altercations. They hear a motorbike pull up outside and Moose and Angel go to the window to investigate. The small, slightly-built motorcyclist dismounts from a modern Harley Davidson and removes his helmet, allowing his long, dark hair to cascade down his back and shoulders. He looks very like Carl from a distance. Noticing Moose and Angel at the window, he smiles and waves as he makes his way to the door. "It's him," Moose smiles as Ronnie goes to welcome another hopeful.

"How ya doin', big chap?" the baby-faced biker greets Ronnie with a very cheery manner and a hearty laugh. Angel and Carl nod and exchange knowing smiles.

"Meet Willie McLarnon, everyone," Ronnie introduces their potential new recruit. "He has come all the way here to study from Glasgow."

"Sorry, pal," Willie shakes his head as he laughs. "The names Wullie. They have Willies in England and in Edinburgh, where they speak with their wee Glasgow Uni accents. We speak properly in Glasgow so we have Wullies."

Wullie buckles with laughter when he notices that Carl and Angel are laughing hysterically at what Marc would call "the Glesga banter."

"On a serious note, Willie, sorry Wullie," says Moose as he tries to compose himself. "How old are you and what brings you to the U.S?"

Wullie's demeanour changes and he is now solemn. "I'm twenty years old, my man," says Wullie. "My wee ma died a few months back after years of ill health and my da thought it would be a good idea to bring the weans here for a fresh start. Losing a parent creates a massive wound that never heals, no matter how well-prepared you think you are…"

"Sorry, dude," Carl says quietly as he fights back the tears. "I've been there too. My mom died two years ago and the pain is still fresh. On a lighter note, I hope you and your family are settling well here. You say you have kids already?"

"Naw, naw, pal," Wullie snaps back to his cheery self as he laughs heartily. "I'm here with my da, my three wee brothers and my wee sister. My plan was to help my da with the weans but they're good kids. They're settling down and doing well here so it doesn't look like they need me after all, which means I can kick back and enjoy life here as well. I'll occasionally need to take my wee sister while my da and my wee brother Tommy work and the other two are at school but she's nae bother. She's six years old going on twenty-six and can play those keyboards as well as me. I swear she's been here before!"

Debbie and the bandmates look at each other in disbelief at that statement. "So she might even replace you when you retire, Wullie?" laughs Moose.

"She could very well, my man," replies Wullie with his usual hearty laugh. "She could very well!"

"Speaking of which," says Debbie. "Are you up for showing us your stuff?"

"Aye, certainly, doll," replies Wullie. "Angel, I'm not much of a singer, pal. Do you fancy helping me?"

"It would be an honour, dude," smiles Angel. "What's the song?"

"A recent chart-topper," laughs Wullie. "You'll know it when I start playing."

"Alright," exclaims Angel as he now feels he trusts Wullie.

Wullie sits down at the keyboard kit and everyone's faces light up as they recognise the famous synthesiser intro. Angel smiles and gives Wullie the thumbs up as he begins to sing the lyrics to "Jump" by Van Halen. Angel and Wullie finish performing their cover and the rest of the band cheers. "Right," smiles Wullie as he claps his hands. "There's no keyboard input in this one yet so I am going to improvise if you could all please bear with me."

Angel recognises the song as Ronnie's composition "Blood, Sweat, Tears" as soon as he hears Wullie play his improvised keyboard intro. It was another Hell Freeze creation that had done well in the charts. Angel picks up his guitar and signals for Carl, Moose and Ronnie to take their places. Delighted with their modified version of an already popular song, the entire band, Papa Joe and Debbie let out a huge cheer. "Whit a joab, man," Carl cheers.

"*WHIT A FUCKIN' JOAB*," Carl and Angel exclaim in unison.

"*YAAAAAASSSS*," cheers Wullie as he runs up to Angel, hugs him and buries his face in his chest before looking up at him. "You guys even speak the lingo. That's crackin'!"

"Well, son," beams Papa Joe. "You've gone your mile today

and really proved yourself. You sure know your stuff, you're very versatile and we would be honoured to have you on board with us."

"Thanks, Mr Martinez," says Wullie with his hearty laugh.

"Please, Willie," smiles Papa Joe. "It's Joe from now on. We're all friends here."

"Sound, Joe," replies Wullie. "On one condition though..."

"What's that, son?" asks Papa Joe.

"It's Wullie," he then buckles with laughter, as do Debbie and the rest of the band.

"That was a great audition, Wullie," exclaims Papa Joe. "The gig's yours if you want it."

"Definitely, Gaffer," laughs Wullie. "I'm looking forward to working with you all. Anyway, good people, I really need to use your toilet before I hit the road. Do you mind if I...?"

"Go to the bottom of the lobby and turn left, son," says Papa Joe.

"Aw, cheers," laughs Wullie. "Two wee seconds, folks."

"Sorry, kids," Papa Joe apologises as he covers his mouth. "I just gave the boy the gig without even consulting with all of you."

"Fine by us," smiles Debbie. "The guy is definitely the best keyboard player I have ever seen in all my years of experience in the business. I think he's fantastic and very funny."

"So it's decided then?" smiles Moose.

"Aye," replies Ronnie as Carl and Angel nod in agreement. "We can't go far wrong with this one."

Wullie bursts back into the room and gives another of his hearty laughs. "Right, lads and lassies," he says as he claps his hands. "It's getting late and I have uni in the morning. Thanks for having me."

"No, thank *YOU*," exclaims Papa Joe. "The pleasure is all ours. Are you making rehearsals tomorrow night, my boy?"

"I sure am, Gaffer," laughs Wullie as he puts on his leathers and picks up his helmet. "I'm looking forward to it. See you all tomorrow after uni."

"Just one thing, young 'uns," Papa Joe says, looking confused as Wullie closes the door. "I'm struggling a bit with the language barrier. What is 'Whit a fuckin' joab'?"

From then on, Hell Freeze become a five-piece as keyboard extraordinaire Wullie officially joins the band.

Chapter 14:
Touring Further Afield

The year following Wullie's recruitment passes in what feels like the blink of an eye as Hell Freeze manage to produce three top ten singles as well as entering the album charts with their new album 'Adrenaline Rush' at number fifteen before peeking at number six. The bandmates are even more excited that Papa Joe has gigs lined up in the United Kingdom due to great demand from British fans. "Have you guys toured in the U.K. before?" asks Wullie.

"No," replies Carl. "The good people of the UK had no idea who we were until fairly recently, now there is a demand for live gigs and they are buying our records. We must have done something right and it looks like we're finally getting to see Glasgow."

"Now that is one weekend I'm looking forward to," exclaims Wullie with his trademark hearty laugh. "They say that if you can get accepted in Glasgow, you will be accepted anywhere."

"It's definitely one of the best places I've ever played," Ronnie nods in agreement. "The last time I was there, we did the Barrowland. What a night! I thought the guys and I were never getting off that stage!"

"I can't believe it is finally happening," enthuses Angel. *"GREAT BRITAIN, HERE WE COME!"*

"Gaffer," says Wullie, hesitantly. "I'm worried about getting away from uni for the tour. The last thing I want is to let you guys down, especially as I'm just in the door."

"Don't worry about it, son," assures Papa Joe. "You're not the first student we've had on board with us. I've arranged the U.K tour dates for when you're on your summer break, the same as when Ronnie and Moose were studying."

"Aw," Wullie says with one of his hearty laughs. "That's a relief! Is it too early for us to see the dates?"

"Never too early, son," replies Papa Joe as he goes into his brief case and produces a piece of paper which he hands to Debbie.

"This is gonna be a blast," enthuses Debbie. "So we start down South in London and we finish up in, wait for it...a big weekend finisher in *GLASGOW!*"

"Aaww, I can't wait to do Glasgow again," laughs Ronnie.

"It's gonna be some buzz," says Carl. "Wullie and Ronnie, you'll need to take us on this well-needed tour."

"Don't worry about that, pal," laughs Wullie as he puts as arm around Ronnie's shoulders. "We will! My brothers will probably put us up while we are there."

"Your brothers?" asks Moose, surprised. "I thought your whole family were here?"

"Naw, pal," laughs Wullie. "My da and my wee ma were busy people and I take it their telly let them down a lot. There's nine of us. I have seven brothers and there's wee Liz. My four big brothers are still in Glasgow. They didn't want to move because they were already settled with careers, wives, girlfriends and everything that comes with life. In fact, you would get on brilliantly with my brother Harry. He's your age and into his fitness and boxing, the same as you. He'll be glad of a gym buddy when we're there."

"We don't want to impose, babe," says Debbie.

"Honestly, doll, you won't," assures Wullie. "They have four good-sized houses in a wee humble place called Giffnock, all within walking distance of each other. It will be peace of mind for them too if they know they can make sure I keep out of mischief. There's lots of space so you will all have your privacy."

"That would be fantastic, Wullie," smiles Papa Joe. "As long as the boys and girls don't mind. We'll look forward to meeting them."

As the weeks pass, Hell Freeze are surprised to learn that all of the gigs planned for their U.K tour have completely sold out already. "It's happening, guys and gals," laughs Papa Joe. "It's finally happening! People are getting to know who Hell Freeze are."

"It's gonna be a blast," enthuses Carl. "I can't wait to do the U.K, especially Glasgow!"

Feeling confident that they have enough rehearsal hours under their belts, the bandmates kick back and relax as they look forward to their long-awaited U.K tour. Even Wullie is feeling confident that he has done well in his exams this year and is looking forward to getting away from the grind of studying for a while.

"How are you finding it all, Wullie?" asks Moose.

"So far so good, my man," Wullie replies with his usual hearty laugh. "I decided to repeat my second year when I moved to the U.S because American law is very different from Scottish law but it's been, surprisingly, a lot easier than I thought it was going to be."

"Just remember to let us know if you need a break," says Moose. "Ronnie and I have already been through what you're going through and it is beyond tough at times!"

"Thanks, guys," smiles Wullie. "I really appreciate your help with this but I think I'll be alright. I hope to be with Hell Freeze for a good long while yet!"

"We're glad of it, babe," smiles Debbie.

"Me too, doll," laughs Wullie. "Me too."

Wullie arrives at Hell Freeze's apartment having finished the last of his exams and announces that he feels he has done well this year.

"So we know where to turn if we end up on the wrong side of the law?" Angel laughs.

"Aye, ma man," replies Wullie as he winks at Angel. "My door will always be open so don't stop being your crazy selves. You're all aff yer nuts and I love it!"

It is now summer of 1985 and Wullie has finished all his exams of his degree year and is confident he has passed everything. He leaves for London with the rest of the band feeling in high spirits and very relaxed. It is now time for Hell Freeze to open their U.K tour as they kick things off in the Eventim Apollo. Debbie arrives two hours before the gig in order to have everything organised for the big night and the friendly, enthusiastic venue staff cannot do enough to help her and they are finished in plenty of time for the concert to open. London is now ready for Hell Freeze's first ever public performance in the capital. The atmosphere is electric as, one by one, the bandmates take their places in order that they joined the band: Angel, Carl, Moose, Ronnie and Wullie. The entire gig runs extremely smoothly from start to finish. The only problem is that every time the band tries to wrap things up, the crowd cries out for yet another Hell Freeze favourite. Before they know it, their proposed ninety-minute gig runs into almost two hours. The guys eventually manage to close the gig with an old favourite "Burn-Out," which had been penned by Angel when he and Carl had not long started their job in Farrell's.

Feeling hot and tired but ecstatic, the bandmates put their tee shirts back on as they go and reunite with Debbie, Papa Joe and the staff who had helped Debbie with the set-ups. "That was some buzz," exclaims Wullie as he cracks open a lager given to him by a member of staff and lets out his trademark laugh.

"It sure was, guv," laughs a middle-aged member of staff as he pats Angel on the back. "Don't be strangers, yeah? You are possibly the lowest maintenance, most down-to-Earth band to have ever graced this place and I hope to work with you again before I retire."

"Likewise, big guy," smiles Moose. "We'll no doubt be back soon now that we know there is a demand for us."

"Can you sign some autographs for us please?" asks a small, dark-haired, female worker as she takes off her leather jacket and hands it to Moose to sign first.

"Sure," replies Moose with one of his gurgling, childlike laughs as he signs the girl's jacket with a silver permanent marker and passes it around for his bandmates to sign.

A young, lively male worker with a blond mohawk does a double cartwheel and announces that he and his colleagues are on their way out to "paint the town red" and invites Hell Freeze to join them.

"Definitely, guys," enthuses Ronnie as he takes Debbie's hand. "We might as well check out the London nightlife while we are here."

"I prefer quiet nights in," the small, dark-haired girl whispers to Moose as she rubs the inside of his thigh. "Do you fancy going next door for coffee?"

"It depends on the type of coffee," smiles Moose.

"Hot and steamy with a bit of a dark side," replies the girl as she straddles Moose and starts kissing him, which Moose doesn't resist.

Noticing this going on, Angel and Carl laugh as they leave Moose to his dirty night in as they join Debbie and the rest of their bandmates and all the venue staff for a night on the town. "Only Moose," Carl chuckles.

As the night goes on, Debbie and the bandmates find that they are suitably merry from all the partying. "We're going back to the hotel," Ronnie tells Wullie as he holds a very drowsy Debbie close. "See you in the morning."

"No bother, big chap," replies Wullie as he continues to dance with some of the venue staff. "See you in the morning."

Meanwhile, Angel and Carl are getting up close and personal with two flame-haired girls. "Do you fancy getting a room for tonight?" Carl whispers to his attractive dance partner.

"You bet, honey," she replies as she grabs Carl by the hand and they rush for the exit.

Meanwhile, Angel continues to enjoy a slow dance with the other attractive red-head as he feels her put her hands up his tee shirt and smooth up and down his body. "I love a toned torso on a man," she purrs into his ear as they kiss passionately.

Suddenly, Angel feels something else that he has never felt in his twenty-five years as intense heat rushes through his entire body. "You OK, baby?" the girl whispers as her hands move slowly downwards, into his jeans and into his underpants but Angel is unable to reply as he gets lost in the moment and feels himself getting aroused.

"Beautiful," the girl whispers seductively as they continue to kiss passionately.

Suddenly, a dreadful thought pops into Angel's head as he has a very harsh sober moment. "Fuck," he thinks to himself. "I don't know what to do!"

"Actually, I don't feel well," Angel stammers.

"Aaww, baby," sympathises the red-headed beauty. "Let me see you home."

"No, no," Angel replies, hastily as he fixes his clothes and rushes towards the exit. "Look I'll see you another time, OK? Ciao."

Confused by what he has just witnessed, Wullie asks the girl what happened. "I don't know," she replies. "Things were going so well and then...well you saw what happened. I'm Bev. Can I have this dance?"

"My pleasure, doll," Wullie replies with his hearty laugh as he and Bev hit the dance floor. "Sorry about Angel. I'll talk to him tomorrow."

"It's OK, darling," smiles Bev. "Come to think of it, I think I know what the problem is. I've seen it before. Your innocent friend got cold feet when things got hot, if you know what I mean?"

"NAW," Wullie laughs. "Surely that's not right? He's our lead singer and a real badass."

"A badass who needs his cherry popped," Bev giggles as

Wullie buckles with laughter at the innuendo.

"Looks like I'm the last man standing, hen," says Wullie as he notices that all his bandmates and all of the workers have gone. "Let's dance."

Early the following morning, Moose and Angel meet up in the hotel gym for a workout before breakfast. "So how was your night?" Angel asks his brother.

"Hot as Hell, bro," laughs Moose. "Let's just say we had a banging start to our U.K tour. How was it for you?"

"Yeah..." Angel smiles nervously and blushes as Moose raises his eyebrows.

"What I mean is," Angel stammers. "I enjoyed it. Yeah..."

"Hmmmmm," says Moose as he furrows his brow and signals for Angel to get onto the bench so he can spot him.

Moose and Angel get showered having had a productive workout then head to the dining room for breakfast as Angel nervously walks a couple of paces behind Moose. Everyone is in high spirits having put on a fantastic show for the people of London then enjoyed a great night of partying among other physical activities. Angel, however, continues to sit quietly as he sips his strong, black coffee and eats his cereal. "I'm going for a walk before we go on the bus," Angel tells his friends. "I'll be back soon."

"Want some company, big chap?" asks Wullie. "I could be doing with some fresh air too."

Angel smiles and nods as he feels Wullie would be one to cheer him up. The two friends are enjoying a walk through the park in the summer sunshine when Wullie asks: "So what happened to you last night, mate? You were right in there and that beautiful lass was really into you."

"I know," replies Angel as he looks at the ground and blushes. "Wullie..."

"Aye, mate?" Wullie whispers as he feels Angel has something very sensitive to tell him.

"Can you keep a secret?" Angel continues as he can feel a

bead of sweat run down his forehead.

"What's up, pal?" asks Wullie as he leans in to listen.

"Please don't tell Moose or Carl because they will laugh," Angel continues. "Wullie, last night…my bottle completely crashed. When it came to it…"

"It's OK, big yin," assures Wullie. "Take your time."

"…I didn't know what I was doing," Angel says hastily as he continues to blush profusely. "I've never done it before. I was scared…"

To Angel's surprise, Wullie doesn't laugh. Instead, he gently squeezes his friend's arm. "It's nothing to be ashamed of, pal," assures Wullie.

"No?" Angel asks surprised. "I am twenty-five years old and…"

"It's alright, brother," reassures Wullie. "You're still young, there's lots of time and there will be plenty more opportunities for you. Remember, you and Moose are very different types of people so please don't feel inferior to him just because you don't have that kind of experience yet. The difference is that he is bolder and a lot more confident in himself than you are in yourself. Also, Moose and Carl are extroverts while you, my friend, are an introvert. You might not have known what you were doing but Bev certainly did and she would have guided you through it *BECAUSE SHE WAS INTO YOU.* She told me herself…"

"She did?" asks Angel, surprised and wide-eyed.

"Aye, ma man," replies Wullie as he stops in his tracks and stands face-to-face with Angel. "You are Angel fuckin' Mancini, our leading man and a good-looking guy with a lot going for you. You just need to learn to go with the flow. Take your time, find a nice girl you're comfortable with and the rest will follow naturally. I promise you, it will happen when the time is right. Just remember, your innocence is nothing to be ashamed of. Moose and Carl wouldn't laugh either because they both know you too well. You're Moose's wee brother and Carl's best pal, after all. I am genuinely impressed that you've held onto it for this long. I just wish I had held off a bit longer myself!"

Both men laugh as they head back to the hotel to get ready to hit the road for their next gig.

"Where to now, dad?" asks Carl.

"We're Nuneaton bound now, son," smiles Papa Joe. "It's another sell-out so I imagine you boys will be as well received there as you were in London."

Hell Freeze arrive at their Nuneaton Hotel following their two-and-a-half hour bus trip and are immediately welcomed by staff and shown to their rooms. After signing some autographs, posing for photographs and chatting with staff and guests Debbie, Papa Joe and the bandmates go to their rooms to relax and prepare for their gig at Queen's Hall. With Debbie being the perfectionist that she is, she leaves the hotel early and makes her way to the venue in order to prepare for the gig. She shows her I.D on arrival and is granted admittance by staff and they help her with the set-up of equipment. "I wish all the bands we had to work with were like you," enthuses a young male member of staff as he hands Debbie a cold can of lemonade. "You turning up early like this and making sure all your equipment is working has made our job so much easier."

"The pleasure is all ours," smiles Debbie. "I think we're good to go."

"Definitely," laughs another male member of staff. "Nuneaton is ready for Hell Freeze!"

Just like in London, Hell Freeze are well-received in Nuneaton as the crowd cheers and goes wild for an encore. Debbie, Papa Joe and the bandmates continue to enjoy their popularity throughout their U.K tour as the perform at other venues in England including Blackpool, Bath and Sunderland until it is time to make their debut as an entire band in Scotland, with their first Scottish date being in Powerhouse Rock Club in Ayr. "We're here, guys and gals," cheers Ronnie as he and his bandmates get off the bus. "We're finally on Scottish soil!"

"Aye, ma man," laughs Wullie. "It won't be long until we do

Glasgow now."

"Three more sleeps," giggles Debbie as she hugs Ronnie.

"Ronnie," says Papa Joe with his serious tone. "I hope you don't mind, son, but I took the liberty of inviting your folks to Glasgow while we're there. I thought it would be good for them to see you play and to catch up with us."

"You didn't," cries Ronnie. "Aaww, Papa Joe, I can't thank you enough! I really miss my wee Ma and Da. This has made the trip even better for me."

"You're very welcome, my dear boy," smiles Papa Joe. "It's the least I can do for you after all your good self, Debbie and the boys have done for me over the years."

Hell Freeze arrive at their first Scottish hotel and are shown to their rooms. "Do you have a phone I can use?" Wullie asks the young female member of staff.

"There's a phone in every room, darlin'," she replies. "Make sure you dial number 9 and it will give you an outside line, then dial your number from there. Please let me know if you need anything else."

"Cheers, doll," smiles Wullie. "Will do." Wullie signals for Debbie, Papa Joe and the bandmates to come into his room. "I'm going to phone Harry and let him know we're here," he tells them.

"Hello?" the caller answers.

"HARRY," Wullie cheers down the phone. "How are you doing, big yin?"

"Jesus, Wullie, how are you doing, son?" Harry replies as he lets out the same hearty laugh as Wullie, which can be heard by everyone in the room.

Angel turns and looks at Moose and Carl. "Bloody Hell," he chuckles, quietly. "The whole family must be like that!"

"Not a bad thing, bro," Moose replies in his deep, gravelly voice as he smiles warmly. "Not a bad thing."

"I'm great thanks, Harry," Wullie continues his conversation. "We've just arrived in Ayr. We're playing here tonight, we're at Livingston tomorrow and we'll come through to Glasgow on Thursday for about lunchtime to get ready for the gig on Friday."

"That's smashing, son," laughs Harry. "Well you know the plan. Come straight to mine and we'll have dinner and decide where you'll all be staying from there. Alec, Jimmy and Hugh will be here with the lassies and they're all looking forward to seeing you all."

"Sounds like a plan, big yin," laughs Wullie. "You're a star. Please tell Wee Anna I'm asking kindly for her and can't wait to see her."

"Will do, son," replies Harry. "Well, you mind and look after yourselves. We've all got tickets for your Friday gig and can't wait to see you play with your new band. I still can't believe my wee brother is playing with Hell Freeze and you're their first ever keyboard player. I've listened to those guys for years and it's going to be great hearing them play live with you as part of the line-up!"

"Thanks, big yin," smiles Wullie. "You won't be disappointed. See you on Thursday."

"See you on Thursday," replies Harry with a final hearty laugh. "Cheerio, son."

Debbie, Papa Joe and the bandmates can't help but laugh. "Is everyone like that in Glasgow?" asks Carl.

"Aye, mate," replies Wullie. "It is the warmest place in the world. We might not be able to promise you the weather but we can sure as Hell do hospitality down to a fine art! My brothers and their wives will definitely look after us. They are a terrific bunch of people."

Again, Hell Freeze prove to be extremely popular in Ayr and in Livingston. It is now time for them to make their commute to Glasgow. It is Thursday afternoon and their tour bus pulls up outside a well-maintained detached house. Waiting outside is a well-groomed couple. The man is tall, muscular and clean-shaven with short dark hair and his wife is a petite lady with shoulder-length, brown, curly hair. "That's them," says Wullie, excitedly. "Big Harry and Wee Anna."

Harry and Anna walk over the the tour bus hand-in-hand to greet Wullie and his bandmates. "*WULLIE,*" Harry laughs, heartily. "So good to have you home, son."

"It's good to be home, big yin," replies Wullie as he gives Harry a handshake and a hug. "It's good to be home."

"*HIYA, HEN,*" Wullie greets Anna as he picks her up and whirls her round. "You are just as stunning as ever."

"So are you, son," laughs Anna. "*AND* we hear you before we see you! Don't be changing though!"

"Never, doll," smiles Wullie. "Anyway, I'd best introduce you to everyone."

"Guys and gals," Wullie addresses his friends. "This is my oldest brother Harry and his beautiful wife Anna. Harry and Anna this is my gaffer Joe, our leading man Angel, his big brother and our lead guitarist Moose, my American twin brother Carl who plays the drums, our oracle Ronnie from the Scottish highlands on the bass and his stunning girlfriend Debbie who does our sound and all the other techy stuff that us dafties can't do."

"Hey, speak for yourself," says Angel.

"Now don't you talk," says Wullie in his voice of authority. "Look what happened the last time you tried to wire up a plug!"

"Wrong hole, Wullie," Angel laughs as he blushes and puts his hands up as Debbie, Papa Joe and all the bandmates laugh. "Literally!"

"Och, that's so cute," smiles Anna. "A lead singer who blushes. What happened with the plug?"

"It's a dinnertime tale, Anna," Angel laughs. "I promise I'll tell it then."

Once inside Debbie, Papa Joe and all the bandmates make themselves comfortable on the large, green velvet sofas as Harry and Anna serve up their home-made vegetable soup with fresh bread while they wait for the rest of the brothers to arrive with their wives. It is now time for Hell Freeze to make their long-awaited appearance at the Glasgow Barrowlands. The bandmates arrive at the venue in plenty of time with over an hour to spare before they go on-stage to perform. They are greeted by Debbie, who was there well in advance in order to get organised and are served cold drinks and snacks by venue staff before they make their long-awaited appearance in Glasgow. "This is exciting," enthuses Angel as he looks at Ronnie and Wullie while be relaxes with an ice-cold lager.

"Told you, mate," laughs Wullie. "It really is the warmest place in the world and the Glasgow Barrowlands is something else!"

"Aye," Ronnie agrees. "Wait until you see the audience."

"Well I make it time," smiles Moose as he stands up and takes his jacket off. "Shall we?"

The audience immediately goes wild as soon as the bandmates walk on-stage one by one to take their places. Moose and Carl start warming up the crowd with the hard hitting intro of an old favourite composition of Carl's "Ecstatic." Before they know it, the Glasgow Barrowlands is in full-on party mode. Hell Freeze are getting well into their performance of a song written by Moose called "Down On Me" when, suddenly, Angel notices something fly through the air and fall at his feet. He picks it up and examines it. "Ladies and gentlemen," he addresses the crowd as he stops the performance. "I take great pleasure in presenting to you my very first bra. Thank you to the well-endowed lady for the gift. It will be a great souvenir for the guys and I to take back with us to the U.S."

By now, all the bandmates and audience members are in hysterical laughter at how Angel handles it. After composing themselves, Hell Freeze carry on performing "Down On Me" as the party gets straight back into full swing.

Having enjoyed a very successful Friday night gig, the bandmates reunite with Debbie and Wullie's brothers and their wives as they decide to check out the Glasgow night life. Papa Joe congratulates the bandmates on their performance before bidding them a good night as he goes home with Ronnie's parents as well as Hugh and his wife Cathy, both of whom have work early the next day.

Hell Freeze are definitely not disappointed in the Glasgow night life as they enjoy an exciting tour around the different pubs and clubs with Wullie's brothers and their wives. As the night goes on, Moose finds he can barely stand. "Have you had enough, big guy?" Harry laughs.

Moose nods as he just manages to reply to Harry through is hiccups.

"Are you two going home already?" asks Anna, surprised.

"Aye, missus," replies Harry as he kisses his wife goodnight. "You mind and keep a wee eye on the boys and I'll see you in the morning. Love you."

Later, Angel and Wullie are partying the night away in The Cat House nightclub when they realise that they seem to have lost everyone. "Bloody lightweights," laughs Wullie. "Anyway, big guy, I think we'd best get up the road too before Big Harry and Wee Anna send out the search parties."

"Isn't it a bit early?" asks Angel.

"It's twenty to four in the morning, ya drunken bum," Wullie replies with his trademark laugh. "Come on. Let's go and get a taxi."

Unfortunately for Wullie and Angel, the roads are deserted. Even the taxis that are on the road are refusing to stop for them when they see how drunk they are. "To Hell," says Wullie. "We'll just have to walk. It's not far now."

"Where are we?" asks Angel.

"This is Shawlands, pal," replies Wullie. "That's Queen's Park. Oh aye, it looks like the shows are on this weekend as well."

"The shows?" asks Angel as he stops in his tracks.

"Aye," laughs Wullie. "They have a carnival for the weans here every summer. Let's go and investigate."

"It's pitch black, Wullie," Angel shudders. "There's nothing to see."

Wullie doesn't listen and enters the park anyway and Angel follows him as he has no idea how to get to Harry's house from there. "I'm getting a souvenir to take home for wee Liz," whispers Wullie.

"*WULLIE*," exclaims Angel. "What the fuck are you up to?"

"*WHEESHT*," says Wullie as he pulls Angel towards the hobby horses by the jacket. "Geez a hawn."

Angel bursts out laughing when he realises what Wullie has in mind. They both pick up a spare hobby horse and carry it back to Harry's house. The following morning, Angel is woken from a drunken sleep by Harry shouting: *"Aaaaaaaargh,* in the name of Jesus Christ. Where the Hell did THIS bloody thing come from?"

Anna peaks round their bedroom door, bleary-eyed and barely able to remember the events of the previous night herself. Moose also emerges from his room, taken aback when he see the huge hobby horse occupying the hallway. Harry knocks on Wullie's bedroom door and he jumps out of bed with the worst hangover. "What the Hell do you call this?" shouts Harry.

"Aaww, naw," groans Wullie as he looks at Angel, who looks back at him wide-eyed when he suddenly has a flash-back from the night before.

"Jesus," gasps Angel. "Was that us? All I can remember is walking through King's Park and..."

"*QUEEN'S* Park, pal," groans Wullie. "And, aye, that was us..."

"Well, you'll have to take it bloody back," exclaims Harry. "You're not getting me a bad name. Come on, you drunken pair of eejits. Get your clothes on and take that thing back where you got it before the polis show up here! It will be good for your hangovers."

"It's awright, pal," Wullie whispers to Angel. "It's Sunday and nobody will see us."

"I bloody hope not," replies Angel. "How embarrassing!"

Once outside, Angel and Wullie can't help but laugh at their antics among other events that occurred the night before as the memories flood back to them in dribs and drabs. They are laughing as they carry the hobby horse through Shawlands until a police car pulls up beside them and a middle-aged police officer and a tall WPC emerge. "Good morning, boys," says the policeman in his voice of authority. "What's going on here?"

"Oh no," Angel whispers as he feels himself begin to cry. "This is it. We're going to prison."

"Just wheesht, will you?" hisses Wullie. "I'll do the talking. Like I said, it will be alright."

"Good morning, officers," smiles Wullie. "My friend and I where just out for our morning papers when we found this fine horse dumped outside one of the shops. Looks like somebody tried to steal it so we were just taking it to Queens Park. I suppose it belongs to the organisers of this year's carnival?"

"Yes, son," replies the policeman. "We did receive a report about a missing hobby horse early this morning so thanks for that. It will save us a job. You are good lads."

"Thank you officer," replies Wullie with his usual hearty laugh. "We'll be on our way."

"WAIT," chimes in the WPC. "I know who you are! You're Wullie McLarnon, the Glasgow boy who just joined Hell Freeze. I would know that laugh a mile away!"

"Aye, doll," laughs Wullie.

"You are the gorgeous Angel," she continues. "You are even more handsome in real life!"

"Aw, shucks," replies Angel as he blushes.

"Would you sign some autographs for us?" asks the policeman. "This will be *REAL* news for us to take back to HQ!"

"Aye, my man," says Wullie as he and Angel fill an entire notepad with autographs before taking the stolen hobby horse back to Queen's Park.

"That was smooth, Wullie," laughs Angel. "REAL smooth!"

Chapter 15:
A Broken Piece

Following another year of sell-out gigs, chart-topping hits and their new album featuring Wullie making it to number one in the charts Papa Joe, Debbie and the bandmates wind down as they prepare to enjoy a peaceful Christmas time with their families. Ronnie, Debbie and Wullie wish their companions a Merry Christmas and a happy new year as they depart for Scotland to spend time with their families and future in-laws.

Ronnie and Debbie arrive back in the U.S. feeling relaxed and rejuvenated as they look forward to getting back to work and gigs. Wullie, however, is not his usual happy self and appears solemn. Noticing Wullie's change in demeanour, Moose decides to speak to him. Following rehearsals one evening, Moose accompanies Wullie to his motorcycle. "Hey, bro," he whispers to Wullie. "Is everything alright at your end? You've been very unusually quiet since you got back from Scotland."

"Just knackered, big yin," yawns Wullie. "Listen, when do you finish tomorrow?"

"Two p.m., pal," replies Moose. "Angel and I are going to see Mom so I've rescheduled my PT clients for the night."

"Have you got time for a coffee before you go?" asks Wullie.

"Sure, pal," replies Moose.

"Great," replies Wullie with a tired smile. "I'll get you in your work's cafe then."

The following afternoon, Wullie meets up with Moose and Ronnie to break some bad news to them. "I'm really sorry to do this to you guys," says Wullie, close to tears. "Things are getting really hot for me at uni and this honours year has just about broken me. I'm afraid I'm going to have to leave Hell Freeze. I'm really sorry..."

"You've got to do what you've got to do, pal," empathises Ronnie. "Moose and I have both been there and we know how tough it is and you have really gone Hell for leather throughout it all."

"Definitely, dude," concurs Moose. "There were times when I came so close to walking away myself. The only thing keeping me there was Angel because I constantly worried about him. You're doing the right thing."

"Thanks for understanding, guys," says Wullie, relieved. "I'll do the gigs that Papa Joe has already organised then I'll call it a day. I'll take you all for a meal to say thanks."

"We'll keep you in mind if you need a good lawyer," laughs Moose as he gives Wullie a few playful biffs. "We'll no doubt need one!"

"You're on," replies Wullie with his trademark laugh. "I'm really going to miss you guys. You have become another family to me..."

"Aw, don't Wullie," sighs Ronnie. "You'll make me cry! Keep in touch, will you?"

"Aye, big yin," smiles Wullie as he embraces Moose and Ronnie.

Following Wullie's departure, Hell Freeze start scouting for another keyboard player. Feeling positive, Angel and Carl go back to the university with the hopes of finding somebody as talented as Wullie. They get several responses and they eventually get a call from one of the university lecturers. "A lecturer?" asks Moose. "How is she going to fit it all in?"

"Time will tell, son," replies Papa Joe. "We'll see how she does at the audition."

The following evening, Julie Hamill arrives for her audition ten minutes late and looking harassed. She is a well-dressed lady in her mid-thirties who teaches scientific subjects including anatomy, physiology and biology as well as being mother to three children. "It sounds like you have an extremely busy schedule," says Debbie.

"I wouldn't have it any other way," smiles Julie. "I love my job, my family and music. I'll make it work somehow."

Julie sits at the keyboard kit and Papa Joe, Debbie and the bandmates are impressed by her covers of "Chain Reaction" by Diana Ross, "Don't Leave Me This Way" by the Communards and "Don't Get Me Wrong" by the pretenders. "That was awesome," cheers Angel. "You have a great voice too!"

"Thank you, honey," smiles Julie. "Like I said, I love music and singing."

"A female vocal will be another great touch," enthuses Papa Joe. "We have two sold-out gigs this weekend. How are you fixed for that?"

"Should be fine," replies Julie.

"What about rehearsals?" asks Debbie, nervously.

"I can only do Friday nights," replies Julie. "I have to take the kids to their clubs and the like. You know how it is..."

The bandmates all look at each other, now feeling doubtful. "It's better than nothing at all," says Papa Joe. "You have already proved you're more than capable so we'll look forward to seeing you do your thing on Saturday."

"Thank you, all," smiles Julie as she bids her new bandmates a good night.

"I'm not sure about this one," sighs Moose as he shakes his head.

"Me neither, bro," says Angel. "I like her but how is she going to fit it all in? She can't even make rehearsals for a start."

"Let's just give her a chance," soothes Papa Joe. "Like I said, time will tell..."

It is Saturday morning and Hell Freeze are loading their

equipment into Debbie's van as they prepare for a weekend of sold-out gigs when they receive a phone call. "Hello?" Debbie takes the call.

"Hi, Debbie," the caller replies. "It's Julie."

"Oh, hi, Julie," replies Debbie. "Is everything alright?"

"All fine, thanks, honey," says Julie. "I'm really sorry I'm not going to make the gigs this weekend. I completely forgot my little Charlotte has a major dance competition today and jack has a football match tomorrow."

"It's very short notice," replies Debbie. "But I suppose family comes first..."

"Thanks for understanding, love," says Julie, relieved.

"No worries," replies Debbie. "I wish you all the very best with your future and I hope all goes well this weekend."

"What?" exclaims Julie. "You're SACKING me?"

"I'm sorry, Julie," Debbie apologises. "We are a professional band who needs somebody we can rely on. With all due respect, you are a busy mom with too many commitments of your own. There's no reason why you can't pick up your music career later when your kids are older..."

"HOW DARE YOU?" cries Julie.

"I can't even apologise, Julie," asserts Debbie. "For one, you are unable to make rehearsals. Now you have let us down at short notice for a gig. Your children need you more, especially right now."

Julie continues to scream unintelligibly down the phone as Debbie calmly hangs up and shrugs her shoulders.

"I knew it," whispers Moose.

"It's alright, babe," soothes Debbie. "We managed as a four-piece before and we can do it again. Sadly, we're just going to have to face the facts that we're never going to get another Wullie McLarnon. He is one of a kind."

"I know," sighs Angel. "For such a little guy, he has left one massive pair shoes for us to fill."

From then on, Hell Freeze continue to perform as produce

new material as a four-piece.

Chapter 16:
Repairing A Broken Piece

The year is 1993 and Hell Freeze have continued to enjoy chart success as well as enjoying their own careers and other successes away from the music scene. It is coming up to Christmas time and Papa Joe has an assignment at one of the local high schools as he records a Christmas jingle for his radio station with the help of the fourteen and fifteen-year-old pupils.

On arrival at the school, Papa Joe is greeted by the head master and his deputy head and they introduce him to the principal music teacher, Miss Galloway. "I can't thank you enough for this opportunity, Mr Martinez," enthuses Miss Galloway.

"The pleasure is all mine, Miss Galloway," smiles Papa Joe. "I really appreciate your help and, of course, that of the students."

Papa Joe and Miss Galloway are walking along the corridor towards the music department when, suddenly, Miss Galloway stops in her tracks and grimaces as she hears the students singing their warm-up scales. "My goodness," she gasps. "Would you listen to that? There's always one who can't sing in tune and I know exactly who that is!"

Miss Galloway throws the classroom door open. "*ELIZABETH*," she shouts. "Your voice can be heard over and above everybody else's!"

"Thank you, Miss," smiles a tiny girl with long, curly, dark red hair and a broad Scottish Glaswegian accent.

"It's not a compliment," scolds Miss Galloway. "You are singing away off-key! Now get to the piano and warm up before you spoil Mr Martinez's jingle."

"Yes, Miss," giggles Elizabeth as she does as she is told and all her friends laugh.

After several takes, Papa Joe is still not satisfied with his recording. Elizabeth puts her hand up. "Honestly, that girl," groans Miss Galloway "What is it, Elizabeth?"

"Miss Galloway," says Elizabeth. "When Mr Martinez plays it back, it sounds abrupt. How about a Christmassy intro before everyone starts singing? Something like this?"

Elizabeth proceeds to demonstrate what she means and Papa Joe's face lights up. "Yes, my dear," he enthuses. "That sounds so much better. Let's try it along with your friends' singing."

Papa Joe presses record and they attempt the jingle another time with Elizabeth's improvisation. "Perfect," smiles Papa Joe. "Just perfect. Thank you so much everyone for your participation."

"Thank you, Mr Martinez," says Miss Galloway. "We'll look forward to hearing your jingle featuring the students' voices. Elizabeth. Would you please help Mr Martinez with his equipment?"

"Aye," replies Elizabeth.

"YES, MISS," Miss Galloway corrects her.

"No, no, no," says Papa Joe. "That won't be nec..."

"It's OK, Mr Martinez," assures Miss Galloway. "The girl may not make it as a singer but she knows sound equipment very well. She is extremely skilled and knowledgable on the technical side of things, which comes in handy for our pantomimes and fashion shows."

"Good show," smiles Papa Joe as he watches young Elizabeth carefully dismantle the sound equipment and assemble it into its correct carry cases.

"Once you've done that help Mr Martinez out to his van please, Elizabeth," says Miss Galloway.

"Yes, Miss," smiles Elizabeth.

Papa Joe thanks young Elizabeth as she lifts the last of the sound equipment into the van. "No bother," says Elizabeth. "Thank you, Mr Martinez and have a nice Christmas when it comes."

"Elizabeth?" Papa Joe asks. "I must say, you are a very skilled pianist. I was wondering, do you play keyboards at all?"

"I prefer keyboards to piano," replies Elizabeth. "But they try to be posh at this school so classical piano music it is. I play keyboards in my spare time and I like writing songs."

"Interesting," says Papa Joe. "Have you ever played in a band?"

"I only get to do it for the school pantomime," laughs Liz. "My big brother taught me how to play when I was only four years old. I love it but all my pals are only interested in boring things like boys so pantomimes are all I get to play at as part of a band."

Papa Joe laughs. "How would you feel about coming for an audition?" he asks. "My boy and his pals are looking for a keyboard player with good technical knowledge and I have a feeling that's you."

"Aw I would love that, Mr Martinez," enthuses Elizabeth.

"Please call me Joe," smiles Papa Joe. "I can pick you up after school tomorrow if that would suit you?"

"That's fine," replies Elizabeth. "Joe, I don't mean to be rude but can you please call me Liz? Everybody does except my dad when I'm getting into trouble and the teachers."

"Certainly, my dear," laughs Papa Joe. "Here is my business card in case of emergencies. Thank you and I'll see you after school tomorrow. I can't wait to tell the boys!"

Papa Joe arrives home and breaks the news to Debbie and the bandmates. "Can the guy definitely play?" Carl asks, nervously. "The last thing we need is another let-down."

"Actually, it's a young girl," replies Papa Joe. "And, yes, I feel she has the skills. All I am asking of you is that you keep an open mind."

"Woah," enthuses Carl. "A young girl? This could be *SO* much fun!"

"'Keep an open mind' though?" groans Angel. "That means there's a catch..."

"I suppose time will tell, bro," says Moose. "We'll see what she does at the audition. After all, we've not had a keyboard player in years. We've nothing to lose."

The following afternoon, Papa Joe picks young Liz up from school and she is excited about meeting her new bandmates as he talks enthusiastically about "my boy and his pals."

"Hello, Debbie darling," Papa Joe greets Debbie as she answers the door. "Meet Liz. She is auditioning for the keyboard player gig."

Debbie doesn't reply. Instead, she stares at Liz coldly. Papa Joe guides Liz into the living room, where the bandmates are enjoying coffee and cigarettes as they wait for Papa Joe to arrive with their potential new recruit. Young Liz smiles confidently as Papa Joe introduces the bewildered bandmates one by one. Liz, herself, is surprised as she had been expecting to meet four teenaged boys around her age rather than tough, long-haired bikers who look to be in their thirties. Still, this does not bother Liz. "OK, my dear," says Papa Joe. "I'll leave you in the capable hands of the boys. Good luck."

"How are you doing, Liz?" Ronnie greets her. "Would you like to tell us a bit about yourself before you do your thing?"

"Aye," replies Liz in her broad accent when she realises she is in the company of a fellow Scot. "Well I'm still at school and I start my exams next year. I'm just trying to get these two years out of the way then I'm hoping to go to medical school. In my spare time I go to the football, boxing and wrestling matches and I like to fix motorbikes and help my brothers in their body shop for a bit of extra money. So if you need any repairs or upgrades, go to MC's Autocycles in the high street, ask for Tommy or Robert and tell them I sent you. They will give you a good discount."

"We're there all the time, Liz," says Ronnie. "Those guys really do know their stuff and they have done extraordinarily well for a small business."

"Thanks, Ronnie," smiles Liz. "I'm proud of my big brothers."

"What about the big game in a few weeks' time, Liz?" asks Moose. "Are you going?"

"Oh, *THE* big game?" laughs Liz. "I wouldn't miss it. My brother John is taking me. I can't wait even though I'm nervous. It's nearly as nerve-wracking as a Glaswegian Old Firm Game!"

"Ah, the Old Firm," smiles Ronnie. "I still get knots in my stomach when I hear it mentioned!"

"Well it sounds like you talk the talk, Liz," smiles Angel. "How long have you played keyboards?"

"I started when I was four years old and got the bug," Liz laughs. "I hope you like what I do today."

"OK, Liz," says Moose in his deep, gravelly voice. "Let's see what you got."

"Aye," smiles Liz. "This song reached number one in the UK charts last year. It's called 'Get Ready For This' by 2 Unlimited."

Young Liz goes on to play a flawless version of the chart-topper with the hard-hitting keyboard-synthersiser melody. All the bandmates, with the exception on Carl, applaud Liz on her performance. "The job's yours, kid," Moose exclaims excitedly.

"Hang on, Moose," yells Carl. "What gives you the right to...?"

"Come on, Carl," Moose shouts back, now standing over him in an intimidating manner. "We've not seen anyone with this much technical knowledge or skill level since Wullie! We *NEED* a good keyboard player for this gig, which is in just three weeks, maybe even permanently. She's a raw talent and we are NEVER going to find anyone else this good!"As a Scottish girl living in the States, Liz cannot hide her amusement at the sound of an American man attempting to say a Glaswegian man's name. She chuckles to herself as the two men continue their argument.

"I'm not afraid of you, you big chunk," Carl yells back at

Moose. "Get away from me! I am talking from a business point of view. She is only a child and she will be a liability."

"I've got your big chunk," growls Moose. "I am talking from a business point of view too! She is a super talented child who will be working with six responsible adults. Sorry, make that FIVE responsible adults and *YOU!* By the way, a gentle reminder that it was your own father who brought Liz to audition in the first place so he obviously sees great potential in her too. His business and all that. Liz, I am so sorry about this..."

"Come on, Moose. Calm down, man," soothes Ronnie as he and Angel guide Moose away from Carl and Angel mouths "sorry" to Liz.

"Do you have anything else for us, Liz?" asks Angel as he and Ronnie sit Moose down away from Carl.

"OK," says Liz. "I'll try this one. This is an experimental piece that doesn't have any keyboard input yet. Here goes."

Angel smiles as he recognises the improvised keyboard introduction as Carl's chart-topping composition "Shattered" and he signals for all the bandmates to take their places. Moose and Ronnie do as they are instructed without question while Carl sits scowling. "Carl," hisses Moose. "Get a fuckin' move on if you know what's bloody good for you!"

Carl grudgingly takes his place and all the bandmates play along with Liz as she performs her improvised keyboard piece. All the bandmates finish with an impressive outro, cheer and congratulate Liz. "That was amazing, Liz," enthuses Ronnie.

"Thank you," Liz smiles.

"I'm still not convinced," says Carl, flatly.

Just then, Debbie bounces into the room with the brightest, most beautiful smile. Liz looks at the tall, blonde beauty with admiration believing that she looks like a supermodel of that era and that smile is her best feature. "My goodness, baby girl," she cries. "Was that you playing the keyboard?"

"Ah, our Debbie," Moose smiles warmly as he sits back in his seat. "The voice of reason."

"Guys, we *HAVE* to have her," exclaims Debbie, hugging Liz from behind.

"There we go," laughs Moose. "The job's yours, Liz. The boss has spoken."

"Thanks," Liz smiles. "Moose? When you were talking about another keyboard player who was with you before, did you mean Wullie McLarnon?"

"*YES*," exclaims Angel. "Have you been following us that long?"

"I suppose I have," replies Liz. "Wullie is my brother. He taught me almost everything I know about the keyboard, the technical side of it and songwriting."

"Oh my God, it's Wee Liz that we kept hearing about," laughs Debbie. "You are quite the legend in these parts, Liz. We've made the right choice. We can't go far wrong if you're Wullie's sister. We've never been able to find anyone anywhere nearly as good as him until you came along."

"Aye," Liz smiles as she looks at Angel. "I've heard lots of stories and I know who you all are!"

"Oh no," Angel groans and blushes as he recalls the incident with Bev following Hell Freeze's debut in London.

"I nearly had a hobby horse," laughs Liz. "Thanks for trying, Angel."

"Ah," Angel smiles, relieved. "We'll maybe look at getting you a real one the way things are going with the band. How is Wullie doing anyway?"

"He's great, thanks," replies Liz. "He's married to a lovely girl called Phyllis who is also a lawyer in the same company as him. They've got two beautiful kids too, a wee girl and a wee boy. They're doing really well for themselves."

"*NOW* we feel old," laughs Debbie. "I just remember Wullie being the baby of the band but he was always wise beyond his years, just like you."

The reminiscing is interrupted by the phone ringing which Ronnie answers: "*Hello?...* Oh, hi, sweetheart. How are you?...

Aw, that's good to hear...Yes, hang on."

Ronnie covers the mouth piece. "Hey, Moose," he whispers. "It's that lass from last night."

"Ooooooooohhhhh," Debbie and the other bandmates chant in unison as Moose jumps up and hides behind Angel and Carl.

"Get rid of her for me, Ron," Moose panics. "That was the biggest bunny boiler I have come across in my entire life! I promise I'll pay you back."

"Only kidding, it's your mum," laughs Ronnie as Moose playfully hits him over the head with his newspaper.

"Hi, Mom," Moose greets his mother. Liz smiles as she gets the warm feeling knowing that her brother's tough ex-bandmate has that love and close relationship with his mother, something that she has missed since she was just six years old. "Yeah, Mom, we've just finished. She's amazing and we're keeping her on...Yeah, she's brilliant and I can't wait for you to meet her... Doing that, Mom...Yeah, Angel is keeping it in his pants too."

Angel covers his face and shakes his head as everyone laughs. "Yeah, here he is...Love you and I'll see you on Friday...Bye for now."

Angel takes the receiver and chats to his mother as Carl scowls and shakes his head. "We'll leave you guys to talk, babe," Debbie tells Ronnie as she kisses him. "Let's go and make some hot chocolate and have a chat with Papa Joe, Liz."

"What the Hell is wrong with you?" Angel asks Carl as he concludes the phone conversation with his mother.

"I told you, dude," groans Carl. "She's far too young."

"How?" asks Moose. "You and Angel were a lot younger than Liz when you were out gigging together. She won't stop us from getting good gigs either. If anything, she'll be an asset because she is every bit as good as Wullie."

"He means she's too young for him to get his leg over," scoffs Angel. "No other reason!"

"Bullshit," yells Carl.

"What is it then?" asks Ronnie. "You said you wanted a

keyboard player as strong as Wullie. Now we have one and your face is still tripping you. What exactly is the problem, pal?"

"Nothing," snaps Carl. "Just bear in mind that I am taking no responsibility if any of this fucks up because you have taken on a child and I ain't babysitting."

"*CARL,*" Moose snaps back. "We're *NOT* babysitting. Liz is very highly skilled, wise beyond her years and more than capable of standing on her own two feet. She knows what she is signing up for and it is going to be great having a full line-up again. The deal is sealed and Liz is staying whether you like it or not!"

Meanwhile Papa Joe and Debbie are chatting to Liz in the kitchen. "Well, young Liz," smiles Papa Joe. "It looks like the boys have made up there minds. Welcome aboard, my dear."

"Thanks, Joe," replies Liz. "I feel as though I have known all of you for years. Wullie has so many great stories about the time he played with you."

"Yes, we definitely had a lot of fun times," laughs Debbie. "I'm sure we'll have many more now that we have our full line-up again."

"I would like to have a meeting with your father," says Papa Joe. "I understand you're only young and it's just so we can keep everything above board and assure your father that you will be looked after. I'll drive you home and touch base with him then. It will be good to see Big Tam again. Do you want to say good night to the boys before we go?"

"Yes please," smiles Liz. "They are practically my family."

Liz bids her new bandmates a good night and, with the exception of Carl, they thank her once again for the audition and welcome her to the band.

"Night, Carl," says Liz.

"Yeah, good night." replies Carl with a very faint smile. "I suppose we'll see you tomorrow..."

"I swear to God, you *BETTER* behave yourself and treat that girl right," warns Moose.

"Fuck off, Moose," laughs Carl. "I still ain't afraid of you."

After what feels like a very long drive, Liz arrives home with Papa Joe and Debbie. "Goodness," gasps Debbie as she marvels over the mansion Liz calls her home. "Is this where Wullie used to bike it to after rehearsals every night?"

"Aye," replies Liz. "He never minded it. He said the ride helped him wind down. He loves his motorbikes. Are you both coming in for coffee?"

"Yes please, Liz," says Papa Joe. "It will be good to see your dad again."

Liz lets herself and her guests into the impressive hallway and pops her head around the living room door. "Hello, my wee lamb," her father greets her. "Well, did you get the gig?"

"I did, Dad," smiles Liz. *"AND* I've brought somebody to see you."

Papa Joe and Debbie enter the living room. "Joe! How are you doing, ma man? Good to see you again, Debbie doll. You look as stunning as ever," Big Tam McLarnon, standing at six foot four, greets his guests.

"Thank you, Tam," replies Debbie. "Good to see you too. You look amazing!"

"Tam," says Papa Joe. "I have come to ask you for permission to employ your beautiful, super talented daughter as my new keyboard player. We had Wullie before things got too much for him and your baby girl is showing signs of being equally gifted and a pleasure to have."

"Well, Joe," replies Big Tam. "My boy did me proud when he was with you and you took good care of him. I would love to see my Liz play for Hell Freeze too. My only concern is that she is planning to go to medical school but I suppose we'll cross that bridge when we come to it..."

"It would be an honour," smiles Papa Joe. "Thank you so much, Tam. You have some very talented, clever kids. Of course, I understand that Liz's schooling comes first."

"That is so kind of you to say that, Joe," replies Tam. "Just as before, if there is anything at all that I can do to help from my end please give me a call. It will be a pleasure doing business with you again."

"Liz, one of us will pick you up after school for rehearsals," says Debbie.

"It's OK, Debbie," replies Liz. "The school is only a short walk from your apartment and I'll always phone in plenty of time if I can't make rehearsals."

From then on, young Liz McLarnon becomes Hell Freeze's new keyboard player.

Chapter 17:
Smoothing
The Rough Edges

The following afternoon, Liz makes her way to the bandmates' apartment. She is enjoying the crisp, autumn sunshine when suddenly she stops. "Aaww, that house," she sighs as she sees a stunning well-maintained, two-story house, which is occupied by a couple who are out on the balcony. The woman is sitting on a chair as the man massages her shoulders and whispering in her ear.

"He is a high profile therapist, just like my Harry," Liz thinks to herself. "She is managing director of a major company which reaches globally. They have three adorable children together, two boys and one girl. They plan to send them to university when they are older. Right now, the couple are laughing and joking with each other as they plan a romantic holiday." Liz continues to gaze at her dream house as she passes it.

"Ach behave yourself, Liz," she chuckles to herself. "You don't know those people at all. They could be squatters for all you know. You can dream…"

From then on, every time Liz passes her dream house she has a different scenario in her head about people who live there and what the house is used for other than somebody's home.

Liz arrives at Hell Freeze's apartment and is welcomed by Moose, who greets her with a hug and offers her a coffee before they start rehearsals. After her first proper rehearsal with the band, the guys and Debbie congratulate Liz and reassure her that she is appreciated and that they are delighted with her performance. "I'm starving," says Carl as he stands up. "Angel, let's put the dinner out. Liz, are you staying?"

"Only if there's enough," replies Liz.

"There's lots," laughs Debbie. "I always make way too much pasta."

"Can you give us a hand please, Liz?" asks Carl.

"Aye," smiles Liz as she follows Angel and Carl into the kitchen.

"Listen, Liz," says Carl. "I owe you a massive apology for yesterday. I got you completely wrong and I'm sorry."

"It's OK, Carl," assures Liz. "Really it is."

"You really proved yourself beyond measure and I hope we can be friends," he continues.

"Aye," Liz giggles as she hugs Carl. "I feel as though I've known all of you for years and I've only done one rehearsal with you."

"Well hopefully we can, at least, enjoy the next two years with you before you go to med school," says Angel.

"Definitely, Angel," replies Liz. "School is a dawdle so rehearsals and gigs won't be a problem."

Everyone is enjoying dinner when the subject of next weekend's big football game comes up. "Aw, don't," groans Carl. "I couldn't get a ticket. I completely forgot to get one and they're all sold out now."

"Aw, babe, I'm sorry," sympathises Debbie.

"Gutted for you, mate," says Ronnie.

"I'll keep an eye out at work," assures Angel. "Everyone will be trying to get that night off and they won't grant it to everyone. Somebody will probably be selling nearer the time."

"I hope so," says Carl. "Anyway, Liz, let's get you home before it gets too late. I'll drive you."

Liz arrives home and is greeted by her gentle giant brother John, who works as a nurse at the local hospital. "Hiya, John,"

Liz greets her brother as she hugs him. "It's so good to see you home. How are you?"

"Not good, pal," sighs John. "I'm really sorry, I'm not going to be able to make the game this week and you can't go without an adult. We've had a massive outbreak of a sickness bug on the wards and we're really short-staffed. I'm going to have to go in. I'm so sorry, hen. I hate doing this to you after I promised."

"It's not your fault, John," replies Liz. "It comes with being a nurse and I'll be in the same boat as you when I'm a doctor."

"I still feel bad, hen," says John.

"John, please don't," Liz reassures her brother. "There will be other...*WAIT!* I know somebody who will buy your ticket."

"Aye?" smiles John.

"Carl couldn't get one because he left it too late," says Liz. "If he buys your ticket, it means I can go with him."

"That's perfect," replies John. "Tell Carl he can have the ticket. His payment is to keep you company and that will do me."

"Thanks so much, John," says Liz as she hugs him and kisses him on the cheek. "You're a diamond! I'll tell Carl when I go to rehearsals tomorrow. He'll be over the moon."

Liz arrives at Hell Freeze's apartment for rehearsals the following evening and breaks the news to Carl. "It would be a shame for it to go to waste," Liz tells Carl. "They're great seats"

"Can't wait," says Carl, excitedly. "Tell your bro I owe him a beer for the next time he's off duty."

"Will do," replies Liz. "The poor soul was more bothered about letting me down rather than making it himself. These things happen when you work in the medical profession."

The weeks pass and Liz continues to enjoy her new role as keyboard player for Hell Freeze as she attends rehearsals after school and performs at Papa Joe's gigs. One morning, Liz is in her art class when she gets a call over the tannoy to report to the head master's office "immediately" and the entire class chants "*ooooooooohhhhhhh.*"

"What's that for?" asks Mr Coyle the art teacher, confused

as Liz has always been one of his star pupils.

"Don't know," replies Liz, who is equally confused. "I'll tell you when I get back."

Liz knocks on the head master's door and is greeted by Mr Burns and her guidance teacher Mrs Devlin.

"Good morning, Elizabeth," Mr Burns greets her. "Please have a seat."

"Is everything alright, sir?" asks Liz.

"Elizabeth, we are very concerned about you," says Mrs Devlin. "I have had several reports from your friends recently that you don't go home after school anymore. Instead, you are going to an older man's house."

"Yes," Liz laughs. "I'm working."

"Dare we ask what the nature of your work is?" asks Mr Burns, concerned. "Your friends are genuinely worried about you and my staff are growing increasingly concerned for your safety."

"I recently joined a band," Liz smiles. "I'm just grateful that I'm getting to do something I love. I walk to the guys' apartment for rehearsals and they drive me home to my dad's house afterwards. We are also out doing gigs most weekends."

"Really?" asks Mrs Devlin. "What is the name of this band?"

"Hell Freeze," says Liz, proudly.

"*NEVER,*" exclaims Mr Burns. "They are a massive band! My children and I have followed those boys for many years and you say you are now playing for them?"

"Yes, Mr Burns," replies Liz. "They've not had a keyboard player since my brother Wullie left in 1986. They like what I do and I love playing for them so it works both ways."

"My concern is that they are wild," says Mrs Devlin. "They are a rough bunch of characters and we are worried that you will get hurt. Elizabeth, it was just a couple of weeks ago that one of those men got completely naked on stage during the performance!"

"Aw, I know," laughs Liz. "Moose did say he had a bit much to drink and I'm sorry I missed that one!"

"It's not funny, Elizabeth," scolds Mrs Devlin. "We really need to speak to your father about this. It's very worrying…"

"It was all part of the act, Mrs Devlin," assures Liz. "Dad knows where I am and he got to know the guys and their manager Jose Martinez when my brother was with them. Honestly, I'm OK and I'm being looked after. I will be doing this job while my friends work in McDonald's and Walmart, that's all. I also still plan to go to medical school when I graduate from here and I am keeping up with my studies without a problem."

"I'd like to talk to your father anyway, Elizabeth," says Mrs Devlin. "I just don't feel it's right that such a young, impressionable girl is keeping such wild company."

"That's fine, Mrs Devlin," replies Liz. "I will give you my dad's work phone number and you will get him there but he is a hundred percent behind me with this, just as he was with my brother."

"Thank you, Elizabeth," smiles Mr Burns. "I'm sorry we had to pull you out of class like this but please be aware that it's only because we care. You are a very highly respected pupil at this school and we just need reassurance that you're safe."

"Thank you, Mr Burns," says Liz as she gets ready to go back to class. "I might even see you at one of our gigs."

"Oh, you will," laughs Mr Burns as Mrs Devlin glares at him in disapproval. "Enjoy the rest of your day and all the very best in your career."

As the months pass and the dark, winter nights draw in, the bandmates are finding the rehearsal hours more and more challenging as they fit them in around work and school. One night, Ronnie is driving Liz home and the drive seems longer than usual. They eventually arrive at Liz's house and she invites him in for coffee, which he gratefully accepts. Ronnie sits chatting to Liz, her father and her brothers Tommy and Robert about upcoming gigs when he feels his eye lids become increasingly heavier. "Ronnie, mate, are you awright?" he hears Robert asking, which jolts him awake.

"Sorry, pal," Ronnie apologises. "I've been on the go since five this morning."

"That's a long day, son," says Tam. "I think you'd better just stay here tonight. You can sleep in the spare room."

"That would be great, Tam," replies Ronnie, relieved. "I really don't think I would have made the drive back home! Do you mind if I phone the guys?"

"The phone's in the hall, son," says Tam. "Help yourself."

"Ronnie, thank God," says Debbie, relieved as she answers the phone. "Are you alright?"

"I'm fine, babe," Ronnie assures her. "Listen, I'm just going to stay with the McLarnons tonight because I'm really going to struggle with the drive home."

"You're doing the right thing, darling," replies Debbie. "At least I know you'll be safe. Well you get a good sleep and I'll see you tomorrow after work. Good night, babe. Love you."

"Night, babe," says Ronnie. "Love you too."

As the nights and rehearsals seems to get longer, Liz becomes increasingly concerned for the safety of her bandmates and Debbie who are all struggling when it comes to the long drive back to the McLarnons' house so she decides to speak to her father.

"Dad?" Liz, now sixteen years old, asks.

Tam: "What is it, my wee lamb?"

"Dad, how would you feel about me moving out?" she asks her father hesitantly.

"It depends what the reason is, hen," replies Tam. "What's brought this on?"

"I'm worried about the guys and Debbie, Dad," says Liz. "They are all working, I am at school, the rehearsals are long and I still need to fit my studying in as well as writing songs. We are all knackered. I just think it would be easier on everyone if I moved in with them."

"I'm not sure about that one, love," replies Tam, concerned. "Are you sure they've got room?"

"I'm sure we could make room," smiles Liz. "I wouldn't even need to worry about travel because the flat is less than a ten-minute walk from the school."

"Let me speak to Joe, doll," says Tam. "In the mean time, you talk to Debbie and the guys when you go to rehearsals tomorrow."

"Will do, Dad," replies Liz as she hugs her father and kisses him goodnight. "Thanks for understanding and for being the legend that you are. I love you."

"Seriously, Liz?" asks Carl when she tells her bandmates her thoughts the following evening. "Yes, it's practical and it would be a lot easier on all of us but what is your dad saying?"

"He said he was meeting Papa Joe for lunch today," replies Liz. "So we'll see what comes out of it."

"Where would you sleep though, Liz?" asks Debbie. "We are all crammed in this apartment as it is."

Moose looks at Angel. "We could put the bunk beds up, get a single bed for Liz and the three of us could share," he suggests.

"What?" asks Angel, shocked. *"OUR room? NO!"*

"What's up, Angel," asks Liz. "Do you guys parade around the room naked or something?"

"No," replies Angel as he blushes, shocked that an innocent girl such as Liz could have such thoughts.

"You'd better not parade around the room naked either," laughs Moose as Angel grimaces. "We'll see what Papa Joe says and we'll get started this week. I don't see it being a problem, as long as you're OK with me leaving early for work? I'm usually up about four o'clock in the morning so I can train."

"I'm fine with it, Moose," replies Liz. "I could sleep through a war!"

The following week, Liz moves into the bandmates' apartment. After finishing his coffee, Moose looks at the clock and bids Papa Joe, Debbie and his bandmates a good night as he has an early rise for training followed by coaching in the morning. Liz continues to sit up later with everyone else as they chat and laugh about various things until the living room gradually empties as everyone retires for the night. Liz goes to her room with Angel to find that Moose, a very light sleeper, is still awake on the top bunk as he reads a nutrition book with a torch. The three of them chat as Angel and Liz get into their beds and Angel falls asleep almost immediately. Liz relaxes, closes her eyes and gets ready to go to sleep when the silence is disrupted. She looks at Angel, startled, then up at Moose. "Uh-oh," says Moose. "Sorry, I forgot to tell you about that."

His brother continues to softly sing a song that neither he nor Liz had heard before. "Is he alright?" Liz asks, concerned.

"He's fine," Moose chuckles. "He does this when he's happy and it worries me when I don't hear it. Does it bother you? I'll wake him and he can sleep on the couch if it does."

"No, Moose, please don't," pleads Liz. "It's actually very cute and it will help me sleep too. I love his voice."

"Me too," Moose smiles warmly as he turns off his torch. "I've listened to this going to sleep since I was any age and it always gives me reassurance that everything's alright with my little brother. Night, Liz."

"Night, Moose," Liz replies as she closes her eyes and falls asleep to Angel's dulcet tones.

The following morning, Liz wakes up on time for school without even an alarm clock and feeling refreshed after a very peaceful night's sleep to find that Moose and Angel have already left for work. She passes the kitchen to find that Debbie is preparing a light breakfast of cereals, toast and coffee for herself, Ronnie, Papa Joe and Liz. "Good morning, sweetheart," Debbie greets her. "Did you sleep well."

"Good morning, Debbie," smiles Liz. "Aaww, I did! I even got the most beautiful lullaby."

"Sorry, Liz," Debbie apologises as she covers her mouth. "Angel does that when he is in a good place. I hope he wasn't bothering you."

"Not at all," assures Liz. "I really enjoyed it. If anything, it helped me get to sleep."

"That's good," says Debbie, relieved. "It looks like things are going to work out just fine with the seven of us. My only worry is that we might need to look for a bigger place soon."

"I'm surprised you haven't by now," replies Liz.

"This place holds so many fond memories for all of us, Liz," sighs Debbie as the feeling of nostalgia washes over her. "I moved in to be with Ronnie after meeting him at our graduation dance when I was just twenty years old. It was love at first sight. Then, of course, I started working for Hell Freeze. Then Carl lost his beautiful mom Antonia, who was a massive influence on all of us and probably the one responsible for Hell Freeze forming in the first place. When she died, we worried about Papa Joe going back to his old house on his own so he stayed here. Then, of course, there was all our achievements as a band as well as our wild nights out together. It's basically our family home..."

"*Wow,*" sighs Liz. "So many memories! I can see why you don't want to leave it. Anyway, like you say, things are working as they are and we all get on."

"Definitely, honey," smiles Debbie.

Liz is enjoying breakfast with Papa Joe, Debbie and Ronnie when the subject of Angel's birthday comes up. "Are you doing anything for it?" asks Liz.

Ronnie shakes his head. "It falls on a Tuesday when we're all working and we have a major weekend of gigs both weekends," he says. "We'll just have a wee night in here for him and we'll spoil him."

"I really want to get him something," says Liz. "But I don't know what. He has been so good to me this year and really looked after me since I joined the band."

"He doesn't really need anything," says Debbie. "He's a low-maintenance boy who only enjoys the simple things."

"Hm," says Liz as she thinks what she can possibly get for him. That afternoon after school, Liz takes a trip into the town centre. She is looking at the various shops when she spots a classy-looking jewellers' shop. She looks at the sign in the window. "Custom orders available," it reads.

Liz goes into the shop to investigate. "Sorry, no children allowed," the elderly shop worker says, firmly.

"Aaww, I was hoping you could design something for me," pleads Liz.

"No," the man says abruptly. "No children allowed. Please don't waste my..."

"Oh, *WOW*," a female worker in her mid twenties cries out from the back. "Liz? Liz McLarnon?"

"Aye," says Liz, nervously.

"It's OK, Dad," the young assistant calls to the elderly worker. "This girl gets served. It's the little girl who joined Hell Freeze last year."

"Good gracious," exclaims the elderly shop worker. "I am so sorry, my dear. I didn't recognise you and I certainly didn't expect to see you in these parts."

"It's alright," Liz smiles. "Thank you for serving me. I am so grateful."

"My name is Arlene," says the young female worker is she shakes Liz's hand. "This is my father and business partner Joseph. I will be your designer. Let's sit down and have a chat."

Arlene fetches her sketch pad and sits down with Liz as she discusses what she wants. "Well I would like a guitar design," says Liz and Arlene proceeds to sketch several rough guitar designs. Within minutes, she has ten thumbnail sketches in total and she shows them to Liz. "Do you see anything that appeals to you here, love?" asks Arlene.

"I really like that one," says Liz as she points to a very unique, classy-looking guitar design.

"Amazing," smiles Arlene. "I can either etch this design into a rectangular background for you, complete, with border or we can make the actual guitar shape."

"I would love the guitar shape," enthuses Liz.

"OK," says Arlene with a serious tone. "I must advise you that due to the amount of work that will go into this particular design, it will cost significantly more than a guitar-embossed design."

"That's OK," smiles Liz. "It's worth it."

"Will you need a chain?" asks Arlene.

"That one, please," smiles Liz as she points to a thick, gold belcher chain on the display.

"That's the eighteen karat gold diamond cut belcher," gasps Arlene.

"Perfect," giggles Liz. "He's going to love it!"

"OK," says Arlene as she writes in her note pad. "I will need a $100 deposit from you today...so your total price for the design and artwork, including the chain comes to $590."

Liz nods and smiles as she hands Arlene's father her deposit. "Is it for somebody special?" asks Arlene.

"Yes, it's for Angel," Liz smiles. "He has been so good to me since I joined Hell Freeze and it's his birthday at the end of the month. I just want to thank him for looking after me and to give him something he can keep and treasure."

"*ANGEL?*" asks Arlene as she almost faints. "Aaww, I wish you had told me sooner! I can't believe I have just designed a pendant for the gorgeous Angel!"

"Yes, and he is going to love it," smiles Liz. "Thank you so much, Arlene. I am absolutely delighted and can't wait to see the pendant finished. I'll call in on Monday after school and give you the rest of your money if that's OK?"

"That's excellent, Liz," smiles Joseph as he shakes Liz's hand. "It was a pleasure doing business with you. See you on Monday."

Chapter 18:
Scaling The Heights

The following Monday, Angel and Carl turn up to Farrell's for their late shift to be met outside by Sharon who is in floods of tears as she carries bags out to her car. "Sharon," Angel calls out. "What has happened?"

"Thirty years of my life I have given this place," Sharon sobs. "Thirty! Now we have been bought over and I have been dropped like a lead balloon and so has Yvonne."

"That's brutal," cries Carl. "What about the union?"

"They say there is nothing I can do," Sharon continues to cry. "It's hopeless. I loved my job and all of you guys. I'm really gonna miss you."

"We'll miss you too, Sharon," replies Angel, now close to tears himself. "I suppose we'd better get in and start."

"Good luck," says Sharon as she dries her tears and hugs Angel and Carl. "It's not a nice place to be anymore..."

Feeling deflated by Yvonne and Sharon's departure, Angel and Carl make their way to the shop floor to start their shift. They arrive to be met by Marc who is dressed in normal overalls, the same as all the other workers. He nods as he acknowledges his workers. "Marc?" asks Angel. "What the Hell is going on?"

"Am no yer gaffer any mare, mate," Marc shrugs. "The new folk demoted me as soon as they moved in and kicked Yvonne and Sharon out. I cannae even afford to leave because I've got a wife and two weans. We're struggling to make ends meet as it is despite ma Gillian workin'."

"I'm so sorry, Marc," says Carl. "What an absolute shit show!"

"Yer no wrang, mate," replies Marc as he goes back to work. Throughout the shift a massive, dark cloud just seems to hang over Farrell's as everyone just works in silence without a single smile and Angel and Carl have never been so glad to finish. They arrive home, take their leathers off and sit down to relax with coffee and a cigarette before bed. "That was the worst shift in the world," groans Angel. "The way those new owners have treated our long-term workers is beyond criminal."

"Right," says Carl. "It just seems nobody is happy there anymore. I'm dreading even setting foot in the place tomorrow."

"Me too, dude," concurs Angel. "Me too."

There is a few moments silence as the two men continue to smoke their cigarettes. "Wait," says Carl. "Maybe we don't have to!"

"What do you mean?" asks Angel.

"Well it's not as if we're broke," laughs Carl. "We have done exceptionally well this year ever since Liz came on board. Let's not go in."

"I want to go in just one last time," says Angel. "Even just to say goodbye to Marc and the other boys and girls on the shop floor."

"Hey, we could take Marc with us," smiles Carl.

"Carl," sighs Angel. "We might be able to afford to walk but Marc can't. He has a wife and two kids, remember?"

"I'm well aware of that, dude," Carl continues to smile. "We could really use a roady now that we can afford one. He could come with us. He is a great worker, it will make things a lot easier on Debbie and he will keep us all laughing. We can't go wrong."

"Great idea, bro," replies Angel. "The three of us could walk out together. No warning. Nothing. After all, we owe the stinking bosses nothing after what they did to Yvonne and Sharon!"

"Let's REALLY go out in style," laughs Carl. "I have the very plan but I need you to drive us to work…"

The following afternoon, Angel and Carl arrive at Farrell's for their late shift. "Awright, bhoys," Marc greets them as he smokes a cigarette in the car park. "How's things?"

"Aaww, Marc," says Carl. "I'm glad we caught you before the shift."

"Aye?" asks Marc. "Whit's up?"

"This is our last day," smiles Angel.

"Aw, gutted, man," says Marc, sorrowfully. "You guys have become my mates an'…"

"No OUR last day, Marc," cries Carl. "We thought you could come with us."

"I telt ye, Carl," sighs Marc. "I cannae afford tae leave."

"The thing is, Marc," says Angel, quietly. "We REALLY need a roady who can drive the tour bus and help us with our equipment now that we are touring further afield. Carl and I thought you could do it. We'll match your supervisor wages for this place and make it worth your while. Come on, Marc. What do you say?"

"I say you've got yourselves a deal," exclaims Marc as he shakes hands with Angel and Carl and embraces them.

"YES," Carl cheers then continues to whisper. "Here's the plan for today…"

Just like yesterday, Angel and Carl can't help but notice the heavy atmosphere on the shop floor at Farrell's as they work. "Now?" Angel whispers to Marc.

"Aye, ma man," Marc laughs quietly. "Let's go."

The three men stop what they are doing, run up all the stairs to the top floor and lock themselves in the top store room. They then proceed to strip naked apart from their boots, burst out of the stock room and run down all the stairs to the reception area as Angel runs at the back with a set of overalls on fire. The entire late shift at Farrell's watches as it erupts with a combination of cheers, laughs and screams at the sight of the three men making their exit in all their glory.

"FUCK THIS PLACE AND FUCK THIS JOAB," Marc shouts as they burst into the reception area, where the new owner and his wife are standing. Angel looks out of his peripheral vision and notices the middle-aged lady boss has fainted and he drops the blazing overalls, allowing them to smoulder on the carpet. The three men jump into Angel's car and make their getaway to Marc's house.

They pull up in the driveway of Marc's detached bungalow where his wife Gillian is waiting. "Gillian, darlin'," Marc calls to her. "Can you bring me ma dressin' goon please?"

Gillian buckles with laughter as she realises the guys' predicament and goes to get her husband's bathrobe. "The sights you see when you don't have a gun," she continues to laugh out loud. "What happened?"

"I resigned from Farrell's, babe," replies Marc as he puts on his robe, gets out of the car and gives his wife a kiss and a hug.

"MARC," cries Gillian. "You know we can't afford for you to leave your job! What are we going to do?"

"It's awright, sweetheart," Marc assures her. "Ma bhoys have hit the big time and am going to work for them. I am the official roady for Hell Freeze."

"There are free concerts in it for you, Gillian," Carl winks at her.

"Well I can't argue with that," giggles Gillian. "I can't believe you were just kids when you just started with Marc, now he works for you!"

"He'll always be Gaffer to us," smiles Carl.

"See you on Friday then, Gaffer?" asks Angel.

"Aye, mate," smiles Marc. *"WHIT A JOAB, MAN. WHIT A FUCKIN' JOAB!"*

"He's back," smiles Carl as Angel pulls away.

Unfortunately for Carl and Angel, the street outside their apartment is unusually busy for a Tuesday afternoon. "We can't get out of the car like this," Angel whispers as he starts to shiver. "There's kids about. Bloody Hell, it's getting cold!"

"That's the trouble with you, Angel," scolds Carl. "You *NEVER* use your head. *EVER!*"

"*NO,*" Angel yells back. "That's because I'm always using *YOUR* head and going along with *YOUR* stupid ideas. That's the problem! All I can say is thank God for tinted windows!"

Just when the guys think things can't possibly get any worse, Angel notices blue flashing lights in his rear view mirror. "Oh no," he groans as he looks at Carl.

"Aw, shit," replies Carl.

A tall police officer emerges from the patrol car and knocks on the driver's side window. Angel rolls his window down slightly, now really shivering with the cold as he does so. "Good afternoon, officer," he greets the policeman. "Is something wrong?"

"Sir, we have reason to believe that this vehicle is stolen and we need you to step out please," replies the policeman with his voice of authority.

"Um we can't do that, officer," Angel says.

"Dare I ask why not," asks the officer.

Angel looks sheepish as he covers his private parts and rolls down the window a bit more. "We've just left our day job," Angel says quietly as he blushes.

The officer immediately goes into hysterical laughter when he finally recognises Angel and Carl. "*SARGE,*" he shouts to his colleague. "You REALLY need to see this."

An older police officer emerges from the patrol car. "*GOOD GOD,*" he exclaims. "Are your record sales SO bad that this is what you guys are reduced to?"

"The exact opposite, officer," Carl chimes in. "They are so good we have just left our day jobs, hence the indecent exposure. Our ex-bosses wanted their overalls back..."

"OK, guys," chuckles the sergeant. "We'll let you go free on the condition that you sign some autographs for us."

"Done and done," replies Carl, relieved. "We'll do that for you on the condition that we borrow your coats? Our apartment is just there and Moose, Ronnie and Liz should all be home."

Carl knocks on the door and is met by Moose who looks bewildered at the sight of his friend and his brother dressed only in police trench coats and boots as they are accompanied by two police officers. "What the," Moose gasps, wide-eyed.

"We resigned," chuckles Angel as he gives his brother a playful punch on the shoulder. "We have a couple of fans here who would like some autographs."

"Moose?" Liz calls out from the living room.

"Liz stay in the living room just now, babe," he replies to her as he turns his attention to the two police officers, Carl and Angel. "Please come in, officers. You two, hurry up and make yourselves decent."

Ronnie and Debbie emerge from the living room and burst out laughing when they realise what's going on as Moose covers his face and muffles his laughter. Ronnie calms himself down and invites the officers into the living room while Debbie and Liz make coffee. The five bandmates then fill two entire note pads with autographs and the policemen leave Hell Freeze's apartment happy.

The following Tuesday is Angel's thirty-fourth birthday. Liz is sitting at breakfast with Papa Joe, Debbie and Ronnie as they chat happily about the surprise party they are throwing for Angel later on. "I'm going to be home late tonight," she tells her friends. "I need to go a message into town after school."

"Alright, baby girl," says Papa Joe. "Just don't be too late so you miss the boy's party."

"I wouldn't miss it," smiles Liz.

After school, Liz arrives at Arlene's shop to pick up Angel's present. Arlene proudly opens the box and reveals the unique, custom-made guitar pendant Liz had requested as a gift for a man she had grown to love like a big brother. "It's beautiful," Liz smiles. "Thank you so much, Arlene."

She arrives home to find the party is in full swing as her bandmates enjoy food, drink and music as they celebrate their friend's birthday. She hands Angel a birthday card along with a small, gift-wrapped box and kisses him as she wishes him a happy birthday. "I'm sorry, I didn't know what to get you," Liz tells him. "It's just to say thank you very much for everything and for being there for me. Love you, big bro."

"I love you too, little sis," replies Angel as he hugs her. "You didn't have to get me anything though."

He opens his gift and gasps when he sees the pendant. "Aw I love it, Liz," he says as he puts it on and hugs her. "I'll always treasure it. Thank you and thanks, everyone, for a great night."

That weekend, Hell Freeze have yet another major out-of-state gig. Like many others, the gig has become a full-blown party until Angel calls for silence. He cues Carl to begin with the unique drum beat of Ronnie's composition "Moon Light." The audience erupts into a massive cheer as they recognise it. From there, Ronnie and Moose join in with their bass and backing guitar and, lastly, Liz plays her unique jazz-piano melody and Angel sings along to it. He is just finishing the first verse then he notices something out of his peripheral vision but ignores it. He begins to sing the chorus when a familiar voice is heard harmonising through the microphone. Angel stares wide-eyed as the legendary Rick Hammer of Moulten Rock, a globally famous band that has been going strong since the nineteen sixties, joins him on stage but he continues to sing the song as a duet anyway. Angel has no idea what to make of this situation as his bandmates stare at Hammer in disbelief, some angry, some confused. Meanwhile, the audience has gone wild and everyone is cheering at the sight and sound of the two rock Gods performing together. Angel's thought process goes into overdrive as he sings: "Somebody has just hijacked my performance of one of Hell Feeeze's biggest hit songs to date and possibly overshadowed me. On the other hand, the so-called intruder is a man I have idolised and endevoured to be as big as since I was a child. Fuck it. Publicity is publicity, right? The audience are enjoying it anyway. I hope this stunt doesn't set us back..."

Hell Freeze finish performing the track with addition of Rick Hammer's distinct vocals and the crowd erupts into another massive cheer. "Ladies and gentlemen," Angel addresses the audience. "The legendary Mr Rick Hammer."

"Ladies and gentlemen," continues Rick. "May I take this opportunity to thank the sensational Mr Angel Mancini and his amazing bandmates for sharing that song with me. It truly is a work of art and one of my favourites of all time. These inspirational guys and that beautiful, talented little girl are going places. Once again, thank you!"

The audience continues to cheer as Rick exits the stage to join his own bandmates who are now watching Hell Freeze perform from the wings.

After the gig, Hell Freeze are greeted backstage by Moulten Rock as all the band members shake hands. "Guys and gals," says Rick Hammer. "I want to thank you all once again for that wonderful opportunity. I really enjoyed performing on-stage with you. I tell you, you guys know how to rock."

"Thank you, Mr Hammer," smiles Angel. "We really appreciate that coming from a huge icon like you."

"Please, Angel," says Hammer. "It's Rick. I'd like to believe we are all friends here now."

"Of course," replies Carl.

"I suppose you're wondering what my entrance was about?" asks Rick.

Hell Freeze nod as they wait for Rick's answer. "Guys and gals," Rick continues. "I have followed you for so many years, since before Wullie McLarnon joined you. I'm glad you have his beautiful little sister working with you now. Liz, you are a real superstar and an asset to Hell Freeze. Anyway, good people, I would like to take this opportunity to invite you to support us at Wembly Arena next year. We are predicting a full weekend of sold-out gigs and it would be a great honour for us if you would join us for that experience."

"*WOW,*" gasps Moose in his deep, husky voice. "We would love to."

"Excellent," smiles Rick as he hands bottles of beer to all the fellow band members and a can of Pepsi to Liz and Miranda Brown, fiancee of Moulten Rock bass player Phil Bryan. "We will look forward to working with you. You are an amazing bunch of talented people."

Debbie, Papa Joe and all the bandmates chat among themselves and continue to enjoy food and alcohol and Miranda introduces herself to Liz. Liz looks at Miranda with awe. She is a tall, stunning woman who works as an actress and model and she is engaged to a musician who plays for one of the most successful rock bands of all time. Liz is even more fascinated that this elegant lady is taking such an interest in her. It is almost midnight and Phil calls Miranda over as they are going home. Miranda kisses Liz goodbye, they exchange phone numbers and Miranda asks Liz to keep in touch. Papa Joe puts an arm around Liz's shoulders and guides her out to his car but not before Moose notices that she is crying. "Are you alright, baby girl?" asks Papa Joe as Liz sits in the passenger seat.

"I'm fine, thanks, Joe," replies Liz with a weary smile as she closes her eyes. "I'm just very tired."

Liz is unable to sleep despite being physically and mentally exhausted. Several hours later, she hears Debbie and her bandmates come home from their star-studded party in the very early hours of the morning. Moose and Angel enter the room and chat quietly as they get changed and into bed. Liz smiles as Angel begins to sing, her indication that her protective adopted older brother is content and relaxed as he sleeps on the bottom bunk. Moose, who still works as a fitness instructor and personal trainer, reads a physiology book with a torch on the top bunk as he winds down after today's excitement. Liz looks up at Moose who happens to take his eyes off his book and is looking at her. "Do you want to talk about it?", asks Moose, his voice hoarse after a busy week of teaching, performing and partying. "Sorry we couldn't take you with us. Did you not enjoy the gig and what about our tour with Molten Rock? Are you not up for it?"

Liz starts to cry again as she climbs onto the top bunk beside Moose, in order not to disturb Angel, and lies on top of the duvet. "It's nothing to do with the party," weeps Liz. "I knew I wouldn't be allowed to go because of my age and I was fine with that. Yes, I loved the gig. It was a buzz and, yes, of course I am up for the Molten Rock tour."

"What is it then?" presses Moose as he puts down his book.

"Did you see Phil Bryan's fiancee?" asks Liz.

"See her?" replies Moose, excitedely. "Fuck yeah! If old Bryan doesn't want her, I'll do her. She'll be due a younger, fitter model soon no doubt.""Really, Moose?" asks Liz, now unable to control her tears. "Put it this way. Would you do me?""Liz, have you gone mad?" Moose grimaces. "I would be on the sex offenders' register as a paedophile and behind bars in the blink of an eye! Even hardened criminals hate those vile beings.""Moose," Liz whispers. "Miranda is two years younger than me! She is just fourteen years old and Phil Bryan must be nearly fifty. That's just not right and I feel so sick with worry thinking about her that poor girl. Where are her parents and what are they doing? Miranda is not being looked after..."

"Listen, baby," he tells her. "We are going to make it big soon and you are going to see some very shady things in this business. The bigger we get the more shady, dirty things you are going to witness. If you want to bail out, now is your time."

"I can't," says Liz. "This is my job now and I don't want to let you guys down after all you've done for me."

"We're all here to protect you," Moose assures her as he gently squeezes her tiny hand. "Please remember that. Now try to get some sleep, baby. Tonight's gig was a tough one and you did really well with everything."

"Thanks, Moose," smiles Liz as she hugs him before going

back to her own bed. "Good night."

Chapter 19:
Taking Shape

The following morning, Liz wakes up to find that Moose and Angel are already up and she can hear all the chatting and laughing from the living room as Debbie and the bandmates recall events from the previous night. Liz gets up, gets into the shower and gets dressed before joining her friends for breakfast. After enjoying some chat and hearing all the funny stories about the late-night celebrations, she finishes eating then gathers everyone's dirty dishes and takes them to the kitchen to wash them. Moose follows her. "How are you feeling, Liz?" he whispers.

"Still uneasy, Moose, but better now that I've spoken to you," replies Liz. "Thanks for listening to me."

"Anytime, baby," smiles Moose as he hugs her. "You know where we are if anything is bothering you."

Just then, a very excited Debbie prances into the kitchen. "That was MegaMetal Clothing on the phone," she tells Moose and Liz. "They want to do an interview and a photo shoot with us to promote their latest lines. They spotted us at last night's gig. Are you both up for it?"

"Sounds good to me," Liz laughs. "I might never be Miranda Brown but at least I'll get my hair and make-up done and get to wear nice clothes."

"No, Liz," affirms Moose. "You are Liz McLarnon, upcoming rock Goddess. Remember you and Miranda are on completely different paths. Please don't compare yourself to her."

"Moose is right again, Liz," says Debbie. "You are carving out your own unique path. Let's enjoy this photo shoot and a good pamper session when it comes."

The day arrives for Hell Freeze's interview and photoshoot with MegaMetal clothing. An assistant takes everyone's measurements before handing them over to the beauticians for their hair and make-up. "Oh, *WOW*," gasps Liz as she catches sight of herself in the mirror. "I never knew I could look this good in make-up and look at the clothes!"

Liz gazes at her outfit of form-hugging leather jeans, paired with a leather bustier top which emphasises her ample cleavage and finished with over-the-knee black patent boots. Debbie looks as elegant as always as she wears a combination of leather hot pants, a cropped leather biker jacket, fishnet tights and ankle boots. Her four male bandmates also look the part in their new leather gear and jeans.

After what feels like forever, Debbie and the bandmates emerge from the studio. "Phew," sighs Moose. "That was hard work! I feel as though I could eat everyone's body weight in food after that."

"Aye, Moose," laughs Ronnie. "Very model-like indeed. You're right, though. We've definitely earned ourselves a good dinner after that! Moose and Angel, we could swing by and pick up your mum. Her house isn't far from here."

"Sounds like a plan, brother," says Angel. "I can't wait to see Mom."

While everyone is waiting for their food, Liz picks up a newspaper and flicks through it. She stops when she sees that Hell Freeze have the main feature in the centre fold of the music section, complete with reviews from audience members. One five-star review in particular hits Liz like a high-speeding freight train. The author had given Hell Freeze a five-star review for their performance and wrote: "OUT OF THIS WORLD. It was an absolute joy hearing Hell Freeze performing old songs from away back when Wullie McLarnon was with them. The chubby little red-haired girl is just fantastic and she has a very distinct voice that will only get better as she gets older. She should think about coming out from behind the keyboard kit and dueting with Angel. Now *THAT* would be powerful!"

Liz sighs and puts the newspaper down. While she realises she should be over the moon that audience members are appreciating her work, the "chubby little red-haired girl" quote sticks in her throat. "I'll talk to Moose later," Liz thinks to herself.

Liz's fears are confirmed the following week when the Hell Freeze interview is published in Strum Magazine along with the pictures from their photo shoot. Everyone is happy with their photos except Liz. "Look at me," she groans. "I didn't realise I had put on so much weight. I'm fat!"

"Liz, you are *NOT* fat," exclaims Debbie. "You still have growing to do and everything will even out in time. You'll see."

"I don't know about that," replies Liz. "I'm plain and dumpy compared to other girls my age who are in the industry."

"Liz, my dear," says Papa Joe. "I've seen most of those girls at my radio station and they are nothing out-of-the-ordinary. What you are seeing are edited, touched-up photos after these kids have had their hair and make-up professionally done."

"Papa Joe is right, Liz," assures Moose. "If you are that worried about it, you are more than welcome to come to the gym with me. I'll work with you and we'll do it safely. How does that sound?"

"Aw, Moose, do you really mean that?" beams Liz.

"Of course," replies Moose. "The last thing we want are eating disorders and everything that comes with those damn things. You will need ALL your energy for our performances. Just promise me one thing: no crazy starvation diets."

"Thanks so much, Moose," Liz replies as she hugs him. "I promise."

The following Monday, after school, Liz makes her way to

Trojans' to meet Moose for her first ever personal training session. Liz finds her session tough but, at the same time, she enjoyed it and feels as though she has achieved something from it. Moose chats with her as he walks her to the changing room. On the way there, they pass another trainer who is busy working with two young clients on what looks like advanced martial arts. The burly Latino trainer waves to Moose as he keeps an eye on his clients and Moose waves back. Liz stops and watches in awe as the athletic teenaged boy and girl go through the motions of a Kata perfectly in sync with each other. "What are they doing?" asks Liz.

"That's Karate, babe," replies Moose. "My good friend Marco has been working with that boy and girl for about six months now and that's the standard they're at already. He's getting them ready for their first competition."

"It looks awesome," enthuses Liz as she continues to watch.

"Why don't you mix up your training?" suggests Moose. "You could come with me on Mondays after school and we'll see what time slots Marco has available and you can go with him too and learn how to defend yourself."

"Are you sure Marco won't mind?" asks Liz.

"Of course he won't mind," assures Moose. "Marco is very passionate about martial arts and will go all out to help anyone who is willing to learn and improve themselves. Would you like me to talk to him?"

"Yes please," beams Liz.

"Great," smiles Moose. "I don't want to disturb his session so I'll catch him at work when I go in in the morning."

From then on, Liz continues to work with Moose on Monday nights and her Saturday mornings are occupied by personal training with Marco then onto a Karate class he runs on his own. It's not long before Liz begins to see the results she wants and so does everyone else.

Following Rick Hammer's publicity stunt during their gig, Hell Freeze see their success sky rocket sky rocket yet again as their re-reliease of "Moon Light" featuring Hammer goes straight into the U.S and U.K charts at number one, as does their album "Bad Blood." Moose and Ronnie decide that now is the time to give up their day jobs so they can fully commit to the band. Their last day of work has arrived and they are sad to go as they have made so many friends at Trojans' over the years. At the end of the shift, Ronnie and Moose are cornered by all the staff. "OK, guys," Lukas laughs, menacingly. "You know how this works."

For many years, it has been a custom for members of staff to jump or dive from the diving dale on their last day of work at Trojans'. It is now Moose and Ronnie's turn.

"Aw, naw," groans Ronnie.

"Oh, yes," chuckles Marco.

"Come on, guys," pleads Moose. "You know I can't stand heights."

"It'll be alright, big guy," assures Ronnie. "Come on. Let's get this over with..."

Moose whimpers as he and Ronnie are escorted to poolside. "Ladies and gentlemen," Lukas addresses his colleagues. "The convicts will now walk the plank."

"I'll go first," says Ronnie. "There will be nothing to it."

Moose says nothing as he looks at the height of the diving dale, which looks to be miles high. Ronnie proceeds to remove his trainers and climb the ladder then jumps, fully clothed, into the pool. He laughs as he surfaces from the water and swims to the side of the pool to be helped out by fellow employees. "Come on, Moose," he smiles. "If a skinny wimp like me can do it, so can a tough guy like you."

That statement from Ronnie was enough motivation for Moose. He removes his trainers and signals with his head for Marco to follow him up the ladder. "It's the one thing I am terrified of," he whispers to Marco.

"You'll be alright, big guy," replies Marco. "Just shut your eyes and it will be over in seconds."

Moose focuses forward the entire time he and Marco climb the ladder as he tries to block out how high off the ground they are. He gets to the top, immediately jumps and feels a sense of relief as he hits the water. Everyone cheers as Moose emerges from the pool. "Oh my God," he beams at his colleagues. *"I DID IT. I FACED ONE OF MY BIGGEST FEARS."*

"Well done, pal," smiles Lukas as he hands Moose a towel. "Don't forget us, eh?"

"How could I forget my two starting buddies?" asks Moose. "I'll still be coming in to train Liz and she'll still want her sessions with you, Marco, so I won't be a stranger."

"Just make sure you're not," says Marco as he pats Moose on the back. "You two will be sadly missed."

"My door will be open too," Ronnie tells the group. "If any of you need a massage or any other treatments, you are more than welcome to come to the house."

Moose and Ronnie get changed into their dry clothes and all the staff cheer and hand them cards and gifts as they all walk out the door and Lukas locks up. They both fight back tears as everyone wishes them all the best for their future as they get into Ronnie's car.

"That's it," smiles Ronnie. "Four of us are full-time rock stars now."

"Yeah," replies Moose with sadness in his voice. "I'm going to miss all my fitness pals though."

"We'll still see them, pal," assures Ronnie. "There's no reason why they can't come to us for dinner and we can still meet them for nights out. The four of us have worked in Trojans' after starting together all those years ago. We'll always be friends."

"I suppose," Moose smiles warmly as he remembers all the good times he had spent with his three colleagues.

One evening, now seventeen-year-old Liz is enjoying her walk home from school in the crisp, autumn sunshine. "Aaww, there's my house," she thinks to herself as she gazes at the impressive house that has brought her so much joy since she moved into

Hell Freeze's apartment. Suddenly, something catches her eye and she gasps. She walks closer to the house to investigate and is excited to realise that it is, in fact, up for sale.

"We could well afford it now," Liz thinks to herself as she let's herself into the tall, cast iron, silver-painted double gate and makes her way up the long driveway, which is occupied by three classic cars and two Harley Davidson motorcycles.

Liz nervously rings the bell and the door is answered by an elderly gentleman. "Hello," Liz greets him. "I noticed your house is up for sale and I was wondering if I could make an appointment for my manager to come and view it?"

"Is this some kind of a joke?" scoffs the man. "You are only a child. What do you know about houses?"

"*LIZ?*" a younger man's voice chimes in. "*LIZ MCLARNON?* Is that really you?"

"Do you know this young lady, Scott?" asks the elderly gentleman.

"Not personally, Dad," replies the younger man. "Although I know who she is. This is the talented young girl who joined the band Hell Freeze two years ago."

"Who?" asks Scott's father.

"Hell Freeze, Dad," replies Scott. "They are an amazing rock band and they are doing really well in the charts just now."

"Never heard of them," scoffs Scott's father.

"Anyway, Liz," says Scott. "What brings you here?"

"I have admired this stunning house ever since I joined Hell Freeze," Liz sighs. "It is my dream home and I was wondering if I could make an appointment for my manager to view and possibly buy it?"

"Certainly," replies Scott. "Shall we say tomorrow at six p.m.?"

"*SCOTT,*" exclaims Scott's father. "Have you gone mad?"

"It's OK, Dad," assures Scott. "I trust Liz is genuine."

"Six p.m. tomorrow is perfect," replies Liz, almost crying with happiness.

"Excellent," smiles Scott. "Here is my business card. Please phone me if you can't make the viewing."

"Thank you so much, Mr Braes," beams Liz. "We'll definitely be here!"

Liz goes home and excitedly tells her bandmates about the appointment she had made. "I hope you all don't mind," Liz tells her friends. "It's a stunning house and I know we need a bigger place, especially with another bathroom or two for the mornings."

"Good thinking, baby girl," smiles Papa Joe. "You and I will go and see it tomorrow and if any of you guys want to come along, you're more than welcome."

"This place," sighs Moose. "I remember having the discussion with our old folks about moving in here away back in 1976. It was originally only intended for myself, Angel and Carl. It has certainly served us well."

"Ah, the memories," replies Angel. "Well I suppose it's time for us to move onto bigger and better things now that we know we can afford to."

"I'm so excited for tomorrow," enthuses Liz. "I've had my eye on that beautiful house for long enough although I'll miss my lullabies."

"It's tough at the top, wee yin," laughs Ronnie.

The following evening Papa Joe, Debbie and Hell Freeze arrive at the Braes' house for their appointment. Scott greets everyone on arrival and proceeds to give them a guided tour of the impressive house that Liz had gazed lovingly at for so long. The ground floor comprises of a generously-sized living room which is adjoined with the kitchen. There is also a patio door which leads from the kitchen to the spacious conservatory. The ground floor also houses a newly-fitted bathroom, two large bedrooms, one of which has a small en-suite bathroom as well as another room which could potentially be their music room. They then ascend the ornate staircase to the upper floor which comprises of another spacious bathroom and four generously-sized bedrooms, one of which has an en-suite bathroom. "It's perfect," gasps Liz. "It's every bit as amazing as I thought it would be!"

"I like it too," whispers Carl as he puts an arm around Liz. "It's still handy for everything and not far from our apartment."

"Well, what do you young 'uns think?" asks Papa Joe. "Are we taking it?"

"It's a no-brainer," exclaims Debbie. "*YES!*"

"Definitely," concurs Moose. "Well done, Liz!"

"I'm not so keen on the conservatory though," sighs Carl.

"It's cool, bro," Angel smiles and blushes. "We can convert it and put in a hot tub and a mini bar. Picture the scene: us bringing home some big-assed blondes."

"You dirty scoundrel," laughs Moose. "I suppose we'll be taking it then..."

"We would like to make you an offer, Mr Braes," Papa Joe says to Scott, an offer which he cannot refuse.

"Thank you so much, ladies and gentlemen," beams Scott. "It has been a pleasure doing business with you. All the very best in your new home and I'll look forward to seeing you in concert soon."

From there Papa Joe, Debbie and the bandmates clear out their tiny apartment. "As much as I love the new house, this is so emotional," sighs Debbie as she glances around the shell that was the first home she had shared with her beloved Ronnie.

"I know, sister," replies Moose. "I still remember enquiring about this place all those years ago. Mrs Sanders is probably not even with us anymore."

"It will be onwards and upwards from here, bro," smiles Carl. "I'm sure we'll make lots of fond memories at our new pad too."

"Of course," says Angel as he tries to maintain his composure. Liz takes Angel by the arm and leans her head against his shoulder as they carry the last of their bags out to Debbie's van.

The months pass and Hell Freeze continue to enjoy their success as full-time rock stars. Meanwhile, Liz quietly sits the last of her exams from which she requires the grades for entry to medical school. One very early Monday morning at around three o'clock Papa Joe, Debbie and the bandmates arrive home from an out-of-state gig to find a brown A4 envelope on the doormat addressed to "Miss Elizabeth McLarnon." Liz opens the envelope and hands her certificate to Papa Joe, her face expressionless. "Congratulations, my baby girl," exclaims Papa Joe as he gives Liz a kiss and a hug. "She has only gone and achieved six straight A passes on her first try!"

Debbie and the rest of the bandmates congratulate Liz as she smiles and her eyes fill with tears. "Thanks go much, everyone," Liz says quietly. "I'm going to bed now. I'm really tired."

"No bother, Liz," smiles Ronnie. "It's been a long weekend but it was nice to come home to that great news. Congrats again, little sis."

Liz hugs Papa Joe, Debbie and her four bandmates as she thanks them all once again before bidding them goodnight. Soon afterwards, Liz receives a phone call from the medical school informing her that she has an unconditional acceptance for her application to study for her PhD. "Thank you so much," Liz quietly tells the caller. "Could I possibly get back to you on that?"

"Of course, Miss McLarnon," replies the male caller. "We will leave your place open for you for the time being but please let us know, one way or the other, whether or not you are accepting our offer."

"I'll call you straight back tomorrow," replies Liz. "I just need to speak to my family."

"Thank you, Miss McLarnon," replies the caller. "I will look forward to hearing from you and hope to work with you very soon."

It is a warm, sunny morning and Papa Joe is sitting in the back porch enjoying coffee and the summer sunshine as he reads a newspaper. "Papa Joe?" Liz asks him quietly.

"Hello, darling," he smiles up at her. "Is everything alright."

"Yes, but I'm looking for a massive favour," replies Liz.

"I'll do my best, my love," says Papa Joe. "What can I do for you?"

"Would you come to my dad's for dinner with me tonight?" asks Liz. "I have something I need to tell him and I really need moral support."

"You're not in trouble, are you Liz?" asks Papa Joe.

"No, no, no," laughs Liz. "Nothing like that, even though it IS something big."

"Do you want to tell me about it?" whispers Papa Joe as he pulls out the chair beside him for Liz to sit down.

"Papa Joe," says Liz, hesitantly as she takes a seat. "I got my unconditional acceptance for med school this morning."

"Excellent, my dear," exclaims Papa Joe. "This is cause for celebration..."

"Papa Joe," Liz says, quietly. "I've decided...I'm not going."

"NOT GOING?" asks Papa Joe, surprised as he removes his spectacles. "Liz, my dear. This is your dream! What's brought this on?"

"We're doing so well as a band right now," says Liz. "I just don't have the heart to leave you and Debbie and the guys at such a crucial stage. Anyway, I'm seventeen years old. I can always go to medical school later if I change my mind. Right now, the band comes first."

"It sounds like you've thought all of this through," says Papa Joe.

"Oh, I have," Liz assures him. "It has kept me awake at night for weeks but I'm definitely sure."

"Alright, my dear," smiles Papa Joe. "As long as you're sure."

Liz gets on the phone to her dad. "Hello, my wee lamb," Big Tam greets Liz. "It's so good to hear from you."

"Hello, Dad," Liz smiles as she hears her father's voice. "Dad, I was wondering if Papa Joe and I could come to you for dinner tonight?"

"Certainly, ma doll," replies Tam. "I've got Wullie and Phyllis coming over with the weans and Tommy, Robert and John will all be there too. We'll make a night of it."

"Amazing," says Liz. "I can't wait to see you. I miss you loads."

That evening, Liz is enjoying a catch-up with her sister-in-law and four older brothers while Papa Joe and Big Tam talk business. "Dad," says Liz, hesitantly as they settle down for dinner. "There's something I need to tell you."

"What is it, my wee lamb?" asks Tam.

"Dad," says Liz. "I got my unconditional acceptance for med school this morning." Everyone cheers at Liz's announcement.

"That's amazing, pal," exclaims Wullie with his hearty laugh. "We'll soon have another doctor in the family then? Our Harry's coat will be on a shaky peg..."

Liz shakes her head. "I'm not accepting it, Wullie," she replies.

"What do you mean you're not accepting it?" asks Tommy. "Liz, this has been your dream since you were any age. Why aren't you accepting it?"

"I'm living another dream right now, Tommy," replies Liz. "I'm seventeen years old and playing with one of the biggest rock bands of this generation. We are doing so well right now and I feel as though this is not the time to walk away. I am young and I have all the time in the world to go back to studying if I change me mind."

There is about a minute's silence as everyone looks at each other and at Big Tam. "You do whatever makes you happy, my wee love," Tam smiles warmly.

"So you don't mind?" asks Liz, very pleasantly surprised.

"Not at all," replies Tam. "Hell Freeze have been doing so well recently that I had a feeling you would have a tough time choosing what to do next. I'm behind you all the way with whatever you decide to do."

"We're all behind you, hen," concurs John. "I'm so proud of you."

"Thanks so much, everyone," Liz sighs with relief. "I was dreading telling you."

Late that evening, Papa Joe and Liz arrive home to find that

Debbie and the rest of the bandmates are in the living room drinking coffee and smoking cigarettes before bed. "Good evening, my young 'uns," Papa Joe addresses everyone. "Young Liz has a special announcement for you."

"Just to let you all know," says Liz. "I got my unconditional acceptance for med school this morning."

"Congratulations, honey," smiles Debbie.

"Debbie," says Liz, quietly. "I'm not accepting it."

"You're not?" asks Moose, surprised. "Why?"

"Moose, I love you guys," replies Liz. "We are doing so well as a band just now and I don't want to leave you at such a crucial stage in our career. Like I've already said to Papa Joe and my family, I am only seventeen years old and I can always go back to studying later."

"Liz, are you sure about this?" asks Angel.

"I've never been surer of anything in my life," assures Liz.

"What about your dad?" Carl asks quietly. "What is he saying?"

"That's why I went home tonight, Carl," replies Liz. "I wanted to run everything past him first but I needn't have worried. He's behind me a hundred per cent and so are my brothers."

"So that's it then?" asks Ronnie. "We are ALL full-time rockers now?"

"Aye," smiles Liz. "I am over the moon!"

"Right," beams Debbie. "Welcome aboard the full-time shuttle, little sister. We'll do something this weekend to celebrate."

"Aw we can't, babe," replies Ronnie. "We're off to Florida for our trip that we've had planned since last year."

"I'm away on a business trip too," Papa Joe chimes in. "Sorry, baby girl."

"That's OK," says Debbie. "You and I will have a girly weekend to ourselves, Liz. We'll do shopping, cinema and dinner. Those clothes are hanging off you now and you could be doing with some new ones."

"Oh, aye," exclaims Liz, surprised as she pulls up her now baggy jeans that had once fitted her snuggly. "Look at that!"

"There you go," laughs Moose. "Didn't I tell you not to worry?"

"Aw, Moose, that's amazing," enthuses Liz as she looks in the mirror at her newly-found abdominals. "I've been so busy with everything that I didn't even measure my progress or look at what I was losing."

"Nor did you have to," smiles Moose. "I'm glad you took my advice too. You got those results just by doing my workouts and whatever you were doing with Marco without even dieting."

"Thank you, Moose," says Liz as she hugs him tight. "This is all thanks to you and Marco."

"You did all the work, Liz," assures Moose. "Well done!"

The following weekend, Debbie and Liz drop their four male bandmates off at the airport before heading into town for their girls day out. With Debbie being the fashion enthusiast and model that she is, she is enjoying trying all the different styles of clothes on Liz with her new, toned figure. However, she notices that Liz is quiet. "Let's go get a coffee, honey," she says to Liz.

The girls are enjoying coffee in one of the mall coffee stands when Debbie asks Liz why she is being so distant. "This is going to sound crazy, Debbie," says Liz. "I know I've lost weight and everything but I still feel very plain and ugly."

"Aw, Liz," sighs Debbie. "You are far from ugly, darling. Maybe it's just that you need a makeover? After all, you've only ever worn make-up to that photoshoot we did and you've worn your hair the exact same way since the beginning of high school."

Liz's face immediately lights up.

"Oh," says Debbie as she realises she has something. "Do you have a look in mind?"

"Yes," enthuses Liz. "Do you know Marie Fredriksson of the band Roxette?"

"Oh my God, yes," exclaims Debbie. "She is a very stunning girl and you could easily carry off that look. Let's get to work."

Back home, Liz giggles as Debbie sits her down and fetches the clippers. She then proceeds to put Liz's long, dark red, curly hair in a pony tail before cutting it off then switching on the clippers and neatly shaving the rest of Liz's hair at the top and sides. "Can I see a mirror?" Liz asks nervously.

Debbie guides Liz to the bathroom and shows her her handy work so far. "I LOVE it," cries Liz.

"Great," smiles Debbie. "Let's get the peroxide on now." Once Debbie has finished, Liz gets into the shower and rinses off all the peroxide before looking in the mirror to see a face she doesn't recognise. She exits the bathroom crying with happiness. "NOW I'm a rock star," she exclaims as Debbie hugs her. "I can't wait to show the guys when they come home on Sunday."

On Sunday evening, Liz and Debbie are lounging around the living room in their pyjamas watching movies as they wait for their male bandmates to come home. "That's them," smiles Debbie as a cab pulls up in the driveway. "Quick. Get changed and show them your new look. They're going to love it!"

Liz goes into her bedroom and picks out a stunning combo of a leather jacket, figure-hugging black jeans and thigh-high stiletto boots, puts them on and does her make-up the way Debbie had shown her. As she does so, she listens for Moose, Angel and Carl going downstairs and closing the door behind them. Once she is sure everyone is settled, she bounces into the living room to reveal her brand new rock star look. Her cheeks puff out as she blows on a lit cigarette without inhaling.

"WOW," gasps Carl as he sees Liz in her new get-up. "Who are you?"

"What the Hell are you doing?" Angel shouts at her as he jumps up, grabs the cigarette out of her hand and stubs it out in the ash tray. "That is a disgusting, filthy habit that will kill you! What are your father and brothers going to say when they see you doing that and about how bad you smell?"

"Hang on, Angel" Liz shouts back. "You're smoking too so don't tell me what to do!"

Sure enough, Angel has a half-smoked cigarette hanging

from his mouth. He rolls his deep, brown eyes as he looks around the room, at the guys and at Debbie and the room falls silent. Angel takes a long drag on his cigarette and holds his breath for a good few seconds before exhaling. He stubs out the cigarette, throws the packet with the remaining ones at Carl and tells the group: "Right. That was my last cigarette."

The room erupts with all the bandmates and Debbie chanting *"Ooooooooooohhhhhhhh"*, as Angel is known to smoke more than forty cigarettes a day. They all sit looking at each other for about five minutes as Angel fidgets nervously.

"How are you feeling, bro?" whispers Moose, anxiously.

"Hellish," replies Angel. "On edge, hungry, irritable, forgetful. Sorry, what were we talking about again?" Everyone laughs. "You've got this," cries Moose as he playfully punches his brother on the shoulder.

"You know what, bro," Ronnie chimes in as he hands his own remaining cigarettes to Carl, shakes Angel's hand and winks at Debbie. "We do this together. I don't want cigarettes in the house for when the wee ones start arriving."

"Oh my God," exclaims Liz as she looks wide-eyed at Debbie. "You're not..."

"Not yet, babe," laughs Debbie as she and Ronnie cuddle up to each other. "We're going to be really busy with gigs, recording and partying over the next few months. We'll start soon, I promise."

"Aw, I can't wait to be Auntie Liz," Liz smiles warmly.

As expected, the paparazzi have a field day over Liz's new look while Hell Freeze are on their summer tour. She catches sight of so many headlines on the front covers of glossy magazines including "Liz Grows Up", "From Chubby To Chiselled", "Superfit Liz" and "Glam Rocker Liz." She even feels better about having her photos taken along with her four hotter-than-hot bandmates.

The weekend has arrived for Hell Freeze to support Moulten Rock and Liz is excited to meet up with Miranda again. That evening, Hell Freeze play a flawless set and it gets even better when they realise that Moulten Rock are on the premises and listening to them backstage. They finish their set and go backstage to meet their showbiz friends. Liz immediately notices how quiet it is. "Rick?" Liz approaches Hammer.

"Hey, girl," he greets her as he shakes her hand and gives her a kiss and a hug. "You look *SENSATIONAL!* How are you, babe?"

"Thank you so much," says Liz. "I'm fine, thank you. Is Phil sick today? I was hoping to catch up with him and Miranda. I've not spoken to them in so long."

"I'm sorry to say, baby," replies Rick, sorrowfully. "Phil doesn't play for us anymore. He is and always will be a great friend and I tried to get him to stay. Sadly, he has too much going on in his personal and professional life at the moment. We have Davy Jackson providing our bass now. He is a great guy and I am grateful to have him."

"What about Miranda?" asks Liz. "I've tried phoning her and the number's not there anymore."

"I'm afraid I don't have any contact details for Miranda as she is a minor," says Rick. "She and Phil have split since we last saw you too. Sorry, darling. I know she was a good friend to you."

Liz feels deflated and tries her best not to cry. "Thanks, Rick," she replies as she hugs him. "Good luck to you and the guys for tonight. See you after the gig."

Chapter 20:
Moulding Together

As Hell Freeze continue to enjoy the success of their career, they are now also enjoying the social aspect of it all, especially Moose, Angel and Carl. The busy nightlife comprises of lots of alcohol and an abundance of sex. Liz, now eighteen years old, lies awake n the small hours of the morning as she waits for her bandmates arriving home. Liz realises that alcohol doesn't agree with her as it disrupts her fitness routine so, as usual, she had left earlier than everyone else along with Ronnie and Debbie. She breathes a sigh of relief as she hears a cab pull up outside followed by a key turning in the lock. However, she hears only Angel and Carl clambering drunkenly up the stairs. Suddenly, she hears a huge bang coming from outside her bedroom followed by Carl laughing hysterically. "Who, in the name of fuck, put the step there?" curses Angel as he slurs his words.

"Get up you drunken, bum," Carl continues to laugh loudly and he and Angel chat and laugh together about their night's antics.

"Where's Moose?" Liz thinks to herself. "I hope he's not... Wait! Why am I thinking like this? He'll never look at me that way. Anyway, he has sex on tap. If he wanted me, he would have done it by now. Hmmmm."

Liz finally falls asleep as she tries to take her mind off Moose. "What happened to Moose last night?" Liz asks Angel at breakfast the following morning.

"You know Moose," Angel chuckles. "He probably got lucky."

Liz sighs and, of course, they don't see Moose at all until Thursday night when he finally arrives home with a tall, leggy brunette whom Moose introduces as his new girlfriend Jennifer. "I don't like her," Liz thinks to herself. "She is giving off a vibe and something just isn't sitting right."

Everyone, with the exception of Liz, enjoys a pleasant evening of dinner, drinks and the hot tub. Liz participates in everything except the drinking but cannot help but draw daggers at Jennifer. It's ten p.m. and Liz leaves quietly and goes up to bed. "Come on, Liz," she tells herself, again. "Snap out if it. He is a work colleague who is old enough to be your father. It would *NEVER* work. Be happy for Moose. The thought of them having sex or even just kissing though..."

Liz cries herself to sleep and it would be the first of many times she does this.

One Saturday afternoon, Liz arrives home from her training session with Marco. She is on a high having won several sparring matches as she prepares for competition and goes to the kitchen to get herself a drink before going to her room to relax. She catches sight of Moose and Jennifer in the health suite enjoying a slow dance together as romantic music plays in the background. Moose wears only a pair of skimpy briefs and the soft, romantic lights emphasise his muscular physique. Jennifer, a model, wears a short, flowy cover-up that clings to all the right places and her long, silky, dark locks fall perfectly over her shoulders and down her back. *"BITCH,"* Liz thinks to herself.

Liz takes one more final glance at the loved-up couple. She hadn't realised just how tall Jennfer was and she is significantly taller than Moose. Liz slips away quietly and is walking upstairs when, suddenly, she erupts into a fit of uncontrollable giggles. "Oh my God," Liz thinks to herself. "It's like that scene in Disney's Fantasia where Mickey Mouse's spell goes wrong and all the brooms end up dancing with the buckets!"

"Ach, stop it," Liz scolds herself. "You're doing yourself *NO* favours with this childishness! Fuck sake! You know Moose is touchy about his height. Still..."

The following week, Hell Freeze go on tour. "At least we will get away from *HER* for a few weeks," Liz thinks to herself.

Hell Freeze kick off their "Burning Up" tour with another wild, successful gig. Afterwards, they decide to go out to a first class, star studded Las Vagas nightclub. Ronnie, Debbie and Liz chat and laugh as they watch all the Z-listers attempting to mingle with the A-listers as well as the antics of the paparazzi who had managed to dodge security. "I'm going out for a bit of fresh air," she whispers to Ronnie.

"OK, pal," replies Ronnie.

Liz gets lost in a happy daydream as she watches the action of the Las Vegas street life when she feels a pair of strong arms hug her from behind. "Oh, hi Moose," Liz giggles, surprised.

"You OK?" asks Moose in his deep, smooth voice that Liz loves.

"Of course," Liz laughs. "Everything is OK as long as I'm with you."

"Oh, fuck," Liz thinks to herself as she blushes. "That was a bit forward!"

"Aw, that's so sweet," Moose smiles as he puts an arm around Liz's shoulders. "Come on. Let's go back inside."

They walk back into the club to the sound of Bon Jovi's "Bed Of Roses." "Can I have this dance?" Moose asks Liz.

"Aye," she replies, excitedly. Liz closes her eyes as she enjoys the slow dance with Moose. She can feel the heat emanating from his lean, muscular body as they dance and she wishes these moments would last forever. At the end of the power ballad, Moose thanks Liz and gives her a peck on the cheek as they sit down together for more drinks, chat and laughs.

After a week of touring Papa Joe, Debbie and the bandmates are feeling tired but accomplished, especially as they read the critics' reviews on their gigs. "Hell Freeze Heaven" one headline reads.

"Solid Rock, Super Solid Stars," reads another one that features photos of shirtless, toned Moose and Angel as well as Liz looking athletic in her custom-made black satin cat suit.

"The energy between Angel and Liz is electric," reads a hard-hitting tagline in one of the glossy magazines.

"I was told I couldn't sing once upon a time," giggles Liz.

"Who told you that?" asks Angel. "Was it a music teacher by any chance?"

"Aye," laughs Liz.

"That's OK," replies Angel. "I was told the exact same thing by my music teacher. I'll never forget the day the headmaster overruled her and asked me and Carl to play a set in front of the entire school."

"I told you," Moose chimes in. "School is not the place for all kids and it wasn't the place for you. You and Carl did ALL your learning outside school."

The following week, Hell Freeze play their final gig of the tour. Yet again it is a wild, energetic one and the fans are not disappointed. "Thank you, beautiful people," Angel addresses the audience of their televised closing gig. "You have been a tremendous audience. Thank you, from all of us, for all the love and support and for being there. Good night, God bless you all and *KEEP ON ROCKIN'*."

"Ladies and gentlemen," Ronnie chimes in through his earpiece. "Not many people do what I am about to do on-stage so I am grateful that you are witnessing this. Debbie, darling, would you please join me centre stage?"

Apart from some murmuring, the audience and the bandmates are silent as all eyes are on Ronnie. Confused, Debbie looks at Liz and joins Ronnie as he has asked. Ronnie drops to one knee and opens a small box to reveal a solitaire diamond engagement ring, still with his earpiece switched on. "Debbie Newton," Ronnie smiles as Debbie begins to cry. "The moment I met you at our graduation dance when we were just twenty years old, I knew you were the only one for me. You are a strong, beautiful woman who has been there for all of us, through our ups and downs and stuck with me, my crazy brothers and my little sister that I call Hell Freeze. Debbie, will you do me the honour of becoming my wife?"

"*YES,*" Debbie cries. "*YES!*"

"Ladies and Gentlemen," Ronnie addresses the audience. "*I GOT A YES!*"

The audience erupts into a loud cheer as the other bandmates play a romantic instrumental as Ronnie and Debbie kiss and then slow dance. Meanwhile, Liz catches herself gazing lovingly at Moose. "Stop," she scolds herself. "He's not for you. Ronnie and Debbie are priority now."

After the gig Marc meets Papa Joe, Debbie and the bandmates backstage as he allows them some celebratory drinks before driving them home. "Congratulations ya pair of nutters," he says to Ronnie and Debbie. "Whit a joab, man. *WHIT A FUCKIN' JOAB!*"

"Cheers, pal," smiles Ronnie. "Moose, I need you to be best man."

"I'd be honoured, dude," says Moose as he embraces Ronnie.

"Liz, honey," says Debbie. "Would you be bridesmaid please?"

"Aaww, I'd *LOVE* to," smiles Liz.

"This calls for celebration, my young 'uns," cheers Papa Joe. "How about dinner tomorrow night?"

"Sounds great," laughs Moose. "Celebrations afterwards too?"

"Sounds like a plan, brother," smiles Ronnie. "You never know, it could soon be your turn next?"

"Uh-uh," Moose laughs. "How about no?" Liz smiles inwardly to herself.

"But you have a stunning girlfriend," says Carl, shocked. "Why…?"

"Girlfriend, yes. Marriage no," Moose replies firmly. "I'm busy enjoying rockstar life right now."

The weeks pass and the bandmates continue to party hard

on their weekends off gigs. As usual, Liz accompanies Ronnie and Debbie home as the rest of the guys stay out. Liz's feelings for Moose are getting stronger and she is even happier that he very rarely stays out with Carl and Angel anymore despite his very quiet split from Jennifer. "Was it getting too hot for you, dude?" Carl jokingly asks Moose.

"You could say that," smiles Moose. "Bachelorville it is and I have other things to concentrate on."

Meanwhile, Hell Freeze have hit a rocky patch in their career. "Papa Joe?" asks Debbie. "What's happening with the new album and our record sales?"

"I don't know, baby girl," replies Papa Joe. "Cameron Barrett is not picking up the phone or returning my calls and Liz and the boys are owed a small fortune in outstanding royalties."

"Nightmare," groans Debbie.

"I know," says Papa Joe. "I have a horrible feeling that Satanic Productions are in trouble..."

"On another note," smiles Debbie. "It's Liz's birthday soon. We can maybe take her out and take our minds off things for a bit."

"Great idea, Debbie darling," enthuses Papa Joe. "I am so proud of the strong, determined young woman she has become."

Liz's birthday night arrives and Debbie organises a night out at a high quality restaurant. After dinner, Liz goes to the bar to buy some drinks for Debbie, Papa Joe and her bandmates. "Good God," exclaims a deep, well-spoken voice. "Liz McLarnon?"

Liz turns around to find that she is faced with Jason Hitchens, one of the biggest music producers in the industry and owner of one of the biggest record labels in the world. "Hello, Mr Hitchens," smiles Liz. "Long time no see."

"Please," replies Hitchens. "Call me Jason and, yes, it has been *TOO* long. You look fantastic. Whatever you've been doing is definitely working for you. Anyway, how are you?"

"Not so good, Jason," Liz replies with sadness in her voice. "Satanic productions are in trouble and I am afraid we are about to be dropped."

"That's definitely not good, baby," replies Hitchens as he looks thoughtful. "I have an idea. Why don't you join me for dinner? I may have the very thing for you."

"That would be amazing," smiles Liz. "When would suit you?"

"Well I am away on business for the next two weeks," says Hitchens. "If we say, three weeks from today?"

"Yes, that would work," enthuses Liz.

"Excellent," smiles Hitchens. "Here is my card. Remember I fly out tomorrow so if anything comes up please leave it with my staff and I'll get back to you."

"Thank you," smiles Liz. "I'll look forward to it."

"The pleasure is all mine," replies Hitchens as he bends down and gives Liz a small kiss on the lips.

From there, Hitchens leaves with his entourage and Liz goes back to her friends. "Right," says Angel as he and Carl get up and put their jackets on. "We're heading out. I would ask you to come with us, Liz, but I see you already have a date." Liz hugs Angel and Carl as she wishes them a good night and thanks them for dinner.

"I'll talk to you tomorrow, Angel," Liz whispers in his ear as she hugs him. "Have a great night and I'll see you then. Love you."

The following morning, Liz is enjoying the warm sunshine as she repairs a motorbike for her brothers Tommy and Robert. Suddenly, a shadow is cast over her as she works and she turns around to be met by a very concerned-looking Angel. She stops what she is doing and greets him with a hug. "How was your night?" asks Liz.

"Honestly?" Angel laughs nervously. "I can't remember! On a serious note, Liz, I'm worried about you. I don't like that guy. He must be in his late forties, at least. He's far too old for you. Not to mention the fact that he's a greasy creep. Are you *REALLY* going on a date with this guy?"

"Angel," exclaims Liz, shocked. "It's not a date! It's a business meeting and I am trying to secure a deal for us. Yes, I'm going to dinner with him but I certainly won't be going back to his house afterwards."

"Aw, I see," says Angel, relieved. "I just worry about you, that's all. I really appreciate what you're doing for us."

"No problem," smiles Liz. "I just hope nobody gets the wrong idea. Even if he doesn't offer me anything worthwhile, at least I'll get a dinner out of it."

"Thanks, little sis," says Angel as he hugs her. "Moose and I are getting ready to go to the gym. Are you coming?"

"Sure," replies Liz. "I'll just get rid of these overalls and I'll be with you."

The weekend of Liz's meeting with Hitchens finally arrives. Papa Joe and Debbie are both away for the weekend. Papa Joe is on a trip with managers and presenters from his radio station as they celebrate winning a major award and Debbie is attending a girlfriend's hen party. Ronnie, Angel and Carl decided to make the most of a very rare weekend off as they plan a wild night out. Moose had been very solemn and unusually quiet all day and it had not gone unnoticed by the rest of his bandmates, who had tried in vain to get him to go on this wild night out. Moose being Moose would not budge, preferring to stay home and do a workout. "What's gotten into him recently?" Carl asks. "He never stays out anymore and he seems to have lost all interest in girls."

"Well he IS nearly forty," laughs Angel. "Maybe he's slowing down in his old age."

"Fuck," replies Carl. "We're not far behind him."

"Maybe he's got a girlfriend and he doesn't want to jinx anything," suggests Ronnie. "You just can't tell with Moose."

"I'll ask him one more time," says Carl. "If he says no, he says no."

"No thanks, Carl," Moose smiles warmly when Carl tries to tempt him one last time. "Honestly, I'm off it. You guys have fun and I'll see you tomorrow."

"Alright, brother," replies Ronnie. "See you tomorrow. Liz, all the very best for tonight."

"Thanks, Ronnie," smiles Liz as she hugs her three bandmates. "Have a great night and I'll see you all tomorrow."

Hitchens arrives at six thirty p.m. in a silver chauffeur-driven Limo to collect Liz. She looks very elegant in a floor-length, sparkly white dress that is cut to show one shapely leg, a white bolero jacket and silver stiletto heels. "I'm off, Moose," she tells him, although he appears to have fallen asleep as he watches the live boxing match on TV so she kisses him on the forehead and hugs him before she leaves.

Hitchens and Liz arrive at the classy restaurant and are seated by waiting staff. Hitchens had already ordered champaign on ice which is ready to serve at their table, which the pair sip as they waited for their food. "Thank you for coming out on this fine evening, my dear," says Hitchens, his toothy smile not quite reaching his eyes.

"Thank you for the invite," smiles Liz, although she feels uneasy and as though something is off.

"My pleasure," replies Hitchens. "I see you are a very beautiful, talented young woman with an abundance of great potential. I have a deal for you that could make you very comfortable for the rest of your life."

"Thank you so much," enthuses Liz. "That will be some well-needed, exciting news for me to tell the guys when I get home. What will be expected of us and what kind of deal are you offering in return?

"Liz, my dear", says Hitchens as he lowers his tone. "You know Annie Lennox, don't you? Another great Scottish artist who is currently doing well in her solo career? I could build you up to be as big as her, if not bigger. However, you *MUST* do it on your own. Why don't you come back to my house after dinner and we can discuss things further?"

Liz grimaces as Hitchens winks at her. "You're asking me to break up my band, *MY FAMILY?*" cries Liz. "I am a multi-instrumentalist and occasional backing vocalist at best. I have no desire to do that kind of work as, unlike the amazing Ms Lennox, I am not a naturally good singer. Please trust me when I say I know my limits. Anyway, I am loyal to my bandmates and to Joe. I wouldn't be where I am if it wasn't for them and I am *NOT* about to betray them."

"Look at it as a promotion rather than a betrayal,"leers Hitchens. "So many doors could open for a sexy, talented young woman like you. You are a very strong woman and a go-getter. I really need more like you. Come with me and I will make you great."

Liz feels Hitchens rub his hand up the inside of her thigh. Disgusted, she throws her champaign in his face and storms out of the restaurant to flag down a cab to take her home.

Meanwhile, back at their mansion, Moose is finishing his workout. He has worked harder than normal as he tries to take his mind off what was going on that night. As he finishes showering in the downstairs bathroom, he realises that his bandmates haven't repaced the towels.

"Damn it," Moose thinks to himself as he walks, naked, into the kitchen to make himself coffee before bed as he's not expecting his bandmates home for hours yet. Just then, Liz lets herself in quietly and walks past the kitchen to see Moose, who is still in his state of complete undress. She smiles and blushes as she enjoys what she is seeing as the kitchen lights highlight his rippling, muscular body. Embarrassed, Moose grabs a dinner plate to preserve his modesty as he apologises profusely.

"It's OK," Liz giggles. "I'll make the coffee and let you get sorted."

Moose and Liz get changed into comfortable gear before settling down for coffee and the live boxing match on TV. "So how was your date?" asks Moose. "I'm really sorry, again, that you saw that. I wasn't expecting you home so early."

"It's OK, Moose," Liz giggles as she rolls her eyes. "Anyway it was a business meeting, *NOT* a date and I was trying to secure a deal for us. Did Angel not tell you?"

"No," replies Moose. "Angel told me nothing."

"I'm so sorry," Liz apologises. "I'm afraid I didn't manage to get us a deal..."

"So you're not seeing him again?" presses Moose.

"Nope," exclaims Liz. "It was never my intention and that's one less greasy creep for us to deal with in the future."

Liz cuddles up to Moose on the sofa and rests her head on his chest as she had often done for the past year. He is a lot happier and more relaxed than she has seen him all day and it's not long until falls asleep, still smiling. Liz watches Moose as he sleeps and his crooked smile fades as he relaxes into his slumber. Right now he looks adorable, angelic and super sexy with his long, dark, curly hair and lightly tanned skin. Even his stomach is perfectly taut as he breathes deeply. "I'll try for a kiss," Liz thinks to herself. "Surely one won't hurt."

She leans over and gently kisses Moose on the lips. However, to her horror, he wakes up.

"I'm sorry," Liz gulps as she thinks Moose will be angry at her bold advance. To her surprise, he lifts her on top of him and continues to kiss her. This is the first time Liz has really been kissed and it feels like nothing she had ever felt in her short life as a sensation of a combination of heat and electricity surges through her entire body. They continue to kiss and remove each other's clothes and there was no turning back now! They go upstairs to Liz's bedroom and make themselves comfortable in Liz's bed.

"Moose," she whispers in his ear between the kisses. "I've never done this before."

"I know," Moose smiles warmly. "I'll be gentle." From there, Liz loses her virginity to a man that she has grown to love and hopes they will stay together forever. Everything feels so right and Liz regrets nothing as they shower and cuddle up in bed together afterwards and drift off to sleep.

The following morning, Liz is woken by shouting which she can hear from the living room directly below her bedroom. She gets showered, dressed and goes downstairs to see what all the noise is about to find Angel shouting, very angrily, at Moose in very fast Italian. Moose nods and smiles as his young brother gets into his personal space and continues to shout at him, his face red and contorted with rage. Moose occasionally smiles at Carl, who is sitting in the huge, leather armchair laughing hysterically at whatever obscenities Angel is shouting. Meanwhile, Ronnie sits at the dining table quietly eating breakfast with his head down as he tries to mind his own business. Leonora, the little, middle-aged housekeeper, puts a hand on Angel's shoulder as she tries to diffuse the situation. "Maybe he was only using the shower, baby," she gently whispers to Angel in Italian as she tries to calm him down.

"No, he *DID NOT* just have a shower," Angel shouts angrily in English. "Maybe a *GOLDEN* one!"

This makes Ronnie burst out laughing too although he doesn't dare disturb Angel while he is mid rant as he continues to yell at his brother in Italian.

"OK," Moose shouts back at Angel. "How about we remember our manners and continue this conversation in English? If you must know I enjoyed my night last night, just like you enjoyed your own night whoring and touring on the tiles. I am hoping to make a go of things with Liz and I am happier than I have been in a long time. Now, if you'll excuse the Hell out of me, I have training to do."

"What's going on?" asks Liz and the living room is now deathly silent. Moose bids goodbye to Ronnie, Carl and Leonora before kissing Liz goodbye, telling her he loves her and that he will see her later.

"Shocking," Angel says to Liz, angrily. "Just shocking. How could you let him do that to you? You realise you're just going to be another notch on that slut's bedpost, don't you? Don't say you weren't bloody warned!"

"Angel…" Liz pleads but he doesn't listen and storms out of the house after his brother.

"Are you alright, baby?" Leonora asks Liz, concerned.

"I've never been happier, Leonora," replies Liz with sadness in her voice. "I just wish Angel hadn't taken it so badly…"

"He's worried about you, doll," Ronnie chimes in. "We all are. Moose is my best pal but, my God, he is ruled by his nuts at times and we don't want to see you get hurt."

"I appreciate your concern, Ronnie," replies Liz. "Really I do. I'll talk to Angel later once he has calmed down."

"As long as you're happy, babe," assures Carl. "That explains Moose's odd behaviour this year. I think the old boy has had the hots for you all this time."

"Thanks for the support, guys," Liz says, relieved as she hugs them both. "I really appreciate it."

Liz checks into Trojans' and she catches sight of Angel with his boxing gloves on as he batters the punch bag. She watches for a few minutes as he is deep in concentration with his workout. "Angel," she calls out to him.

He turns around, picks up his towel and quickly dries himself off, looking a lot calmer than he was earlier. "Can we talk?" Liz asks him.

"Sure," he says quietly. "I'm going to get showered. I'll get you in the cafe when I'm finished."

"Alright, babe," smiles Liz. Angel cleans himself up and greets Liz with a hug and a kiss before sitting down with coffee that Liz had got for him.

"Sorry about earlier," Angel apologises. "As much as I love Moose, I know what he's like because I have seen him get up to all sorts of shit with girls since I was a kid. I love you like a sister and I just don't want to see you get hurt."

"That's so sweet of you, Angel, and exactly what Ronnie and Carl said," replies Liz. "I really appreciate that you all care but all I ask is that you be happy for us."

"Have you told your father yet?" asks Angel.

"No," replies Liz. "Not yet. I don't see it being a problem though. Dad will give us his blessing as long as Moose proves himself and doesn't fuck around. I'll need to tell him before he sees it in the papers though. I think I'll pay him a visit tonight and get it over with."

"Now that I think of it," sighs Angel as he looks at Liz with his warm, deep brown eyes. "I've not seen Moose show an interest in anyone since his split with Jennifer and there have been no more wild nights out or one-night stands that I know of. Dare I say it but I think my big brother has finally grown up and he really is ready to make a go of things with you like he said…"

"Hey," a deep, gravelly voice calls out.

"Hello, babe," Liz greets Moose with a kiss and a hug. "Are you joining us for coffee?"

"Sure," he smiles warmly as he greets his young brother with a few playful biffs.

Just as Moose, Angel and Liz arrive home, the house phone starts ringing. "Hello," Liz answers.

"Hello, my wee lamb," says Big Tam.

"Oh, hi Dad," Liz greets her father. "I was just about to call you."

"Great minds, hen," laughs Tam. "Great minds. Anyway, my wee love, I was hoping you could come over for your dinner tonight. I have some great news and all the boys and girls are going to be there."

"Sounds amazing, Dad," smiles Liz. "I can't wait to see you."

"He's in a good mood," Liz whispers to Moose when she concludes her phone call. "If you can come with me, we'll break the news to him then."

"Great," says Moose. "At least your brothers, their wives and girlfriends will all be there in case he doesn't take our news well…"

That evening, Moose and Liz arrive at Big Tam's house and are greeted by Wullie, who looks totally different from his days as a rock star with his short back and sides and sporting a smart but casual shirt and jeans, a far cry from his long, curly hair and leather gear. *"MOOSE,"* Wullie exclaims with his trademark hearty laugh as he embraces his former bandmate. "Great to see you again, ma man. How are you doing?"

"All good here, thanks, dude," smiles Moose as he puts a strong arm around Liz. "Great to see you too. I can't wait to catch up. It's been a while!"

Everyone settles down to eat in the living room as Liz helps her father and her brother John put the dinner out. "Well, folks," smiles Big Tam as he looks at everyone with his sparkling, piercing blue eyes. "I've called you all over so I can announce my retirement. I was going to carry on until I was at least seventy but I really want to see more of all of you and my grandkids."

"Congratulations, Tam," cheers Phyllis. "Wullie and I really appreciate that but hope it won't be too much for you?"

"Never, hen," laughs Tam. "Just remember my door is always open for all of you."

"To Dad," says John as he proposes a toast.

"To Tam," everyone says in unison as they raise their glasses.

"Dad," Liz says, nervously. "I've got news too…"

"You're NOT…?" Liz's brother Robert asks, wide-eyed.

"Naw, naw," laughs Liz. "Nothing like that, Robert. Dad, I wanted to tell you before you see it in the papers…"

Tam looks at Liz and Moose over his spectacles with his piercing blue eyes.

"Dad," whispers Liz as she nervously holds Moose's hand. "Moose and I are going out."

The room is silent as everyone anticipates Tam's reaction.

"Elizabeth McLarnon," Tam says with a serious tone. *"I KNOW!"* He then bursts out laughing, picks Liz up and whirls her around.

"How…?" Liz asks, surprised as she looks at Moose and he shrugs his shoulders and shakes his head.

"I know you better than you know yourself, hen," Tam

continues to laugh. "I know you've been fond of the big fella for a while now. You do what makes you happy, ma doll."

"Aaww, thanks, Dad," Liz sighs with relief.

"I know you'll keep my wee girl safe, big chap," Tam says to Moose as he shakes his hand. "You have my blessing."

"This calls for double celebrations," exclaims Liz's brother Tommy as he pops open a bottle of champagne and hands a glass to everyone.

"Jesus," laughs Moose, having lost count of the glasses of champagne he has had. "I won't be able to drive home at this rate."

"There's plenty of room for you here, mate," assures John. "After all, you're part of this mental family now. God help you!" The celebrations continue into the early hours of the morning as everyone parties the night away.

The following afternoon, Moose and Liz arrive home and a very concerned Debbie watches from the window as they get out of Moose's red Rolls-Royce and kiss before walking up the driveway hand-in-hand. "What...?" Debbie gasps, shocked.

"Sorry, babe," Ronnie apologises. "I wanted you to hear it from Moose and Liz."

"OH MY GOD," Debbie cries as Moose and Liz enter the living room. "When did *THIS* happen?"

"Saturday night," smiles Liz as she and Moose cuddle up together on the sofa. "I've wanted Moose for so long and I have not been this happy in ages."

"But...but, I thought you had a date?" stammers Debbie.

"It was more of a business meeting than a date," sighs Liz as she hangs her head. "I failed and I am so sorry. Hitchens only wanted sexual favours from me and I would probably still have got nothing in return..."

"JASON HITCHENS?" cries Debbie. "That guy is a crook and a slimeball."

"I know," replies Liz. "I found that out the hard way and I'm glad I had the guts to walk away."

"So are we, honey," smiles Debbie.

"So you approve?" asks Liz, surprised.

"As long as you're both happy, babe," says Debbie. "I'm happy for you."

"While we're on the subject of your meeting, Liz," says Ronnie as he puts an arm around Debbie. "Debbie has news for all of you too."

"Aye?" smiles Liz.

"Yup," replies Debbie. "I was going to wait until everyone was home but I may as well tell you just now. I've been working away quietly behind the scenes and have started my own record label. I've had my plans in the works for a while and now the wheels are finally in motion. I am already working with several established bands, including Hell Freeze under my new name Newton's Law Media Productions."

"*WOW,*" says Moose as he jumps up and hugs Debbie. "Congratulations, sister. That's excellent news!"

"Absolutely brilliant," Liz congratulates Debbie. "Papa Joe and the boys will be over the moon!"

"Oh, there's more," smiles Ronnie. "Papa Joe told us he is taking his retirement from Golden Plus FM so he can concentrate on managing us full time. Probably just as well because we are going to be crazy busy!"

"It'll be full steam ahead from on," enthuses Debbie.

The months pass quickly for Hell Freeze as they continue to work under their brand new record label Newton's Law Media Productions. The bandmates are busy with various different projects including gigs, recording of new material, television and movie appearances and modelling contracts. Angel opens a well-established, glossy magazine and flips to the centre fold that features an interview with him talking about the band's ups and downs, featuring a shirtless photo of him looking superfit in a pair of form-hugging leather jeans as his long, curly dark hair flows down past his sculpted shoulders. "You look gorgeous, bro," smiles Debbie as Angel blushes. "All the healthy eating, exercise and giving up the smokes looks good on you!"

"Thanks, sister," Angel laughs timidly. "It was a lot easier than I thought it was going to be and I'm sorry I didn't do it sooner."

"I have one more favour to ask you while you're in a good mood, babe," says Debbie.

"Anything for you, good mood or not, sister," replies Angel. "Fire away."

"Ronnie and I are on the countdown to our wedding now, honey," says Debbie.

"Uh-huh..." replies Angel in anticipation.

"We don't want any presents because we are the couple with everything we need," Debbie continues. "So there will be no wedding list."

"OK..." replies Angel.

"There is just one little thing I would like from you though..." Debbie says quietly.

"Sure, sis," smiles Angel. "What's that?"

"Do you remember a song you wrote many years ago and we didn't record it?" asks Debbie.

"Debbie, there have been so many over the years," replies Angel. "If only the general public realised how much we work behind the scenes for material not to be produced..."

"Angel," Debbie interrupts. "*YOU* banned us from recording this song in particular. I was so disappointed because I loved it the moment I heard it."

"Really?" asks Angel, surprised. "Which song was that?"

"It was called 'Hold Me Forever'," says Debbie. "I would love you, the guys and Liz to perform it as my wedding song when I walk down the isle with Papa Joe."

"No," Angel replies flatly.

"Angel," exclaims Debbie. "I am only asking for *ONE* gift and that's it!"

"Debbie," cries Angel. "Everyone laughed at it..."

"You mean *CARL* laughed at it because he was too immature

to understand the meaning of romance," affirms Debbie. "I certainly didn't laugh at it because, like I say, I loved it as soon as I heard it. Ronnie wasn't laughing at it because he thought along the same lines as me. He told me himself. Moose didn't laugh at it because he has always recognised you as the great artist that you are, whether you are his brother or not, and Wullie didn't laugh because he admired you as an artist as well as the beautiful soul that you are. I bet Carl won't laugh now that he has grown up and experienced his share of romance and Liz will love it just as she loves all your work. You need to look at the bigger picture and be proud, babe."

"*Wow,*" whispers Angel. "I never thought of it like that."

"There you go," exclaims Debbie. "What do you say?"

"It's your wedding though," replies Angel as he feels himself begin to perspire. "It's one of the biggest days of your life in front of all your family and friends."

"Exactly," beams Debbie. "It will be perfect. Anyway, Angel, it is only a small, intimate wedding. I only want you guys, Marc, Leonora, Papa Joe, Big Tam, Ronnie's parents, your mom and any of Liz's brothers and their partners who can make it."

"For you, sister," smiles Angel. "Anything."

"Amazing," exclaims Debbie as she kisses Angel. "Thank you *SO* much. It's going to be stunning!"

As expected, Ronnie and Debbie's wedding date arrives in no time. "It's going to be a busy one for us," says Moose as he, Angel and Carl get dressed up in their Tuxedos.

"You're a real dark horse," Carl says to Angel. "How did you manage to pull such a power ballad out of the bag?" Moose and Angel exchange looks and laugh.

It is now time for Ronnie and Debbie to get married. The remaining members of Hell Freeze take their places at the front of the chapel as Ronnie waits, nervously, at the alter with Big Tam by his side. Finally the door opens, Debbie walks elegantly down the isle arm-in-arm with Papa Joe as he prepares to give her away and Hell Freeze proceed to play Angel's power ballad.

The minister does his speech and Ronnie and Debbie exchange their vows. "You may now kiss the bride," the elderly minister smiles at the happy couple as everyone cheers.

Ronnie joins the minister at the front of the chapel. "Thank you so much to everyone for coming to our wedding," he addresses all their close family and friends. "My beautiful wife and I would be honoured if you would join us for food and drinks back at our house. Once again, thank you."

Back at Hell Freeze's mansion, everyone enjoys food prepared by the Macinis as well as drinks to celebrate Ronnie and Debbie's union. "Congratulations, my darling Debbie," smiles Margaret as she embraces her new daughter-in-law.

"Welcome to the family, love," says Donald. "You look sensational and we wish you and our boy all the happiness"

"Thank you so much for being here, Donald and Margaret," says Debbie. "Ronnie and I are so glad you made it and we really appreciate it."

"We have all of you to thank for making it all possible," smiles Donald. "Especially Maria for her hospitality."

"It has been such an amazing day," enthuses Debbie. "Although poor Ronnie is stuck with me for good."

"He won't be complaining," replies Margaret. "He fell head over heels in love with you the moment he laid eyes on you and I can understand why. We are honoured to see you as the new Mrs Buchanan."

As Hell Freeze are busy with many up-coming projects, Ronnie and Debbie opt for a spa weekend away rather than a full honeymoon. "Everything is just perfect," Debbie reflects as she and Ronnie relax in the hot tub of their hotel. "Ronnie Buchanan, I love you so much."

"I love you too, Mrs Buchanan," replies Ronnie as he kisses his new wife. "Thank you for becoming my wife. I can't wait to build our future together."

Chapter 21:
Full Steam Ahead

Ronnie and Debbie are no sooner home from their weekend away until they are plunged back into work along with their bandmates. Within a matter of weeks, Hell Freeze have compiled a new album under Newton's Law Media Productions, featuring Ronnie and Debbie's wedding song, penned by Angel. The band are ecstatic when they get the news that their power ballad has gone straight in at number one in the U.S and U.K charts. "You see," Debbie whispers to Angel as she hugs him. "I was right, wasn't I?"

"Thank you so much, sister," smiles Angel. "You know me..."

"I do indeed," replies Debbie. "You need to have more confidence in yourself. You are gorgeous and a very talented writer and performer. You will be around forever."

Angel blushes. "Thanks, sis," he says quietly. "I really appreciate all you do for us."

It's not long before Hell Freeze's brand new album "On Fire!" reaches number one in the album charts too.

"This is the business," cries Carl. "I can't wait to get out and perform all of these great songs live!"

"Some buzz, bhoys and lassies," exclaims Marc. "Whit a joab, man. *WHIT A FUCKIN' JOAB!*"

The weeks pass and Hell Freeze continue with their regime of recording, gigs and staying in shape for their on-stage and television appearances. Very early one morning, Marc drops the bandmates off after yet another wild, energetic gig. "Night night, bhoys and lassies," he bids the bandmates, Debbie and Papa Joe goodnight. "See yeez…hey are you awright, Liz."

"Just tired, darling," replies a very flushed-looking Liz as she yawns.

"You better take that lassie tae bed, big chap," Marc says to Moose with a cheeky smile. "Nothin' too energetic noo."

"I have every intention," Moose winks at Marc. "Don't worry about that!"

"Aw I always find energy for that, Marc," giggles Liz as she takes Moose by the hand. "Night, mate. Tell Gillian we're all asking kindly for her."

"Will do, wee yin," says Marc. "You take care noo and I'll see ye soon."

The following morning, Moose wakes up and gets ready for his workout. He comes out of the shower to find that Liz is still fast asleep. "She can catch up with it later," he tells himself as he pulls the duvet over Liz and kisses her.

He looks into Angel's room to see if he is up for an early morning sparring match but he is out for the count too and unusually quiet. "Looks like I'm on my own then," Moose says to himself, concerned, as he goes downstairs and out the door.

Moose returns home to find that everyone is in the living room, still in their nightwear, except Angel who is still in bed. "I think I may have pushed him too hard," Debbie says sorrowfully. "This isn't like him."

"Don't sweat it, sister," says Carl. "As the old saying goes: it's tough at the top. He probably just needs a lie-in or two. He did run around like a thing possessed on that stage last night." Moose remains quiet as he looks at the floor.

"I'm going to see how he is," he tells Moose as he puts a hand on his strong shoulder.

Carl pops his head around Angel's room door and Angel wearily opens his eyes. "You alright, brother?" Carl asks him.

Angel shakes his head. "Come in and shut the door please,

pal," he says, close to tears.

"Aw, Christ," groans Carl as he sits on the bed. "Dude, you don't look well."

"I ain't," replies Angel. "As much as I love working under Debbie, I am exhausted. I don't know how long I can keep this up."

"We're all in the same boat, pal," concurs Carl. "Everyone except Moose, that is."

"Of course," Angel laughs timidly. "I don't know how he does it."

There is a few moments silence. "Angel," says Carl.

"Mm-hm?" Angel replies as he continues to fight sleep.

"How about I get us some gear for our next gig?" suggests Carl.

"WHAT?" asks Angel shocked as he sits up. "CARL, Moose would go ballistic man! Are you out of your God damn mind?"

"Dude," says Carl as he rolls his eyes. "It wouldn't be anything heavy. Just a bit of whizz to get us through the gigs."

"Whizz?" asks Angel, quietly.

"Yeah," enthuses Carl. "It's great stuff. It keeps you awake for hours on end, we'll get a lot done and we won't even have to stop for food. It'll be the answer to all our problems *AND* it will be good for our figures."

"Sounds great," smiles Angel as he lies back down. "If you can get us some for the weekend…"

"Oh, I will," laughs Carl. "We'll be kicking ass in no time."

"Carl," Angel calls his friend back. "Not a word to Moose, OK?"

"Our secret, dude," assures Carl. "Leave it with me."

The next three weeks see Hell Freeze being extremely busy with sold-out gigs and other work the bandmates had taken on away from the music scene. One afternoon, Angel and Ronnie take a very rare break from writing as they sit chatting in the living room drinking strong, black coffees. "Guys," Carl whispers as he signals to them to follow him.

They go to Carl's bedroom and he closes the door tightly behind him. "What's up, pal?" asks Ronnie.

"I got us a little something to help us through our workload," says Carl with a cheeky smile. He proceeds to share out tiny samples of powder for himself and his two bandmates.

"What now?" asks Angel.

"We snort it and let it do its job," smiles Carl as he takes his share and Angel and Ronnie take theirs.

"I don't know if I like this," grimaces Ronnie.

"Let it kick in, dude," says Carl. "Rhea assures me that it's worth it."

"Rhea?" Angel asks, surprised.

"The drug dealer, pal," replies Carl. "She says she can get me anything I want. I just need to call her."

Later that evening, Hell Freeze are in high spirits as they prepare to go on-stage. "Glad to see you looking better, bro," Moose says to Angel.

"Yeah," he replies. "I must have really needed that extra sleep. I feel like a new man."

"Alright, kiddo," Moose says in his deep drawl. "Let's go get 'em!"

Throughout the gig, Moose watches as Angel and Ronnie put on an extremely energetic show. "Bloody Hell," Moose chuckles to himself. "I thought I was the fit guy in the band but these two are putting me to shame!"

Papa Joe congratulates the bandmates on yet another successful gig when he is reunited with them backstage. "What the Hell came over you two tonight?" Moose asks Angel and Ronnie. "That was the most entertaining gig we've put on in a long time!"

"Definitely," replies Ronnie. "I felt as though I had a new lease of life out there."

"Long may it last," smiles Carl as he is unable to stay seated any longer and neither are Ronnie or Angel.

Papa Joe, Debbie and the bandmates arrive home at just before two a.m. "Well done for another great gig tonight, guys," says Moose as puts an arm around Liz and bids everyone else a good night. "See you when I get back from the gym."

"Night, pal," replies Ronnie. "Have a good sleep."

"It's late," says Papa Joe, concerned. "You young 'uns had better get some well-needed shut-eye."

"Doing that right now, Joe," Debbie yawns as she signals for Ronnie to join her. "Come on, babe."

"I could stay up all night," Angel says to Carl. "But I suppose we'll best get in so we don't look suspicious."

"I suppose," says Carl as he reluctantly heads for his room.

Angel lies down and curls up to sleep but, with the best will in the world, he can't. He tries reading but can't focus on the story so he puts his book down and continues to toss and turn in bed. "Bloody useless," he curses to himself as he gets back up and gets dressed. He fills a bucket with hot, soapy water and stands on a footstool to clean the Venetian blinds in the living room. It's not long before Ronnie joins him and gets the iron board and laundry ready then Carl joins them and starts dusting and polishing all the brass work on the windows.

Moose's sleep is suddenly disturbed and he can't think what woke him as he sits up, startled, in bed. "What's wrong, babe?" asks Liz.

"Ssshhhh," he whispers. "I think we're being burgled. Wait here." He gets up, picks up a baseball bat and runs downstairs to confront the intruders. He bangs the door open and startles his three bandmates. "*WHAT THE FUCK ARE YOU ALL DOING?*" he shouts when he sees his three bandmates are all doing random household chores at the very ungodly hour of the morning. "I thought we were being burgled and almost shit myself! I mean what the fuck, guys?"

The three bandmates burst out laughing at the sight of a very angry Moose as he stands naked wielding the baseball bat. "Well I'm just glad you didn't confront a burglar dressed like that," Carl laughs loudly.

"Well, as you can see, I have other ways of getting myself and my girl to sleep," yells Moose as he grabs a cushion and sits on the sofa to preserve his modesty. "Seriously, though.

What did you all take? Come on, I'm a fitness professional and I can spot drug use when I see it. Now what the fuck was it?"

The three guys exchange looks. "Just a bit of whizz, bro," Angel confesses. "You saw how we've been struggling recently."

"Yes," says Moose. "It's nothing that healthy eating and decent sleeping patterns wouldn't fix. You guys are eating shit, staying up late drinking and gossiping like bloody sweet wives *THEN* you complain that you're tired. Clean up your bloody acts and stop putting that shit up your noses!"

"Sorry, Moose," says Ronnie as he hangs his head.

"Please don't do it again?" pleads Moose. "Stop it now before it becomes a real problem and get to your beds or Leonora will have nothing to do when she turns up for her shift tomorrow."

Liz wakes the following morning to find that Moose is still in bed having changed his mind about going to the gym for once. She also can't help but notice that Moose is unusually quiet and not his usual jocular self. "Is everything alright, babe?" asks Liz as she cuddles up to him.

"Just tired, Liz," Moose says quietly. "The guys were all on the whizz yesterday and that was what the noise was last night."

"They were speeding?" asks Liz, shocked. "Did they admit it?"

"They could hardly deny it," replies Moose. "You saw what the three of them were like at the gig. It was all fun and games until their heads wanted to sleep and their bodies didn't. I just hope they keep their promise to me to stay off that stuff. It's bloody dangerous."

"Babe, I know it's hard after all you've seen already," says Liz. "But try not to worry. The guys aren't daft and they surely won't be that easily led."

"I hope you're right, Liz," replies Moose. "Those dealers can be manipulative bastards and performers and artists are easy targets for them. I'll be keeping a close eye on those three just in case..."

Meanwhile, Carl pays another visit to Rhea. "Hello, gorgeous," Rhea greets him with her deep, raspy voice as she towers over him. "How did you get on?"

"We love it, Rhea," enthuses Carl. "It really is magic stuff and the answer to all our problems."

"More of the same then?" Rhea winks at Carl as she licks her lips. "I can sort you out with some extras too while you're here. I could really be doing with a good salt solution to help this bad throat of mine."

"I'm sure I could sort you out with that," Carl chuckles. "After all, one good turn deserves another..."

Rhea grabs Carl by the wrist, pulls him into her mansion and kisses him passionately before leading him to her bedroom. Carl lies on the huge, Queen-sized bed and relaxes as Rhea gives him oral sex before they go on to have full-on, wild, energetic sex. "That was your endurance test," she winks at Carl as they lie relaxing afterwards. "That performance shows that it really does work and I'm sure I'll be doing business with you again very soon."

"If business is always as pleasurable as that then it'll be a definite," exclaims Carl.

"Glad to hear it, honey," purrs Rhea as she gets up and gets dressed. "Let's sort you out with your gear."

"Thank you, Rhea," beams Carl as she hands him his package.

"Same again tomorrow?" asks Rhea.

"For sure," enthuses Carl. "We have one more gig after today so yes..."

"Great," smiles Rhea. "See you tomorrow, cutie. "It was a pleasure doing business with you."

Carl gets back to Hell Freeze's mansion and Ronnie and Angel join him in his bedroom for another hit. "I feel kind of guilty," says Ronnie. "We promised Moose..."

"What works for Moose doesn't work for us," says Angel. "With the best will in the world, I've tried to do what Moose does since I was a young teenager and I just never got it right because we are very different people. Our audience loved what we did yesterday and that's all that matters."

"That's true, brother," replies Carl. "Well I suppose we'd better get ready for the gig."

The following Monday, Moose and Liz decide to pay a visit to Big Tam to find that he is at home alone. "Where is everybody, Dad?" asks Liz. "There's usually somebody here..."

"You know what happens, my wee lamb," Big Tam replies with sadness is his voice. "Weans have this terrible habit of growing up and once they do, they don't need their auld Da anymore and they leave. I only see Wee Irene and Wee Grant the very odd time that Wullie and Phyllis have to work at the same time but they're lawyers and can usually be there for their weans. I can only clean the house so many time and play so much golf. Retirement isn't what I had planned it to be at all."

Moose and Liz look at each other. "We could use your help, Tam," says Moose.

"What with son?" asks Tam. "You already have a housekeeper who does all your cooking and cleaning for you."

Moose laughs. "Tam, what I mean is Papa Joe could use your help," he replies. "He has been crazy busy to the point where I am worried about him since we started working under Debbie. The pair of you get on famously, he could do with an extra brain as well as a pair of hands, you need something to keep you busy and Debbie and the guys like you. You and Papa Joe would be the ideal management team!"

Big Tam's full cheeky smile lights up his piercing blue eyes. "I would love that, son," he tells Moose. "It would mean I would see more of my baby girl too."

"You're a genius, babe," cries Liz as she kisses Moose. "Dad, why don't you come to us for dinner tonight and we'll tell Papa Joe our plan. He'll be so relieved."

From then on, Big Tam comes on board as a manager for Hell Freeze."

Chapter 22:
Crumbling Artwork

O ne stormy Wednesday morning, Moose and Liz are sitting at breakfast with Debbie and Papa Joe. "Where is everyone?" asks Liz.

"Still in bed with their hangovers," groans Moose. "Nice to know they listened to me…"

"I'll talk to Ronnie, babe," says Debbie. "I'm getting sick of the three of them and their antics. They should have outgrown this stupid behaviour when they were in their early twenties."

"I just hope it's not too late," says Moose. "I don't care much for that new girlfriend of Carl's."

"I've not met the woman, Moose, but me neither," replies Debbie.

"Debbie?" asks Liz. "Have we got anything planned for this week?"

"No, babe," replies Debbie. "I was planning on taking Ronnie away to get him away from all this for a bit."

"Great idea," smiles Liz. "Moose, I think we'll go to your mum's and take Angel with us. Your mum has been worried as she's not seen him in a while. Papa Joe, could you possibly have a word with Carl? I'm worried about all three of them."

"I will do, baby girl," says Papa Joe. "Thank you."

Just then, Big Tam arrives and reports for duty. "What's on the agenda, compadre?" he asks Papa Joe.

"I'm afraid we're having issues with some of our band members, my friend," sighs Papa Joe. "The boys have managed to get themselves into a vicious cycle of drink and drugs."

"That's bad news," replies Big Tam. "Very bad."

"It is indeed," concurs Papa Joe. "We have a full weekend of sold-out gigs this weekend but, with your permission, I'm going to reschedule it. The health of my boys is priority right now."

"We'll do what we need to do," says Tam.

Angel can be heard singing from upstairs and it makes Big Tam smile. "He's either awake or about to wake up," says Liz. "I'm going to see him."

"Thanks, babe," says Moose as he pulls Liz close and kisses her.

Liz pops her head around Angel's bedroom door but he is still asleep so she enters the room, closes the door and sits on the bed. "Angel," she whispers.

Angel stirs, smiles and turns to look at Liz with his tired, deep brown eyes. "Are you OK, big bro?" Liz asks him.

"Hi, little sis," he greets her as he yawns. "What day are we on?"

"Oh my God," groans Liz. "It's Wednesday. You've slept almost all of that time since the wee small hours of Monday morning. You'll have to come off that shit you've been taking. We're all worried about you."

"Sorry, babe..." replies Angel. "Nobody told me how brutal the come-down was going to be."

"Nobody ever does," affirms Liz. "That fucking cow that Carl calls a girlfriend has a lot to answer for. Anyway, we're going to your mum's tomorrow. Moose and I thought we would get you away from here and away from the clutches of that scabby bastard Rhea for a bit."

"Have you said anything to Mom?" asks Angel, nervously.

"All I've told her is that we've all been busy and that you're exhausted from all the running the on stage," assures Liz. "Make that your story."

"Thanks, babe," replies Angel with a tired smile.

"Well I'll let you get back to sleep and let you recover for tomorrow," says Liz as she gives Angel a kiss and a hug. "See you then."

"Well?" asks Moose as Liz sits back in her seat.

"I think we may well have caught them on time," she replies with a sigh of relief. "One thing's for sure, we'll need to get Carl away from Rhea. She's bad for him *AND* us!"

"Who's that?" asks Tam.

"She's a drug dealer that Carl has somehow got involved with," replies Liz. "She is only seeing the dollar signs and she does not have Carl's best interests at heart..."

"Leave it with me, baby girl," assures Papa Joe. "I'll take my boy away on a fishing trip. That will get him away from her for a few days."

"She's fucking toxic," Liz yells angrily. "I just want to go to her house and stick a knife in her!"

"She's not worth it, ma doll," soothes Big Tam. "We'll handle this our way."

The following morning, Moose and Liz get back from their gym workout to find that all the bandmates are now present. "Thank God," Liz sighs with relief. "Is everyone packed and ready to go?"

"We certainly are, honey," smiles Debbie as she hugs Ronnie. "I can't wait to spend some quality time with this one."

"You didn't even have a honeymoon, Debbie," gasps Moose. "Why don't you both make this your time? It's not as if we can't afford it now and we all need to recharge."

"Good idea, brother," smiles a very tired, gaunt Ronnie. "Tell your wee mum we're all asking kindly for her and we'll see you in a couple of weeks."

Ronnie and Debbie arrive at their luxury hotel for their spa week and Debbie is quick to lay down some ground rules for a recovering Ronnie. "This stupidity stops right now," she commands. "If we're serious about trying for a baby, we can't have that shit in our lives or it will destroy us."

"I'm sorry, babe," Ronnie replies as he fights back the tears. "I didn't realise we would deteriorate so quickly. How could

I have been so naive?"

"It's water under the bridge now, darling," smiles Debbie. "Let's just kick back, relax and enjoy our vacation." They proceed to strip down, get into the jacuzzi in their room and make love.

Meanwhile Moose, Angel and Liz arrive at Maria's house and she greets them all with a kiss and a hug. She gasps in shock as she hugs Angel's rail-thin body. "What on earth has happened to you, baby?" she asks, close to tears. "You're so thin!"

"We've just been busy, Mom," assures Angel. "Sometimes there's not enough hours in the day."

"I get that, son," replies Maria. "But you can't neglect your health. If you don't make time for your health your body will make time for your sickness. I'm sure Mario has told you that."

"Every day," groans Angel as he and Moose exchange looks.

That evening, Liz and the Mancinis stay at Maria's and eat a healthy meal prepared by Maria herself. They sit up late chatting although Moose omits to mention Angel's drug use. "I think we'll take a trip to the shooting range tomorrow," suggests Maria.

"Great idea, Mom," enthuses Angel. "I've not been there in so long!"

"Aaww, I've never shot a gun before," gasps Liz. "I can't wait to try it."

"You're in for a treat, little sis," Angel chuckles.

"I suppose we'd better retire for the night then," says Moose. "We'll need to get there early."

Moose, Angel and Liz settle down for the night in Moose and Angel's old room and it's not long until Angel has fallen asleep. Liz smiles as he begins to sing. "Thank God," Moose says, relieved, as he cups Liz's breast in his hand and cuddles up to her.

"Just what we all needed," whispers Liz as she kisses Moose.

"Yeah," he replies. "I just hope the three of them stay off that shit."

The following week, Hell Freeze go back to work feeling

refreshed after some well-needed time-out with loved ones as they endeavour to make it up to the fans who had to have their concerts rescheduled. The weeks pass and neither Ronnie, Angel nor Carl have taken any amphetamines of any kind. It is a Friday evening and Debbie and Marc arrive at one of the venues they had rescheduled a gig for. "I need a favour, Marc," says Debbie. "Can you plug in this equipment for me if I tell you where everything goes? I've really hurt my back."

"Whit have ye done?" Marc laughs.

"My own fault, babe," replies Debbie. "I've lifted something that's far too heavy and now my lower back has gone. It's agony!"

"Nae bother, Debbie doll," says Marc. "If you just keep me right, I'll do it."

"Thanks, sweetheart," smiles Debbie. "I knew I could rely on you."

It is now time for Hell Freeze to go on-stage and perform. Liz hugs Angel from behind as he sits on one of the low stools with a beer. "How are you feeling, big bro?" she whispers in his ear.

"A million times better, little sis," he smiles as he turns around and hugs her. "I should go home more often. I left it too long that time."

"Definitely," says Liz. "You don't want to lose touch with your mum. I just wish mine was still here. Anyway, shall we?"

"Yeah," replies Angel as he takes Liz by the arm.

"Good luck, baby," Debbie says to Ronnie as she kisses him before he goes on-stage.

"Debbie, my darling," smiles Ronnie. "Thank you so much for everything and for being such a wonderful wife to me. I love you so much."

"I love you too, babe," whispers Debbie. "Get out there and keep doing me proud."

As usual, Hell Freeze do not let their adoring fans down as they put on yet another hard-hitting, energetic show. "Thank you, beautiful people," Angel addresses the audience after the show. "Apologies, once again, for rescheduling but thank you *ALL* for coming back to us and supporting us. See y'all again soon. We love you. Good night, God bless and *KEEP ON ROCKIN'!*"

Backstage, Moose and Ronnie dry themselves off and change their clothes while Angel waits as he shivers with the cold. "Are you alright, big bro?" asks Liz as she gently puts her arms around him.

"I'm OK, thanks, babe," replies Angel. "I think I might be in for something though. I couldn't warm up at all tonight."

"You need to get some of that good Italian food doon ye, ma man," Marc says with an unusually serious tone. "It's comin' in tae winter and you'll need tae get your muscles back."

"Sure, pal," Angel nods as he continues to shiver. "Cheers."

"Come on, big bro," says Liz as she holds Angel's ice-cold hand. "We'll hit the jacuzzi when we get home."

"Hey, Carl," Angel whispers to his friend. "What's the story with you and Rhea? Are you still able to get us decent gear?"

"Sure, pal," replies Carl, who is also shivering with the cold. "Although I think we need stronger stuff."

"That's what I thought," says Angel. "Can you sort it for us?"

"Leave it with me, dude," smiles Carl. "I'll see what she's got for us tomorrow."

The following morning, Liz and Moose rise early for their morning workout. They go downstairs to find that Debbie is already preparing breakfast. "Good morning, Debbie," Liz greets her. "You're early this morning."

"Yeah," enthuses Debbie. "I was going to join you both at the gym but I've changed my mind and I'm going to take advantage of the mild weather and go for a run instead."

"Oh, that sounds good," replies Liz. "I think I'll join you."

"Great," smiles Debbie. "I could use the company." The girls bid Moose goodbye as they head out for their run. They get about half a mile into their run when, suddenly, Debbie stops.

"Are you alright, Debbie?" asks Liz.

"I don't know," says Debbie. "There's something wrong with

my hips."

"Are they sore?" Liz asks, concerned.

"There's no pain," replies Debbie. "They just feel weird and as though they are out of alignment. It's hard to explain. Sorry, babe, I'm going to have to turn back. I'm scared to carry on in case I do any damage."

"I'll come with you," says Liz as the two women walk back home.

Later, Moose arrives home and asks them about their run. "I don't know what's been wrong with me lately," Debbie complains to Moose. " I have been absolutely riddled with injury for a good couple of months now and for no apparent reason. My lower back has been sore for weeks, then I hurt my ribs now my hips are playing up. It has just been one thing after another. I'm constantly very tired too. Man, I *HATE* being forty!"

Debbie lifts everyone's dirty dishes, takes them into the kitchen and Moose follows her. "Debbie?" he whispers. "You wouldn't be pregnant, would you?"

"I doubt it, babe," says Debbie. "We've been really busy and we've all been going hard at it since I started my new record label. Maybe I just need to kick back and relax."

"Please take a test before you do anything else," Moose begs. "If you are pregnant, we don't want you doing any damage to yourself or the little one."

"I will," assures Debbie as she hugs Moose. "Thank you, brother."

That night, Moose is struggling to sleep as feelings of uneasiness hit him again. "What's wrong, babe?" asks Liz as she senses his change in demeanour over the past few weeks.

"Too many things going on just now, Liz," sighs Moose. "I know Angel and Carl are still doing shit and I suspect Ronnie is too. Now I'm worried about Debbie..."

"Debbie?" asks Liz, surprised.

"I have a feeling she is heading for a terrible fall," replies Moose.

"Moose, you're *REALLY* freaking me out," cries Liz. "What did she say to you earlier?"

"It's alright, babe," sighs Moose as he kisses her and tries to settle down. "I'm probably imagining things."

Moose hasn't long fallen asleep until he is woken by a very tearful Ronnie standing by his bed. "What's wrong, dude?" asks Moose.

"Can you please take me to the hospital with Debbie, pal?" Ronnie whispers as he tries not to disturb Liz. "I think she's miscarrying and I feel as though I have too much alcohol in my system to drive."

Moose jumps up, throws on a pair of jeans and a sweater and he and Ronnie support Debbie as they take her to Moose's car.

Moose and Ronnie wait nervously outside the ward where Debbie is being cared for until, eventually, a doctor asks to speak to Ronnie. "I'm afraid the baby couldn't be saved, Mr Buchanan," the Doctor informs Ronnie. "Mrs Buchanan suffered from many complications in the very short time that she was pregnant. I know you are busy people but I strongly advise that you and your wife rest. Also, sorry if this sounds impertinent, please give your bandmates the same advice from a concerned fan."

"Thank you so much, doctor," replies Ronnie as he fights back the tears. "We'll pass on your regards. Can we see Debbie now please?"

"Of course," replies the doctor.

Moose and Ronnie enter the private ward to find Debbie looking exhausted. "I'm so sorry, baby," Debbie apologises as she cries.

"It's not your fault, doll," assures Ronnie through his tears. "The doctor said there were lots of complications."

"I knew that," replies Debbie. "I just hoped it was the effects of turning forty and I didn't expect to fall pregnant to quickly. I'll know better next time."

"I know it's hard," says Ronnie. "But please try not to beat yourself up about it. We'll take some time off and think about getting somebody in to help you for when you come back."

"That might not be a bad idea, babe," replies Debbie with a tired smile.

"Anyway, Moose and I will let you get some sleep," says Ronnie. "I'll come back and see you later on."

"Thanks for being there, honey," says Debbie. "Moose, thank you so much for all you've done for us. We really owe you one."

"What are friends for?" asks Moose as he kisses Debbie. "Get well soon, sister. We'll see you later."

Back at Moose's car, Ronnie breaks down. "I'm sorry, pal," he apologises to Moose.

"Dude, you've just had a bereavement," empathises Moose. "It's normal."

"I just feel so helpless," sobs Ronnie. "I should have done more for her."

"You did all you could, Ron," assures Moose. "You didn't know Debbie was pregnant. Dude, even Debbie didn't know. I'm just glad you came and got me rather than attempt the drive."

"One thing's for sure," affirms Ronnie. "I am *NEVER* drinking again. I've let it become too much of a habit so no more after today."

"I am beyond proud of you, pal," Moose smiles warmly. "Just remember I'm always here if you need me."

"Actually, there *IS* something else," replies Ronnie. "Can I join you and Liz for some sessions? I need to get myself fit for when the wee one joins us and I don't want to be one of those wimpy daddies who can barely lift the phone book."

"That will never be you, pal," Moose laughs as he embraces his friend. "I've known you since our uni days and you are one of the strongest characters I know. Of course, it would be an honour if you would join us. Anyway, we'd best get home before Liz sends out the search parties."

"Thank God," exclaims Liz as she throws her arms around Moose and Ronnie. "I've been worried sick. Where's Debbie?"

Moose puts a strong arm around Ronnie's shoulders. "Debbie miscarried last night, babe," Moose tells Liz. "We've been at the hospital most of the night."

"Aw, Ronnie, I'm so sorry," sympathises Liz. "I had no idea she was pregnant so that explains all those injuries. How is Debbie and are *YOU* alright?"

"I'm OK, thanks, babe," Ronnie replies wearily. "I'm just worried about Debbie. She is exhausted and heartbroken so she is being looked after at the hospital just now."

"You should get some rest, buddy," Moose advises Ronnie. "We'll go back to the hospital and see Debbie again later, once we've all had some sleep."

"Thanks again for everything, pal," Ronnie says with a weary smile. "If I'm not up by five p.m. will you please wake me?"

"Will do," replies Moose as he signals for Liz to follow him to their own bedroom.

"Dare I ask where Carl and Angel are?" he asks Liz as they get into bed.

Liz hangs her head. "I've not seen them all day," she replies. "They were still asleep when I went to the gym and they were gone by the time I got back."

"Shit," groans Moose. "They will be with that fuckin' skank Rhea and I dread to think what she's feeding them now..."

Presently, Carl and Angel are at Rhea's mansion for their daily fix. "I have something new for you beauties to try," she purrs in her deep, raspy voice.

She then proceeds to put out two lines of cocaine. "It's magic stuff," she winks. "Try it. You won't look back."

"COKE?" asks Angel, shocked.

"You're a big boy now, gorgeous," Rhea winks at him. "Go on. You know you want to."

Carl snorts the white powder without question. "It's good stuff," he whispers. "It works a treat right away!"

"Moose will go fuckin' tonto," Angel thinks to himself. "Fuck it. He won't know..." He proceeds to take his share of the addictive stimulant.

"Let it do its job and go knock their socks off," exclaims Rhea. "Right now, any chance of a three-way with you two studs?"

Angel grimaces inwardly. "Not with you, you butt-ugly brown-bagger," he thinks to himself.

"Sorry, Rhea, I really need to get going," stammers Angel. "Carl, have fun and I'll catch you later."

Angel arrives home to find the house unusually silent with only Papa Joe and Big Tam sitting in the living room organising recordings and upcoming gigs. "Where is everyone?" he asks his managers.

"They're in bed, son," replies Big Tam. "That was a sin what happened to Debbie."

"What happened?" asks Angel.

"She had a miscarriage early hours of this morning, son," Papa Joe tells him. "She and Ronnie are heartbroken and she's resting at the hospital."

"Shit," exclaims Angel. "That's bad news, man."

"Tragic, son," says Tam. "Liz is going up with Ronnie and Moose later. Why don't you go with them?"

"Aw, I will," replies Angel. "Right now, I need to take my mind off it. I'm going to the gym. I'll be back later."

"OK, son," says Tam. "Just watch you don't do too much. You don't want to get too skinny."

"No, Tam," assures Angel. "See you later."

"Why the Hell did I take that stuff today?" Angel curses to himself. "I should have waited until the weekend when we have gigs. I feel as though I've wasted it. As long as Moose doesn't find out."

Angel arrives at Trojans' and is greeted by Marco who is busy washing down the gym equipment. "How are you doing, buddy?" Angel greets him.

"Bored out of my mind, pal," groans Marco. "I had three last-minute cancellations now I don't have another client until six p.m."

"Sorry to hear that, dude," replies Angel. "Are you up for making a quick buck?"

"Sure, kid," enthuses Marco. "What do you want to do?"

"Something as energetic as possible," replies Angel. "We had a bit of bad news at home today and I need to take my mind off it."

"Want to talk about?" asks Marco, concerned.

"Debbie miscarried, dude," replies Angel. "Nobody even knew she was pregnant."

"So sorry, pal," empathises Marco. "Please pass on my deepest condolences to Ronnie and Debbie. I can see why you need something high energy and I have the very thing for you. Get changed and we'll do some Kung Fu and a bit of sparring."

"Sounds great," enthuses Angel. "Thanks for listening, man."

"Now I'll have an alibi," he thinks to himself.

As expected, Moose confronts Angel as soon as he gets home. "I was with Marco, bro," he tells his brother.

"Don't lie to me, kid," warns Moose. "I will find out and where is Carl?"

"I don't know," replies Angel. "I told you, I was at the gym doing a session with Marco. Ask him yourself if you don't believe me. I've not seen Carl."

Moose looks Angel straight in the eyes. "I suppose Papa Joe and Tam told you about Debbie?" asks Moose.

"Yeah," Angel replies with sadness in his voice. "She and Ronnie will be devastated. Are we going to the hospital tonight?"

"Sure, pal," Moose smiles warmly. "Debbie would love to see you. She's been worried about you."

"Honestly, bro," assures Angel. "I'm fine and there's no need. I'm just trying to stave off the middle-age spread, that's all."

"Just be careful then," replies Moose. "Remember you'll need those gains for when you're on stage."

The bandmates arrive at the hospital, with the exception of Carl, to find that Debbie is up and dressed. She greets them all with kisses and hugs as they enter her private room. "It's so good to see you all," she says, almost in tears. "Thank you for coming."

"What are you doing up, babe?" asks Ronnie "The doctor said you had to rest."

"I can't stay in that bed any longer, honey," replies Debbie. "I just want to go home and have company. I'm going to speak to the doctor."

"Fine," says Moose. "As long as you take time out and let your body and your mind recover."

"Thanks, babe," replies Debbie. "I promise I will. I've slept long enough and being cooped up in this room by myself in a maternity ward is doing me no favours. I just want to go home to my own bed and my family."

"As long as you're sure," says Ronnie as he kisses her. "Let's go and see the doctor."

Moose holds Liz close as they wait for Ronnie and Debbie to get back. "Let's go home," smiles Debbie as she and Ronnie re-enter the room.

That night, Debbie is enjoying a relaxing night in with the bandmates and her management team. "How are you feeling, Debbie doll?" Tam asks her as they make coffee together.

"I'm very sore, Tam," replies Debbie. "But I suppose that's normal and it will take me a good few weeks to recover."

"Aye, hen," says Tam with sadness in his voice. "My wee Mary went through the exact same thing three times before our Liz. We had almost given up hope, then a miracle happened. She went full term with Liz, despite working all through the pregnancy and our wee girl was born weighing a very healthy eight pounds. I would advise you to take some time out just now, darling, especially if you and Ronnie are planning on trying again."

"I can't to that, Tam," gasps Debbie. "What about the tours?"

"We'll take on somebody temporarily," suggests Tam. "Your job is a heavy one and we don't want to see you go through this kind of pain again. You could still come to the gigs and help train the new engineer but let them do all the heavy lifting with Marc."

"Sounds like an idea, Tam," smiles Debbie. "Thank you so much."

"You're very welcome, sweetheart," replies Tam. "I'm sure Joe knows somebody from the industry that could come on board with us. It would suit a strong, retired person or a graduate looking for experience. We'll see what Joe says."

From there, Papa Joe recruits an old associate Danny Walker to assist Debbie. Danny is a burly, retired man in his late fifties who is grateful for a bit of adventure with one of the biggest rock bands of that generation. Danny's abilities are challenged just weeks later when he turns up to set up for a gig but Debbie is sick and can't attend. "What's wrong with your girl, son?" he asks Ronnie.

"She's not been well for a few days now, big chap," sighs Ronnie. "She's still in a lot of pain since her miscarriage too. If she's not any better tomorrow I'll be taking her to hospital."

Meanwhile, Angel and Carl are high having paid a visit to Rhea very early in the morning. "As much as I love it," Angel says to Carl. "I still feel guilty about doing this."

"Dude, it's alright," assures Carl. "We can stop taking it any time we want. Let's just get this busy spell out of the way."

"OK..." Angel replies, not convinced.

Another very busy weekend passes for Hell Freeze. By Monday, Angel and Carl are restless as they feel the effects of the cocaine wearing off. "I'm going to see Rhea," says Carl as he fidgets nervously.

"OK, pal," Moose says without looking up. "See you later."

Carl makes a sharp exit and Angel follows him. "I have the very thing for you boys," smiles Rhea when they arrive at her mansion. "It will help you relax and unwind."

"What's that?" asks Carl.

"A very special smoke, honey," she purrs.

"No," says Angel, flatly. "I gave up the smokes a long time

ago and would *NEVER* go back to it."

"You and your God damn pride," sneers Rhea. "Is it because of *HER?*"

"Fuck up, Rhea," Angel barks at her. "If you mean Liz then yes. I feel better having given up that shit and I am loyal to my little sister...something you know damn all about..."

"Listen, asshole," growls Rhea. "Do you want a downer or do you not? I'm doing *YOU* the favour here and don't you ever forget it. Anyway, it's only a smoke and the little pug and your meddling, nerdy brother don't need to know."

Angel shakes his head and says nothing as Rhea produces two spliffs. She gives Carl and Angel one each, lights them up and watches as they both relax into a trance-like state. "It's good," slurs Carl, unable to keep his eyes open any more.

"How about you, sexy?" she asks Angel as he closes his eyes and slumps backwards into the couch.

"Mm-hm," Angel just manages to mumble.

"Very good, honey," whispers Rhea as she rubs up and down his thigh to his crotch and he sees her wink at him through his blurred vision. "Better than sex." She proceeds to lie Carl on the floor then straddles Angel and kisses him passionately.

Several hours later Moose, Ronnie, Liz and the Hell Freeze management team are worried about the whereabouts of Angel and Carl. "Does anyone have a number for Rhea?" asks Liz.

"No," replies Moose. "I've already tried phoning but the number on our phone leads to a call box. Typical drug dealer. I knew that woman was poison. There's no point in us even involving the police because they won't get involved unless they've been missing for a certain amount of time."

"Any sign of them?" Debbie asks as she pops her head around the door.

"Still, nothing babe," sighs Ronnie. "Come on, you'd best get to bed if you're still not well."

"Why don't you turn in for the night, Ron," suggests Moose. "I'll let you know if I hear anything."

Just then, there is a knock at the door. Moose answers the door to be met by a burly, latino man in his forties. "Sorry to bother you so late, dude," the man apologises. "I have two of your bandmates in the back of my car. Can you help me please?"

Moose goes out to the waiting taxi and the driver helps him peel Angel off the back seat. Moose then effortlessly carries Angel upstairs to his bed before collecting Carl. "Dear God," groans Papa Joe as he breaks down in tears.

"Thanks so much, big guy," Moose says to the driver as he presses $50 into the palm of his hand. "Sorry for the trouble."

"It's OK, Moose," assures the driver. "I just hope your brother and his buddy get the help they need before it's too late. Can I also be really cheeky and ask for an autograph from you? My girlfriend loves you."

"Sure," smiles Moose as the driver hands him a small Hell Freeze poster.

"Can you make it out 'To Stefano and Claire' please?" asks the driver.

"There you go, dude," Moose smiles warmly as he hands the signed poster back to the driver. "Thanks again and enjoy the rest of your night."

Moose goes back indoors to find that Liz is crying as she is comforted by her father and Papa Joe. "Everything's going wrong," she sobs.

"It will be alright, my wee lamb," Tam tries to assure her. "You get yourselves to bed and Joe and I will keep and eye on the boys."

"Come on, babe," whispers Moose as he takes Liz by the hand. "Thanks so much, Tam and Papa Joe. You are legends."

"See you in the morning, son," says Tam as he and Joe prepare for the bedside vigils in order to ensure that Angel and Carl are as safe as they can be under the circumstances.

Early the following morning, Moose and Liz check on Ronnie and Debbie before relieving Tam and Papa Joe of their duties. "Why the Hell did you do it, Angel?" Moose asks frustrated as his brother lies in bed unresponsive. "After all the times we spoke about this. *WHY?*"

Meanwhile, Liz sits in the next room with Carl as she goes over everything in her head. Debbie is sick, now two men that she classes as brothers are on a slippery slope with their health due to drug addiction. "We need to get you away from Rhea," she whispers to Carl as she holds his hand, even though she knows it is fruitless. "She doesn't give a shit about you. You know she doesn't…"

The weeks pass and Hell Freeze continue with their strenuous regime of gigs and recording despite Angel and Carl's deteriorating health. "I may as well tell you now," Debbie whispers to Moose and Liz as they go out to the back porch for some fresh air. "I'm pregnant."

"How far along are you?" asks Moose, anxiously.

"Just over the twelve weeks now, babe," smiles Debbie. "I'm very tired though and my back is still very sore."

"Congratulations, big sis," says Liz. "I still think you're doing far too much though. Remember we've got Danny on board with us now as well as Marc and your health has to be priority at this time."

"Thanks, my loves," replies Debbie. "I'm just so worried about Angel and Carl."

"Leave them to us," says Moose as he puts a strong arm around Liz.

That night, Moose and Liz are both woken by the front door closing. "It's Ronnie," Moose tells Liz as he watches him assist Debbie into his car. "He must be taking her to the hospital. I hope to God it's not another miscarriage."

"I hope not," replies Liz. "It's the last thing we all need right now."

"Try to get some sleep just now, babe," soothes Moose as he cuddles up to Liz in bed. "I hate to say it but the guys and Debbie are relying on us more than ever now."

"Aye," replies Liz, although she can't stop her silent tears.

Moose, Liz and the management team are relieved when Ronnie arrives home mid morning. "What happened, son," asks Papa Joe, concerned. "Debbie took a heavy bleeding last night and is in a lot of pain, Joe. The doctors have assured us it's not a miscarriage and that the baby is fine but they're keeping Debbie in for observation. I came away because she was going to sleep."

"You'd best get some sleep too, son," advises Tam.

"I can't, Tam," sighs Ronnie. "What if I miss the visiting times?"

"It's alright, babe," assures Liz. "We're all here and we'll visit Debbie if you're tired. You must be exhausted after all the stress."

"I am, doll," replies Ronnie. "I can't thank you all enough for everything."

"Any time, dude," says Moose. "Try to get some sleep. You've done enough today."

Meanwhile, the bandmates have barely seen Angel and Carl. One evening, Moose has a horrible feeling in his gut and can't sleep so he goes downstairs, flicks through a newspaper and gasps in shock at what he sees. Angel had been snapped walking alone through the busy town centre looking ill, emaciated and as though he no longer cared for his appearance as his long, dark hair appears to have lost its condition and his clothes look at least two sizes too big. "Oh, God, please no," Moose sobs as he drops the newspaper on the floor.

His fears are confirmed when Carl and Angel both turn up for the bus ride to their Friday evening gig looking haggard and ill. Even Marc is speechless as he stares wide-eyed at the two sickly-looking rock stars. "Whit, in the name of fuck, happened to those two?" he whispers to Moose in his broad Scots Glaswegian accent.

"They're sick, Marc," Moose says with sadness in his voice. "I don't even know if I can help them now."

"Looks like a joab for the professionals, mate," replies Marc. "We'll need tae get they bhoys help before it's too late."

"Yeah," says Moose as he walks away trying to fight back the tears.

"You don't look too hot yersel', hen," Marc says to Liz.

"I'm OK, thanks, babe," Liz replies with a faint smile. "I'm just stressed out with everything just now."

"It's yer big birthday soon, hen," smiles Marc. "It might be a good idea for you to get the big guy tae take ye away for a wee spa weekend and get away from all this for a wee bit."

"I don't know if we'll have time, Marc," replies Liz as she hangs her head. "Not with things the way they are."

"Come on, wee yin," says Marc. "You'll be twenty one, not fifty. Enjoy it while you can. Mind we're all still here."

"Thanks, Marc," Liz smiles as she hugs him. "I promise I'll talk to Moose later."

Despite his shocking appearance, Angel doesn't disappoint the audience as he puts on yet another dazzling performance with Hell Freeze. Moose, Ronnie and Liz look at the audience and notice that people are upset, with many crying as they can see that their idol is clearly unwell. Liz can't help crying either as she has been worried about the welfare of her beloved friends for several weeks now. After yet another energy packed performance, Hell Freeze close their gig with their massive trademark outro before Angel addresses their fans. "Thank you so much, beautiful people," he slurs as very much of the audience descends into an unhealthy combination of murmuring and gasps. "Thank you for being a terrific audience, for your support and all the love. Good night, God bless and *KEEP ON ROCKIN'*"

Moose notices Carl slumped at the drum kit. "Wait here, buddy," he whispers to him. "I'll be back in a minute, OK?"

Carl manages to lift his head but he is unable to open his eyes and collapses back onto the drum kit. Members of the audience who had remained watch in horror as Moose effortlessly picks Angel up and carries him backstage before going back out to get Carl, with many of the adoring fans crying and pleading with him to get help for his bandmates. Of course, the press reports and reviews regarding Hell Freeze's weekend performances are more geared towards the welfare of the bandmates rather than on the performances themselves. "Health Fears For Hell Freeze," "Drug Problems," "Hell Freeze Splitting?" and "Hell Freeze In Crisis" are among the headlines.

In spite of all the bad press, Angel wins a record deal with Magnetic Records in order to pursue a solo career as well as remaining front man for Hell Freeze. Much to the enragement of the media and the general public, he also wins a modelling contract with Me2U, a high-profile unisex clothing brand aimed at the eighteen to twenty-five age category. Despite being barely able to walk or assemble a full sentence most days, Angel is called for photoshoots where his photos are very rapidly published in magazines, newspapers and billboards. Even though he has had his hair and make-up professionally done, rather than look sexy, the observation of the general public is that he looks lost and childlike in the photos with his hollow cheeks, protruding ribs and sunken stomach. Even his distinct deep brown eyes look vacant, giving the impression that Angel has lost the will to live. Me2U come under fire for the images. "It's bad enough that the so-called supermodels are glamorising eating disorders for the girls," one critic rages. "NOW we have Angel Mancini doing it for the boys! Congratulations Me2U. You have really out-done yourselves!"

A spokesman for the clothing brand, however, defends their decision by stating "Heroin chic is fashionable and Angel Mancini is hot property."

The heavy criticism doesn't stop Angel and he continues to work as a model and actor while still writing and performing music while having severe problems with alcohol and narcotics.

One afternoon, Moose is in the music room composing a new song as he plays his guitar when there is a knock at the door. "Yeah?" Moose asks.

"Hello, my son," Tam smiles as he enters the room quietly.

"You know it's the wee yin's birthday soon, big guy?"

"I know, Tam," sighs Moose. "It's her big one too and I have no idea what to do for her."

"She's not been very well lately, son," whispers Tam. "She's very fragile."

"I'd noticed that," sighs Moose. "We've had a lot going on and she's put up with a lot more than she should have, especially with Carl and Angel. She's so ahead of her time that people, myself included, forget how young she is and they expect a lot more from her than they should. "

"Why don't you take her away for a relaxing weekend?" suggests Tam. "Just the two of you."

"Marc and Danny suggested that too," replies Moose. "But..."

"It's alright, son," assures Tam. "Joe and I will keep an eye on the boys and Debbie and we'll hopefully get the two weans into rehab if we can pin them down. Anyway, this trip is for your own health rather than just a present for Liz. Go on, it's on me."

"Thanks, Tam," Moose smiles warmly. "I'll touch base with Liz and see where she wants to go. I really appreciate it."

"Thanks, big chap," Tam smiles as he embraces Moose. "You're so good to my wee girl and please don't think for a minute that my boys and I don't see it."

"I'm a very lucky man, Tam," replies Moose. "Things happened for us at just the right time. I couldn't be more grateful for the stunning, selfless girlfriend that I call mine."

"I'm glad of it, son," smiles Tam.

A few weeks later, Liz turns twenty one and everyone is becoming increasingly concerned about her health. As organised by her father, she and Moose enjoy a relaxing weekend away. "This trip is just what I needed," she tells Moose as she strips off and joins him in the jacuzzi.

"Sure is," replies Moose as he kisses her. "Happy birthday, babe." The couple go on to enjoy a passionate weekend of good food, movies and romance. Sadly, their happiness is short-lived.

They arrive home to find that Debbie, now eighteen weeks into her pregnancy, has been rushed to hospital yet again. To make matters worse, Carl and Angel's drug addiction is out of control and they are constantly ill despite still managing to produce excellent recordings for the fans.

"I can't deal with much more of this," Liz thinks to herself as feelings of extreme nausea wash over her.

"I'm going to bed," she tells Moose, Tam and Papa Joe. "Can you wake me when we're going to the hospital please?"

"You need to try and eat something, my wee lamb," says Tam, concerned.

"Sorry, Dad," Liz apologises. "I just can't. Not just now..." Liz closes her bedroom door tightly, goes into the bathroom and does a pregnancy test. She can't remember when her last period was as she and Moose had continued to enjoy a very active sex life despite her deteriorating health. Liz breathes a sigh of relief when the test result is negative, lies on top of the bed and closes her eyes. Later, she spends another traumatising evening at the hospital as she awaits news of Debbie's well-being with Moose, Ronnie, Tam and Papa Joe.

"Mr Buchanan?" the doctor calls for Ronnie. "Your wife is experiencing several complications. We advise that she stays for observation and further treatment if needed."

"Thank you, doctor," replies Ronnie as he fights back the tears. "Can I see her now, please?"

"Certainly," says the doctor. "Please come this way."

Ronnie is led to a private room where Debbie is lying in bed feeling weak, exhausted and in a lot of pain. "Thank you for being here, my darling," she says quietly with a faint smile. "Please stay strong."

"Please hang in there, babe," sobs Ronnie. "Get plenty of rest and I'll see you tomorrow. I promise."

"Night night, my love," Debbie whispers. "See you tomorrow."

As they make their way through the multiple corridors on the way back to Moose's car, a very exhausted Liz is struggling to keep up with her management team and her two bandmates as she lags further and further behind the more they walk. Moose picks her up and carries her the rest of the way and she falls asleep in his arms almost immediately.

The weeks pass and press reports show more and more disturbing photos of the Hell Freeze bandmates looking frail, ill and exhausted as the pressure of being in the spotlight mounts. Very early one morning, Liz wakes up experiencing chest pain and she is having difficulty breathing. "Moose," she manages to utter as she fights to catch her breath. Moose doesn't hesitate, gets up and rushes Liz to the hospital while trying to reassure her as he drives. He waits anxiously in the waiting area of the coronary care unit as doctors carry out several tests on Liz.

"Mr Mancini?" the doctor calls Moose.

"How is she?" he asks nervously.

"Mr Mancini," the doctor begins. "Your partner is suffering from anorexia nervosa stemming from high levels of anxiety. She appears to have lost a lot of weight in a short period of time and I have advised her to stay here and rest for now."

"Thank you so much, doctor," Moose says, relieved. "Can I see her before I go?"

"Of course," smiles the doctor. "I trust, with your expertise, you will ensure Miss McLarnon stays in line."

"Sure," replies Moose with a weary smile.

Moose enters the private room to find that Liz is crying. "I am so sorry to have put you through this, baby," she apologises.

"Hey," soothes Moose. "You're not putting me through anything. We are a team and we do this together. OK?"

"Aye..." Liz whispers through her tears as she has other plans. "Whatever happens, babe, please remember that I love you very much."

Moose leaves the hospital, makes sure nobody is watching then bursts into tears. He calms himself down enough to get on the phone to his mother. He lifts the receiver off the pay phone and dials her number. "Hello, son," Maria greets him. "It's so good to hear from you. I've missed you so much. How are you?"

"I'm OK, Mom," replies Moose as he tries to remain calm. "Mom, do you mind if I come home?"

"You know you're welcome here any time, my love," says Maria. "Is everything alright?"

"I've got too much to tell you, Mom," replies Moose. "I just need to to get away from here for a bit. I'll fill you in when I get there."

"Alright, my darling," says Maria. "You take care, drive safely and I'll see you very soon."

Moose arrives home and is greeted by his mother with a long, tight hug before she escorts him into the living room and sits him down. "What's happened, son?" she asks him.

"Everything is going wrong, Mom," says Moose as he fights back the tears. "Debbie is in and out of hospital and I am worried she is going to lose the baby. Carl and Angel are in serious trouble with drink and drugs and I've just left Liz at the hospital. She has been suffering from anorexia for God knows how long and I don't know if I can help her. I think our days as a band are coming to an end. Mom, I've never felt so helpless in my life."

"It's all part and parcel of being a strong person, son," soothes Maria.

"I don't feel very strong right now, Mom," says Moose as he starts to cry. "I feel as though I have failed everyone including my own brother and my girlfriend."

"None of this is your fault, darling," assures Maria as she hugs her son. "As difficult as it is, you need to accept that you've done your best. You can't control how others react to different situations. It just so happens that Angel, Carl and Liz are cracking under the pressure of being high-profile rock stars and drink, drugs and eating disorders are their coping mechanisms. You can't help that, son. All we can do is support them if they want us. I'm just glad you came home to me and I hope you keep doing so."

"I am so grateful for you, Mom," replies Moose with a weary smile as he dries his tears.

Unsurprisingly, Moose has difficulty sleeping as he goes over in his mind what his plan of action will be. "I'll ask Lukas and Marco for a job," he thinks to himself as he settles down to sleep in his old bed. "I'll ask Liz to marry me and I'll look after her while she gets her treatment. I'll do extra personal training and classes so I can get Angel into rehab too. Everything will be fine but I'll need to work extra hard."

The following morning, Moose makes the journey back to the hospital to take Liz home following her discharge. "I love you so much, baby," she whispers as she cannot stop the tears. "Thank you…"

"We're going to see Debbie, my wee lamb," Tam tells Liz later. "You mind and get plenty of rest."

"Thanks, Dad," replies Liz. "Please tell Debbie I send my love and I'll see her soon." She watches as Moose's car pulls away. Once she is sure everyone is a safe distance away, she phones her brother Harry who is a well-respected consultant psychiatrist.

"Hello, wee sis," Harry greets her with his usual hearty laugh. "How are you doing?"

"Harry…" Liz begins before bursting into tears.

"It's not like you to cry," says Harry, concerned. "What's the matter, love?"

"Harry," says Liz as she tries to compose herself. "I really need your help."

"It's going to be alright, hen," soothes Harry. "What do you need?"

"I need help with anorexia, Harry," says Liz. "I am ill. But I can't stay here. I'm going to need to come home."

"Well I can do that bit for you, love," replies Harry. "You can stay here with myself and Wee Anna until I get you the help you need. I'm sorry eating disorders are not my strong point but I know people who can definitely help you."

"Thanks so much, Harry," says Liz, relieved. "I feel as though a giant weight has been lifted from me. It breaks my heart to leave like this, especially Moose. I just wish I could have it all ways."

"You're doing the right thing, pet," assures Harry. "Moose is a good egg and I'm sure he'll understand."

"I hope so," says Liz as she begins to cry again.

"Leave it with me, hen," replies Harry. "If I don't phone you tomorrow, it will be the day after."

"Thanks, Harry," sobs Liz as she concludes the phone call. "Love you."

The following afternoon, as promised, Harry phones Liz. "I have great news for you, hen," he tells her. "My good pal Tom O'Donnell at Leverndale Hospital says he'll be more than happy to help you. He specialises in eating disorders and you'll receive in-patient care for as long as you need and out-patient care afterwards."

Liz breaks down. "It's all starting to feel very real now, Harry," she sobs. "The break-up of my band and having to leave Moose. I know I should be happy that I'm getting help but I'm heartbroken about everything."

"You're being extremely brave, my doll," says Harry. "I know this isn't an easy decision for you but I can assure you, it's the right one. At least you'll get peace to recover over here."

"I know, Harry," replies Liz. "I'm trying to look on the bright side but it's so hard. Poor Moose. I have treated him so badly yet he is still loyal to me. He deserves better."

Chapter 23:
Shards Of Porcelain

In the week following, Papa Joe and Big Tam have a serious talk concerning the future of Hell Freeze. "We can't go on the way we are, Tam," says Papa Joe. "The kids are sick and every one of them needs help."

"You're right, Joe," concurs Tam. "I think the best plan I'm of action is to have one more tour to let them say goodbye to the fans then split up the band."

"It's the only way," replies Papa Joe. "Otherwise, we're going to have death on our hands."

"Sounds like a plan," says Tam. "One final push then we'll call it a day."

Shortly afterwards, Moose arrives home with Ronnie having picked him up from his visit to Debbie, Liz comes slowly downstairs still feeling cold, ill and exhausted from the constant crying and Angel and Carl make a very rare appearance as they make themselves as comfortable as possible on the sofas. Liz cuddles up to Moose on the sofa, cherishing the moments she still has with him and hoping he will understand her heartbreaking decision to move back home to Scotland for her treatment.

"Good morning, folks," Papa Joe addresses the bandmates. "Tam and I have an important announcement to make."

"We understand that you are all ill and in need of professional help," Tam continues. "Joe and I have decided that the best course of action is to take an extended break from touring and recording so that you can go to rehab and concentrate on your other personal issues."

"You mean you're breaking up the band?" slurs Carl.

"There's no other way, son," says Papa Joe. "If we keep going the way we're going, the six of you will end up in an early grave and we don't want that."

"So what now?" asks Ronnie, nervously.

"We do one final farewell tour so you can all say goodbye and thank you to your fans," says Tam. "Then we finish up."

Carl and Angel get up and leave. "Guys," Liz tries to shout them back but only a whisper and silent tears escape her tired body.

Just then, the phone rings and Papa Joe answers it. "It's the hospital, son," he whispers to Ronnie.

A wave of nausea washes over Ronnie as he takes the receiver. "Right now?" he asks, panicking. "Yes, I'll be right there. Thank you, doctor."

"I need to go," says Ronnie. "Debbie has gone into labour."

"Shit," Moose panics. "Come on, dude. Papa Joe and Tam, can you phone Ronnie's parents and get them over here please?"

"Aye, son," assures Tam. "You take care now."

Moose takes Ronnie to the hospital and waits patiently in the waiting area as Ronnie attends the birth of his baby. Just under five hours later, Ronnie emerges looking tearful and exhausted. "It's a wee girl," he whispers to Moose. "Debbie gave birth prematurely at twenty nine weeks and the baby only weighs two pounds and nine ounces."

"So sorry, dude," replies Moose as he fights back his own tears. "I wish there was more I could do to help."

"Mr Buchanan?" the doctor calls Ronnie. "Your wife has taken a turn for the worse. I'm afraid she suffered a series of complications during that very difficult birth and lost a lot of blood. She has gone into a coma and your daughter is critical."

"Can we see them?" asks Ronnie.

"Of course," replies the doctor.

Moose puts a strong arm around Ronnie's shoulders as they enter the private room where Debbie lies unresponsive. "I'll take you to see your daughter," whispers the doctor. "This way please."

The doctor points to an incubator where Ronnie and Debbie's new daughter lies fighting for her life with all sorts of tubes inserted into her tiny body. "She's beautiful," whispers Ronnie.

"She is, brother," soothes Moose as he gently squeezes Ronnie's arm. "Does she have a name?"

"Caitlin," affirms Ronnie. "Debbie has always loved that name. Caitlin Elizabeth Buchanan, after her Auntie Liz."

"Liz will be thrilled," smiles Moose. "Let's go and sit with Debbie for a bit."

"Thanks, brother," whispers Ronnie through his tears. "Thanks for all you do for us."

Presently, Tam calls Ronnie's parents to tell them what he knows so far. "We're going to be grandparents right now?" Donald asks, surprised.

"You are indeed, my good man," replies Tam.

"Whatever happens, your boy and his wife need you. Please make your way over, we'll see you when you get here and help you with your finances."

"We're on our way, Tam," assures Donald. "Thank you."

"I have news too," Liz whispers as Papa Joe hangs up the phone.

"What's that, love?" asks Tam.

Liz breaks down. "Dad," she begins. "I've not said anything to Moose and I have no idea how I am going to tell him…"

"Tell him what, Liz?" whispers Papa Joe.

"Dad, Papa Joe," Liz sobs. "I'm going home to Scotland. I'm going to have to break up with Moose and it is killing me. I love him more than anything in the world."

"Why?" asks Tam, shocked. "I know things are tough but we'll get through it."

"Harry is organising treatment for me at Leverndale, Dad," Liz tells him. "His pal has already agreed to treat me because he specialises in eating disorders. It's the only way I'll get through it."

"It's a very brave thing you're doing, my wee lamb," says Tam as he hugs Liz. "I know it wasn't an easy decision for you as all your friends and your boyfriend are here."

"I know, Dad," says Liz. "But I won't get peace to do my treatment here. You know what the press are like. It's bad enough that my weight loss is all over the papers and magazines. What will it be like when I gain weight? I am terrified of gaining weight as it is without everybody and their granny scrutinising me. I just hope Tom O'Donnell can help me. I know everyone is saying things about Angel and Carl but I feel as though I am worse than them and poor Moose is picking up the pieces for all five of us. It's not fair on him and he deserves better."

"You need to take the help when it's going, baby girl," assures Papa Joe. "Your big brother knows what he's talking about and, you've said it yourself, at least you'll get peace to recover over there."

"I just don't know how I'm going to tell Moose," says Liz as she continues to cry uncontrollably.

In the week following, Liz still hasn't summoned the courage to tell Moose of her intentions to move away. Amid hospital trips to visit Debbie and Baby Caitlin, Angel and Carl with their troubled times and Liz, herself, being so ill all the time now, there just doesn't seem to be a right time to tell Moose of her heartbreaking decision.

One evening, Tam is in a meeting with Papa Joe organising Hell Freeze's farewell gig when the phone rings. "It's your son Jimmy, Tam," says Papa Joe as he hands him the receiver.

"Hello, son," Tam greets Jimmy. "How are you?"

"Not good, Dad," replies Jimmy and it is obvious he has been crying. "I have dreadful news and we need you to come home as soon as you can. Our Hugh has been involved in a serious multi-vehicle car accident. He is critically ill in hospital and he's just gone into a coma..."

"Try to stay calm, son," soothes Tam. "I'll be home as soon as I can. Which hospital is he in?"

"The Southern General, Dad," replies Jimmy. "Alec and Harry are there right now and Ellen and I were there all last night."

"I'm on my way, son," assures Tam. "You mind and get some sleep. Our Hugh is a strong lad and he won't give up without a fight."

"I need to go home, Joe," Tam informs his partner before proceeding to tell him his worrying news.

"It never rains but it bloody pours," groans Papa Joe. "Have a safe journey, my friend, and I wish your boy a speedy recovery. Please keep me posted on how he is doing."

"Will do, Joe," replies Tam. "Thank you."

"Let me come too, Dad," says Liz.

"No, love," replies Tam. "You're not well enough for two long plane trips and I want you to do the farewell gigs. After all, we owe it to the fans."

"I know, Dad," replies Liz as she starts to cry. "I hope Hugh is going to be alright and that I can see him soon. I just feel so helpless."

That evening, Moose and Ronnie arrive home from their hospital visit to Debbie and Baby Caitlin to find that Angel and Carl have made a very rare appearance home. Their fatigued bodies are there although their minds are elsewhere. A very exhausted Liz makes her way downstairs, wearing several layers of clothes to beat the cold, to greet Moose and Ronnie. "OK, my young 'uns," Papa Joe addresses the bandmates. "I am going to break the news to you now, while you are all here. Our final weekend of farewell gigs is scheduled for two weeks on Friday. We will play for the full weekend then we will call it a day as a band. Every one of you needs professional help and I hope you all make the effort to get it before others have plans for your fortune. This industry can be extremely cut-throat and I want you *ALL* to do the right thing for yourselves."

Liz nods and quietly goes back upstairs, closes the door

behind her and Moose follows her. He closes the door tightly after himself and holds Liz in a warm hug, which she takes the time to relish and hugs him back as she knows it will possibly be the last time he will do it. "Liz," he whispers to her. "I know this has probably been the toughest day for all of us as a band and it's all starting to feel so final. We can all survive this and I really want to help you through everything the best I can. Liz McLarnon, will you marry me?"

Moose gets down on one knee and opens a small box to reveal a solitaire diamond engagement ring. Liz covers her mouth as she bursts into tears and shakes her head. "I'm so sorry, baby," she whispers. "I can't marry you. Not the way things are. I am going home to Scotland for treatment. It's the only way I can do it. Please try to understand."

Moose doesn't even look at Liz, closes the box and storms out of the house without even saying anything to Papa Joe or his remaining bandmates.

That evening, Liz goes to bed and waits in vain for her beloved Moose to return home and she eventually cries herself to sleep. She wakes up at one thirty the following morning and goes to the spare room which was Moose's, hoping he had come home and gone to sleep in there. To her dismay, he is neither there nor on the couch downstairs. Liz cries as she gets dressed and calls a taxi to take her to the hospital. "Good morning," the receptionist greets her as she arrives at the hospital. "Can I help you?"

"Is John McLarnon working tonight?" she asks through her tears.

"Oh my God," the receptionist gasps. *"LIZ?"*

Liz nods and continues to cry uncontrollably. "John's on duty tonight, Liz," says the receptionist as she sits Liz down. "I'll call his department."

Within minutes Liz's gentle giant brother John, who works as a cardiac nurse, arrives at reception. "Oh my God, Liz," he gasps when he sees his sister. "You look a fright! What on

Earth is going on?"

"Moose and I split up yesterday, John," Liz manages to string together between her sobs.

"Did he hurt you, hen?" John asks angrily. "I'll stiffen the wee bastard!"

"John, no, please," Liz begs. "It was me. I had no choice. It's the last thing I want to do but I'm going home to Scotland for treatment. Harry is organising it for me and I am waiting for word back from his friend about a date for when I start."

"You're doing the right thing, hen," John assures his little sister as he hugs her. "It couldn't have been an easy decision for you as I know you think the world of that big guy and I know he's mad for you. I just wish there was more I could do for you but eating disorders are away out of my depth and I have no idea what to do or where to start."

"John...Oh my goodness," gasps a deep female voice and a tall, well-built woman stands in the doorway covering her mouth. "Just a quick word please, John."

"I'm sorry, John," Liz apologises, believing she has gotten her brother into trouble with his matron.

"John, you'll need to take your sister home," advises the matron.

"Are you sure, Fiona?" asks John. "I don't want to leave you short."

"Honestly, John, there is enough of us here now that we have supply nurses helping us," assures Fiona. "I was shocked when I saw your sister there. I would never have recognised her had she not been with you. The poor little mite is obviously in a very bad way."

"She is, Fiona," replies John. "She knows it and she is organising treatment for herself."

"Well I'm glad she recognises it and she's taking steps," smiles Fiona. "Go on. Take your sister home and the rest of the night off. Phone us tomorrow if you're making work one way or the other."

"Thanks, Fiona," says John, relieved. "I'll ask my three brothers to sit with Liz tomorrow so that should let me get back to my duties. Thank you very much for everything. You're a pal."

"Come on, hen," whispers John as he scoops Liz up in his arms. "I'll take you to Dad's."

"I hope I didn't get you into trouble," slurs Liz.

"Not at all, pal," assures John. "Fiona is a good lass and a massive Hell Freeze fan. She's very worried about all of you and is constantly asking after you and the guys."

"Please tell her I said thank you," Liz yawns as she falls asleep in her brother's arms.

Liz wakes up late the following morning with her usual burning thirst, headache and still feeling exhausted despite her long sleep. She forces herself to get up, showered and dressed. "I need to go home," she tells John as she goes downstairs.

"You don't have to go back there if you don't want to, love," John assures her as he puts a small bowl of porridge made with water and a cup of black coffee down to her.

"I need to," sighs Liz. "The guys and I still have rehearsals to do. I just hope Carl and Angel aren't too bad today."

"Just remember to come back here if it gets too hot for you over there," says John. "Just pick up the phone and one of us will come and get you."

"Thanks, John," replies Liz as she is unable to stop the tears. "I'm dreading going back over there but we've got a job to do before I go back to Scotland. I promised Dad."

Determined to get through their final two weeks together Hell Freeze power through rehearsals despite illness, exhaustion and tension among the members. Moose has barely looked at Liz since they split and it breaks Liz's heart.

The morning of the final gig of the band's farewell weekend arrives. Ronnie and Moose had risen early in order to make their daily trip to visit Debbie and Baby Caitlin before doing a final rehearsal before going on stage for the very last time. Ronnie checks on Liz as she had asked him to wake her as she also wanted to visit Debbie and offer him moral support. However, he finds that she is still fast asleep and probably too ill to cope with another traumatic hospital visit so he decides against disturbing her. Ronnie had received more bad news the previous night that Debbie now has pneumonia, Caitlin isn't feeding properly and it is now unclear that whether or not mother or baby will survive.

Again, Liz rises late with a blinding headache after yet another broken sleep due to severe malnutrition. She goes downstairs to find that Moose and Ronnie are just arriving home from the hospital and that Carl and Angel are already drunk and it is only ten thirty in the morning. Liz goes into the kitchen for some paracetamol and Moose offers her some breakfast without even looking at her to which she refuses. She feels she is unable to eat or even take a glass of water as she knows she will bring it straight back up again. She doesn't even get the same high when she weighs herself and the scale shows yet another loss and she can't even confide in her father because he is attending to her brother Hugh, who is still critically ill following his accident. Liz watches helplessly as Angel and Carl leave the house for more drink and drugs, Ronnie falls asleep on the couch with tears in his eyes and Moose goes back to his old room and locks the door behind him. All she can do is cry quietly to herself because she feels as though her hands are tied and she is too ill and weak to help anyone with anything.

It is seven p.m. and time for Hell Freeze to make their final public appearance as a band. Everyone is silent backstage as they wait for Papa Joe to announce them one last time. Angel and Carl feel dazed having been drinking and taking different types of narcotics all day. Ronnie is lost in his thoughts of Debbie and Baby Caitlin, both of whom he fears he will lose. Liz's illness is not helped as she watches every one of her bandmates suffer, she has hurt Moose whom she loves very much and now she has the added worry about her beloved older brother whom she fears she will never see again. Even Moose feels himself cracking under the pressure of being the "tough outer shell" of the band as his fears of his little brother's fate are coming true as well as that of Carl, he is unable to do anything for his best friend except stand with him and he has lost his beautiful girlfriend to anorexia which could potentially kill her. Still, he refuses to let his guard down and for anyone to see him cry. *"LADIES AND GENTLEMEN,"* Papa Joe addresses the audience. "Performing for you one last time for their farewell concert, please welcome *THE LEGENDARY HELL FREEZE."*

One by one, the members take their places in order that they joined the band: Angel, Carl, Moose, Ronnie and Liz.

Unknown to the bandmates, Maria is watching in the audience as she is hoping to catch her sons after the gig and take them home. She can't help but cry as she watches helplessly and fears for the safety of both of them. As his mother, only she knows how vulnerable and fragile Moose is. She is the only one, apart from Debbie, to have ever seen him openly shed tears and he had done it several times during his time with the band when he was worried about his loved ones and even Elvis Presley. She had also been worried about Angel following his visit to her several months ago when she had noticed his drastic weight loss and how tired he was. Now it is obvious what caused it. "My poor babies," she thinks to herself as she weeps quietly.

As usual, despite their illnesses and addictions, Hell Freeze do not disappoint their adoring fans, many of whom cry from start to finish of the show and the last gig seems to pass in a blur for the bandmates and audience members alike.

Hell Freeze are about to perform the final song of their farewell weekend tour, the grand finale as they play their biggest hit song to date. After six years of working tirelessly together in this line-up the time has now come for the five bandmates, their managers and their engineer and other staff members to go their separate ways. The atmosphere of the audience looks electric but as Liz scans the stage looking at her band mates, it is a totally different story altogether. Liz is exhausted and feels so much older than her twenty one years. She can't remember the last time she had eaten or slept properly, her weight has plummeted and the custom-made cat suit that once hugged her petite figure now hangs loosely on her. Her band mates also look frazzled with the only one who appearing to be holding it all together being Moose. But then, that's Moose with the tough guy image he tries his best to uphold.

Liz looks at the rest of her bandmates. Angel and Carl both look emaciated and ill. Their once strong, athletic physiques are now ravaged by drink and drugs, yet they carry on being the perfect showmen that they are for the sake of the audience despite being absolutely wasted on stage. Ronnie had cried for almost the entire gig as his thoughts are with critically ill Debbie and Baby Caitlin who are still showing no signs of improvement. It is understandable that Ronnie does not want to be there, yet he has the fans' best interests at heart and has turned up to play to the best of his ability one last time. Liz's thoughts are also with her brother Hugh who is still critically ill in hospital back in Scotland.

Throughout the gig, Liz keeps catching eye contact with an older lady in the audience. She is a maternal-looking lady in her fifties and she looks at Liz with pity in her eyes as she knows fine what is really happening on stage. "If those were my kids, I would be worried sick," Liz hears her say to a younger woman, possibly her daughter, during a break in the music.

Liz can't control her tears as she had been crying since long before the start of the gig and for days running up to it. There was no point in her even trying to do her make-up tonight as it would have just run straight off.

The end of the gig is now upon the band as all the members play the massive outro of their instruments and finishing in unison to a massive, roaring cheer from the audience with many of the devotees in tears. "Thank you so much, beautiful people," slurs Angel as he holds onto Moose's shoulder for support while Moose continues to prop him up. "Thank you, so much, from all of us for being there for us and making our band what we are. Love you all. Please take good care, stay safe and *KEEP ON ROCKIN'. GOOD NIGHT AND GOD BLESS.*"

Moose and Ronnie help Angel backstage, where he immediately blacks out. Liz takes Carl by the arm, allowing him to steady himself as they walk awkwardly backstage. Carl just makes it to the toilet where he projectile vomits before staggering out and collapsing on the floor beside Angel. Meanwhile, Ronnie continues to cry quietly to himself as Moose comforts him while wondering where he is going to start and which of his bandmates he can help.

Paramedics burst through the back door, take details from Papa Joe and Carl was rushed to hospital. "I'll take care of Angel," Liz whispers to Moose through her tears.

Moose nods and mutters "thanks" without making eye contact with Liz, puts a strong arm around Ronnie's shoulders and guides him out the back door in order to avoid as many eyes and cameras as possible and takes him to hospital to reunite him with Debbie and Baby Caitlin as he had promised. "I hope I'm doing the right thing here," Moose thinks to himself as he drives in silence, allowing Ronnie to cry quietly to himself. "Carl is already being taken care of by medical professionals and Liz is going to Scotland for treatment, which I really hope will work. I just hope Angel gets the help he so badly needs. Aw, I'm sure Angel will be fine. He's a clever, talented guy. He has his record deal, modelling contracts and other work in the music industry. He'll be able to get help for his addictions...I hope. He will. He definitely will and he won't want me hanging onto his coat tails. He doesn't need me anymore. None of them do. "

Moose can't stop the tears any longer as he thinks about the uncertain future of his former bandmates. He weeps quietly, knowing that Ronnie is lost in his own thoughts and not paying attention to him.

Meanwhile, Liz crouches down beside Angel who is still

unconscious on the floor and cradles his head. "Can somebody please help?" she pleads with the venue staff.

A steward eventually manages to get Angel to stir. "Mom," he whimpers as the excruciating pain and nausea suddenly hit him.

"It's alright, big guy," the steward assures Angel. "You're gonna be alright. Easy does it." Two stewards take an arm each and carry him out to the tour bus, where Danny effortlessly lifts him on board while Liz follows behind carrying Angel's treasured guitar.

During the drive home, Liz's thoughts are rushing through her head at a million miles an hour: her beloved Moose that she has lost forever, Ronnie and his sick wife and baby, Carl and Angel who both have their demons to contend with and her brother Hugh, whom she prays will continue to fight for his life and win.

Meanwhile, Maria goes backstage to collect her sons. "They're gone, ma'am," one of the stewards informs her.

"Have you any idea where to?" asks Maria.

"Moose said he was taking Ronnie to the hospital and Little Liz took Angel onto the tour bus, hopefully to the hospital too," he informs her. "They all look like they need a stay in hospital, even big Moose, bless him. The demon drink and drugs have a lot to answer for."

"Thank you," replies Maria. "I'll try the hospital."

As soon as they arrived home, Danny carries six-foot-plus Angel off the bus and into their mansion as though he is a small child and lies him, gently, in the recovery position on the only bed left. The magnificent house that had been the bandmates' home for the past four years had already been sold and was almost cleared out for the new residents who are due to move in the following week. "Can I take you anywhere, love?" asks Danny.

"No thanks, darling," replies Liz. "I'm going to stay with Angel. I'll keep an eye on him and take him to the hospital if he gets any worse."

"As long as you're sure", says Danny as he reluctantly heads for the door. Liz puts $100 into Danny's shirt pocket and hugs him to say thank you for helping as she wishes him all the very best for the future. Once Danny leaves, Liz tries in vain to get Angel's leather jacket off but he is a dead weight. She barely has the strength left to keep her own eyes open let alone lift her unconscious bandmate.

Liz lies on the bed beside Angel, still fully clothed, pulls a duvet over them both and cuddles up to him for heat as she can hear the rain lashing heavily on the window and the howling wind outside. As tired as Liz is, she is too afraid to go to sleep as she is worried about Angel's worsening condition. She has no idea what kind of concoction of alcohol and narcotics he and Carl had taken prior to the gig. Angel's breathing is now very shallow, his lips and hands are tinged blue and Liz wishes she had asked Danny to take them to the hospital rather than bring them home. She holds Angel's cold hand as she calls 911, willing him to keep breathing. The paramedics are there within minutes and ask Liz several questions that she is unable to answer. "He was drunk early this morning," she tells the female paramedic while her male colleague attends to Angel. "He's been doing heroin, coke and other heavy stuff too for weeks now. I'm really sorry, that's all I can tell you."

"We have enough information now, love," the female paramedic assures Liz. "Angel is very bradycardic, though, and he needs urgent medical attention as he has overdosed on whatever he has taken, which was a potentially deadly combination. It looks like you contacted us just in time and saved his life."

Liz stays with Angel at the hospital until the doctors take him away for his treatment. She feels helpless but there is nothing more she can do for the gentle soul who had held her hand and supported her ever since she had joined the band. She asks a member of hospital staff for a pen and a piece of paper while she waits. "My darling Angel," she writes. "I brought you to the hospital because you overdosed. I am begging you to please get help and either go to your mum's or to my dad's house when you feel better. Somebody will be able to help you. I wish I could do more for you but I need to go home as I need help as much as you do. Please stay strong, take care and look after yourself. All my love. Your little sister, Liz xxx"

Liz gives the letter and Angel's pay cheque from Papa Joe to the doctor who would be caring for him. She can't wait any longer. All she can do is hope that Angel will come out of this and follow the instructions that she had left him. "I'm so sorry, my dear Angel", Liz thinks to herself as she weeps quietly. "Please keep fighting this."

Liz is almost too exhausted to walk or keep her eyes open anymore as she gets into a waiting cab and makes her way to her father's house. This is the less glamorous side of being a rock star. The media coverage is every bit as harsh and Liz McLarnon is named among the most hated women in showbiz as she is blamed for the demise of Hell Freeze, one of the most beloved rock bands in the world.

www.ingramcontent.com/pod-product-compliance
Lightning Source LLC
Chambersburg PA
CBHW031952040426
42448CB00006B/326